Leonard Woolsey Bacon, père Hyacinthe

The Family and the Church

Advent Conferences of Notre-Dame, Paris, 1866-7, 1868-9

Leonard Woolsey Bacon, père Hyacinthe

The Family and the Church
Advent Conferences of Notre-Dame, Paris, 1866-7, 1868-9

ISBN/EAN: 9783337162733

Printed in Europe, USA, Canada, Australia, Japan

Cover: Foto ©ninafisch / pixelio.de

More available books at **www.hansebooks.com**

AND

THE CHURCH.

Advent Conferences of Notre-Dame, Paris,
1866-7, 1868-9.

BY THE REVEREND

FATHER HYACINTHE,

Late Superior of the Barefooted Carmelites of Paris.

EDITED BY

LEONARD WOOLSEY BACON.

WITH AN INTRODUCTION BY JOHN BIGELOW, ESQ.,
Late Minister of the United States at the Court of France.

NEW YORK:
G. P. PUTNAM & SON,
LONDON: S. LOW, SON & MARSTON.
1870.

PREFACE.

THE two volumes of Father Hyacinthe's Discourses, of which this is the second, contain, together, with one insignificant exception, everything that has been written or revised by him for publication.

In addition, we give herewith the rough and unrevised reports of his last series of "Conferences" at Notre Dame, on The Church. In reading them no small regret will be felt at finding them evidently so incomplete. But containing as they do their author's doctrine of the Church, and especially his enunciation of that doctrine of "the soul of the Church," which has been remarked as one of the chief characteristics of his preaching, they could ill have been spared from this volume.

It would be an interesting study to discover wherein this Catholic doctrine of "the soul of the Church," as enunciated by Father Hyacinthe in Rome and Paris, with the approval of the highest dignitaries of his Church, differs from that doctrine of "the Church invisible" which is cherished by evangelical theologians of various schools; certainly, not in the declaration that there is no salvation outside of the visible Roman

Church for one who clearly recognizes the duty of entering therein. Doubtless all sincere theology would declare that there was no salvation for any man in the way of the wilful disobedience of his own conscience. But when Father Hyacinthe, obeying the voice of an honest conscience, went sorrowfully forth into excommunication from the Church which he had passionately loved, and illustriously served, he set forth, with an emphasis to which not even *his* eloquence could have attained, the necessary corollary of his doctrine, to wit: that there is no salvation *in* the Roman Church for one who clearly recognizes the duty of leaving it.

It is a great pleasure to the editor of this volume to prefix to it an Introduction from the distinguished pen of Mr. Bigelow.

The authorization which Father Hyacinthe has conceded to Mr. Putnam's edition of his works, should not be understood as making him in any degree responsible for the work of the translator and editor.

LEONARD WOOLSEY BACON.

NEW ENGLAND CHURCH, Brooklyn,
January, 1870.

N. B.—It appears, from the blunders of one of the critics of the former volume of Father Hyacinthe's Discourses, to be necessary to reiterate the statement prefixed to that volume, that the Notre Dame Conferences are translated from incomplete short-hand reports; and to inform, not readers, but those who criticise without reading, that the passages within brackets contain the French editor's summary of the portions of the argument omitted, and not the translator's comments on the portions presented.

TABLE OF CONTENTS.

	PAGE.
INTRODUCTION	9
THE FAMILY—Six Lectures in Notre Dame, 1866–7	53
LECTURE FIRST—Domestic Society in the General Scheme of Human Society	53
The Bonds of Society	56
The Forms of Society	61
Relative Importance of Domestic Society	64
LECTURE SECOND—Conjugal Society the Foundation of Domestic Society	70
Conjugal Society as related to God the Creator	71
Conjugal Society as related to God the Redeemer	82
LECTURE THIRD—Corruption of Conjugal Society by the Immorality of the present day	92
Corruption of Conjugal Society in its Essence	92
Violation of the Law of Marriage	98
Violation of Marriage in its supernatural consecration as a Sacrament	102
LECTURE FOURTH—Fatherhood	106
As a means of the Reproduction of the Individual	108
As a means of the Propagation of the Species	115
LECTURE FIFTH—Family Education	125
The Agents of Education	126
The Laws of Education	136
LECTURE SIXTH—Home	145
Possession of the Home	146
Transmission of the Home	151
Occupation of the Home	158

	PAGE.
THE CHURCH—Six Lectures in Notre Dame, 1868-9....	165
LECTURE FIRST—The Church under its most Universal Aspect...................................	165
LECTURE SECOND—The Church of the Patriarchs.....	179
LECTURE THIRD—The Church in the Family.........	192
LECTURE FOURTH—The National Church of the Jews.	209
LECTURE FIFTH—The Jewish Church in its relations to the Christian Church.........................	225
LECTURE SIXTH—Conflict between the Letter and the Spirit in the Jewish Church....................	244
SPEECH on the Education of the Working-Classes, delivered at the Catholic Congress of Malines, September 6, 1867..	263
MEMORIAL LETTER on Bishop Baudry...............	289
APPENDIX.—Pastoral Letter of Bishop Dupanloup, on the Proposed Definition of the Dogma of Papal Infallibility...	293

INTRODUCTION.

FATHER HYACINTHE AND HIS CHURCH.*

On the 18th day of October last, the Superior of the Monastery of Barefooted Carmelites, in Paris, was landed from a French steamer upon the wharf at New York. Instead of wearing the usual garb of his order, however, he was clothed in the ordinary dress of a private gentleman; instead of availing himself of the hospitality provided in most large cities for the religious mendicant orders, he drove with his baggage directly to one of our popular hotels. His arrival was promptly telegraphed to the extremities of the continent; it was the subject of comment in every newspaper in our land. Every source of information was ransacked for details of his life; his hotel was thronged; he was interviewed by reporters; he was deluged with invitations; shop-windows and illustrated journals were radiant with his portrait; the mails were loaded with expressions of interest and sympathy for him; in fact, Pius IX. himself, if he had executed the purpose at one time attributed to him, of taking refuge in the United States, could hardly have produced a greater sensation.

The name of the monk, whose extraordinary reception among us contrasts so widely with that usually given to

* From Putnam's Magazine for January, 1870.

monastic visitors, is Charles Loyson, to which was added that of Brother Hyacinthe, by the religious order of which he had taken the vows. Father Hyacinthe—for it is by that name that he is now known to the world—is a French gentleman about forty-two years of age, a graduate of the Theological Seminary of St. Sulpice; for the past four or five years the favorite pulpit orator of Paris, and in his form, carriage, and general appearance, bearing a singular resemblance to the first Napoleon. But it is not for any of these distinctions that his name is now on every tongue, and his praises are echoing from continent to continent.

The day Father Hyacinthe left Paris, he renounced the position he held as Superior of the Convent of Carmelites, and laid aside the garb of his order without permission; thus provoking the solemn penalties of excommunication from his Church, that he might the more effectually vindicate the rights of conscience and the "liberty of prophesying."

It was this daring protest of the most illustrious orator of the Latin communion against the growing pretensions of the Papacy, that has awakened in this country a degree of interest, not easily exaggerated, in the person and history of its author.

Of the origin and history of the rupture between Father Hyacinthe and his Church but little is generally known. Till his departure for the United States was telegraphed from France, his name had rarely been heard outside of his own religious communion, and the impression naturally prevails that some sudden misunderstanding had resulted in an explosion, the immediate effects of which have become familiar to the public. This is a mistake. The antagonism between Father Hyacinthe and the Papal government, or its ultramontane section, has been developing for years, though hitherto successfully concealed from the secular public. Nor have the real grounds of their differences yet transpired. About all that is known of them is, that his Catholicism is broader than that of Rome, and that he prefers to defy the thunders of Rome to those of his own conscience.

We feel, therefore, that we cannot render a more acceptable service to the public than to give a brief history of a religious dissension which, in view of the approaching Council, threatens to take serious proportions, and which can hardly fail, in any event, to produce a profound impression upon the Latin Church.

In the summer of 1864, Father Hyacinthe was invited to deliver an address before a club of young people organized under the name of the *Cercle Catholique*, or Catholic Club, at Paris, corresponding to some extent with our *Young Men's Christian Association*. He accepted their invitation, and in the course of an address, conceived in fullest sympathy with the progressive thought of his age, he referred to the first French revolution in the following terms:

"1789 est un fait accompli, et s'il n'était pas, il faudrait l'accomplir."*

As Father Hyacinthe was already as well known for what was regarded by a certain class of his co-religionists as his too comprehensive Christian charity as for his eloquence, this phrase aroused a great deal of feeling in Paris; he was violently attacked by the *Monde*, an organ of the Ultramontanists, and a cabal was speedily organized to limit the infection of his dangerous eloquence as

---

* "1789 is an accomplished fact; and if it were not, it would be necessary to accomplish it."

much as possible by destroying his influence.* It did not, however, succeed in poisoning the mind of the Archbishop of Paris, who, regardless of their remonstrances, invited Father Hyacinthe to preach the Conferences of Advent that year at Notre-Dame. This pulpit for years, I might say centuries, has been reserved for the most popular orator in the Gallican Church. Several attempts had been made to revive these conferences since the death of Lacordaire, but they had proved unsuccessful. None of the preachers designated for that duty since the decease of the famous Dominican had come up to the traditional standard. They preached, but they failed to attract hearers. Some discourses delivered by Father Hyacinthe during the summer immediately previous, led the Archbishop to hope that he, if any one, could revive the ancient glories of Notre-Dame. Nor was he destined to be disappointed. Their success was complete, though the *Monde* did not see fit to announce them. They fixed his position as the worthy successor, not only of Lacordaire, but of any of his predecessors in that famous temple.

It was at these conferences that the writer first saw Father Hyacinthe. The solemn old cathedral was crowded with all that was socially most distinguished in Paris, and hundreds hung around the doors, unable to gain admission, but seeking to catch a casual

* It will possibly astonish some of those censors of Father Hyacinthe to be reminded of the following avowal made by Thiers in the Corps Legislatif in 1845:

"Wherever an absolute Government ceases to exist in Europe, whenever a new liberty is born, France loses an enemy and gains a friend. Understand me well. I am of the party of the Revolution, as well in France as in Europe. I desire that the Government of the Revolution rest in the hands of moderate men. I will do what I can to continue it there. But if this Government shall pass into the hands of men less moderate, of ardent men, even radicals, I shall not abandon my cause for that. I shall always be of the party of the Revolution."

phrase as it fell from the burning lips of the hermit-preacher.

The following entry, made in the writer's diary immediately after, will give an idea of the impression left upon the mind of a foreigner and a Protestant, whom curiosity, mainly, had brought under the magical influence of his eloquence.

Sunday.—Went to hear Father Hyacinthe, the Carmelite, at Notre-Dame. Paid a franc for my seat; Berryer sat just in front of me. Great crowd. The speaker middle-sized, plump, round-faced, well-conditioned man, with the faculty of kindling from his subject until he gets into a blaze of eloquence. His movement is exceedingly graceful—as perfect as possible. I would go to hear him again, if I had a chance. The Archbishop was present, and after the sermon was finished, left his seat below, mounted the pulpit, and made a short speech and pronounced the benediction."

La France, a semi-official journal of the Government, and one of the organs of the Gallican Church in Paris, gave a brief account of this conference, which closed as follows:

"When Father Hyacinthe had descended from the pulpit, where we hope he will soon reappear, Monsignor the Archbishop of Paris took his place, and addressed the immense audience, an allocution admirable for its noble thoughts and Christian views. He at first thanked and congratulated the young and brilliant orator who had so early placed himself in the ranks of the great masters of speech, and confirmed his teachings with all his authority as a bishop and his charity as a pastor.

"The effect produced by this unexpected discourse was great, and the crowd dispersed profoundly impressed."

To measure the importance of the Archbishop's presence and remarks on this occasion, it is necessary to know something of the relations then subsisting between the French or Gallican and Ultramontane Catholics.

It will be remembered that when the famous popular demonstrations were made in Europe, in 1848, the Pope gave them his sympathies, and popular meetings were held all over the United States to hail the omen. That tendency was followed by a violent reaction, and since then the Roman Church, under the counsels of the Jesuits, has been striving in every possible way to centralize its power in the hands of the nominal head of the Church. Its first trial of strength on a large scale was made in the proclamation of the Pope, in 1854, without the aid of any council, of the Immaculate Conception of the Virgin Mary as a dogma of the Church. The audacity of this proceeding shocked large bodies of French and German Catholics, and provoked many publications designed to throw doubt upon the validity of the new dogma. The leading liberal Catholics of France were astonished, and many were alarmed; but Rome was to them too important an ally in the warfare they were waging with the Imperial Government, to contest the growth of an authority which, in view of their pressing exigencies, they were disposed to increase rather than diminish. They therefore quietly accepted the dogma, but they became only the more zealous in their efforts to liberalize the Church and reconcile it with the civilizing tendencies of the age. These very efforts tended to divide them as a class more and more from the Ultramontanists. To give power and organization to the reactionary influence, the Liberals, prominent among whom were the Archbishop of Paris, the Bishop of Orleans, the Count de Montalembert, Bordas Dumoulin, Arnaud de Ariege, the Prince de Broglie, A. Cochin, Falloux, and, during their lives,

Lammenais, Lacordaire, and Ozanam, with the *Avenir* and later the *Revue Correspondant,* for their organs in the press, held a sort of Liberal Catholic Congress at Malines, in August of the year 1863, at which they gave formal expression to their distinctive sentiments and aspirations. It was at this Congress that the Count de Montalembert made two speeches, which were widely circulated in France as a faithful reflection of the feelings of the Congress. A paragraph or two from these discourses will disclose at once the spirit and significance of this movement.

" Of all the liberties of which up to this time I have undertaken the defence, the liberty of conscience is in my eyes the most precious, the most sacred, the most legitimate, the most necessary. I have loved, I have served all the liberties, but I honor myself more than all for having been the soldier of this. Again to-day, after so many years, so many contests, and so many defeats, I cannot speak of it without emotion. * * * Yet I must admit that this enthusiastic devotion for religious liberty which animates me, is not general among the Catholics. They desire liberty for themselves, and in this there is no great merit. In general, everybody wishes all sorts of freedom for himself. But religious freedom in itself; freedom of conscience to every one; that freedom of worship which is contested and resisted, that it is which disquiets and alarms many of us.

" I am, then, for freedom of conscience, in the interest of Catholicism, without reserves or hesitation. I accept freely all its consequences, all which public morals do not reprove and which equity demands. This conducts me to a delicate but necessary question. I will meet it boldly. Can one to-day demand liberty for truth—that is, for himself (for every one acting in good faith thinks he has the truth)—and refuse it to error (that is, to those who do not think as we do)?

" I answer boldly, No. Here I feel, indeed, *incedo per ignes.* So I hasten to add again that I have no pretension to give more than my individual opinion. I bow to all the texts, all the canons which may be cited. I will not contest or discuss any of them. But I cannot trample under foot to-day the conviction which rules in my heart and conscience. I declare, then, that I experience an invincible horror for all those punishments and violences visited upon humanity, under the pretext of serving or defending religion. The fires of persecution, lighted by Catholic hands, shock me as much as the scaffold on which Protestants have immolated so many martyrs. The gag in the mouth of any one preaching his belief with a pure heart, I feel as if it were between my own teeth, and I shudder with the pain of it. The Spanish inquisition saying to the heretic, 'The truth, or death,' is as odious to me as the French terrorist saying to my grandfather, 'Liberty, fraternity, or death.' No one has the right to subject the human conscience to such hideous alternatives."

These were new doctrines to come from any large body of eminent and representative Catholics. They were regarded as deliberately hostile to the Jesuits, and generally unfriendly to ultramontane Catholicism. These proceedings had barely time to get to Rome, when Europe resounded with the famous Encyclical Letter and Syllabus of 1864, which was a formal protest from Rome against pretty much everything that had been accomplished for the social and political improvement of the human race since the dark ages.

The following paragraph from this famous document leaves no doubt that it was designed as a formal rebuke of, as well as reply to, the Congress of Malines.

"You are not ignorant, venerable brothers, that there are not wanting men in our day who, applying to civil society the impious and absurd principle of naturalism, as they call it, dare to teach 'that the perfection of government and civil progress require that human society be constituted and governed without taking any more account of religion than if it did not exist, or at least without distinguishing between the true and the false.' Besides, contrary to the doctrine of the Scriptures, of the Church and the holy fathers, they do not fear to affirm that 'the best government is that which recognizes no objection in itself to repress, by legal penalties, the violators of the Catholic faith, except when necessary to maintain social order.' Parting from this absolutely false idea of social government, they do not hesitate to favor this erroneous opinion, fatal to the Catholic Church and to the safety of souls, characterized by our predecessor of happy memory, Gregory XVI., as a delirium, ' that the freedom of conscience and of religious worship is the proper right of every man, which ought to be proclaimed by law, and secured in every well-constituted State, and that citizens have a right to the fullest freedom in expressing their opinions, whatever they may be, by printing or otherwise, without any limitation from civil or ecclesiastical authority.' Now, in sustaining these rash affirmations, they do not think nor consider that they preach the freedom of perdition, and that if it be permitted to human opinions to contest everything, men will not be wanting who will dare resist the truth, and place their confidence in the verbiage of human wisdom, a pernicious vanity which faith and Christian wisdom ought to carefully avoid, according to the teaching of our Lord."

Attached to the Encyclical Letter was a Syllabus, or list of popular errors upon which the Pope wished specially to place the seal of his condemnation. We will quote a few of these proscribed errors; a few will suffice, for from them the rest may be inferred—as with a telescope all objects may be seen within its range by simply changing its direction.

" Every man is free to embrace and profess the religion which he shall regard as true, according to the light of his own reason."

The reader will please not forget that the propositions we are citing are condemned, not approved, by the Syllabus.

" The Church has no right to employ force.
" The Church should be separated from the State, and the State from the Church.
" In our time, it is not useful that the Catholic religion be considered the only religion of the State, to the exclusion of other modes of religious worship.

"In some Catholic countries, the law has wisely provided that foreigners coming there to settle should enjoy the public exercise of their religion.

"It is false that the freedom of all religious worship propagates the pestilence of indifference.

"The Roman pontiff can and should put himself in harmony with progress, with liberalism, and with modern civilization."

The appearance of this extraordinary proclamation from Rome was, of course, hailed with jubilant enthusiasm by the Jesuits and the Ultramontanists. "It was their hour and the power of darkness." The Pope had come to the support of their favorite doctrines with the consecrated weapon of his Infallibility, and the apologists of Passive Obedience and of the Inquisition were proclaimed to have most correctly divined the policy of the Church.

It was in the heat of this contest between the liberal Catholics of France and the Ultramontanists, that Father Hyacinthe vindicated the Revolution of 1789, and was invited to preach the Conferences of Advent at Notre-Dame.

We have already spoken of the efforts made at this time to bring his teachings under discipline at Rome.

To disarm his adversaries, or to neutralize their influence, he was sent for by the General of his order to come to Rome, in 1865, under the pretext of assisting at the beatification fêtes of a Carmelite Nun of the name of Marie des Anges. He was then for the first time presented to the Pope, by whom he was received with the greatest kindness, and so far from being censured, or even questioned, was treated with special consideration.

Meantime the war went on, modified more or less by the various exigencies of the Papacy on the one hand, and of the liberal Catholics on the other, until 1868, when Father Hyacinthe was again sent for to come to Rome, ostensibly to preach the Conferences for Lent in the church of St. Louis of France, but really to counteract by his presence, if possible, the prejudices which the Ultramontanists were still sedulously propagating against him. His subject for these conferences was "The Church," which he treated in a most comprehensive and liberal spirit, and with scant respect for mere sectarian distinctions. He sought to trace the plan of a universal church which should conciliate God's children in all Christian communions, while he specially denounced the Pharisaism which in our Lord's time was constantly seeking to entrap Him in His words, as it is now seeking to entrap His disciples.

His success was something marvellous; it was almost, if not quite, unprecedented. He was received on this visit, also, in the kindest manner by the Pope, who testified his pontifical affability by a most gracious pun upon his name. He called him "*Hyacinthe, fleur et pierre précieuse.*"

Father Hyacinthe left Rome again, triumphing, it may be, over his enemies, but with impressions of the Holy City and government painfully unsettled. Like Luther when he returned from his first visit to Rome, he felt as if he were awakening from a painful dream. He had not found the dignitaries there assembled to receive the oracles of God, as exempt from human infirmities as he had been educated to believe them. He encountered ignorance often where he looked for wisdom, intolerance where he expected charity and brotherly love; double-dealing, selfishness, and worldly-mindedness where ingenuousness and devotion to the Church, to humanity, and to God were promised. With all his success, he left Rome more troubled in mind than when, almost in the character of a criminal, and uncertain of the reception that awaited him, he set out for the Eternal City. Suspicions had been planted there which reacted upon many of the most pleasing and endeared associations of his life.

In December of 1868 he was again invited to preach the conferences at Notre-Dame. He treated of the same subject, "The Church," which had been the theme of his conferences at Rome, and from substantially the same point of view. His portrait of what he regarded as the true idea of a Universal Christian Church, contrasted so broadly with the Church of the Encyclique and the Syllabus of 1864, that it greatly increased the irritation of the Ultramontanists, which was aggravated to exasperation by the closing discourse on Pharisaism, the aim of which could not be mistaken. The Archbishop of Paris listened also to this discourse, and at its close made a public acknowledgment to the orator.

The following extract from a despatch of Cardinal Bernis, when French Minister to Rome, addressed to the Minister of Foreign Affairs, in 1779, is calculated to leave the impression that Pharisaism, in the eyes of French Catholics, is a chronic vice with the Ultramontanists, and that that phrase in the mouth of Father Hyacinthe had a traditional significance, which is almost necessary to account for the bitterness which, in this instance, it will be found to have engendered:

"They think, at Rome," he writes, "that the Catholic Courts do but their duty when they favor the Court of Rome, and that they fail of their duty when they do not blindly everything it pretends to have the right to decide. The habit of seeing these things does not prevent my being often revolted by it. I have not to reproach myself with not having expostulated upon the subject on more than one occasion, *but the evil is incurable.* I content myself, therefore, with making the best of a country where *Pharisaism*, if I may permit myself to use such a term, prevails more than anywhere else."

While descending, as it were, from the pulpit of Notre-Dame, on the occasion to which we have just referred, Father Hyacinthe received a summons to repair at once to Rome, to explain a letter which had recently appeared over his signature in an Italian Review, and which was reported to have filled the heart of the Holy Father with a degree of wrath generally supposed to be unknown to celestial minds. And what offence, what crime, could have been committed to have provoked the Pope to such a humiliating, such a degrading procedure against the most popular preacher in the Church, at the very moment when the lofty aisles of Notre-Dame were yet ringing with his matchless eloquence?

We will explain as briefly as possible. In one of the Paris Clubs, Father Hyacinthe had been accused by a popular orator of having invoked the aid of canister-shot against atheists and free-thinkers. Though nothing was farther from the thoughts or character of the preacher, he thought it his duty to reply to the charge, in a letter which was read at the next meeting of the Club. In the course of this letter he said:

"I did not think it was necessary to separate my cause from that of certain Catholics who, without appealing to canister, yet mourn the loss of the Inquisition and the Dragonnades. They have taken care to separate themselves from me by attacks of which I have been the target since the beginning of my ministry, and which assail, I admit, the most deliberate and unshakable convictions of my reason and of my conscience."

This letter was bitterly assailed by the ultramontane press, and provoked a second reprimand from the General of his order.* It was followed shortly by another, written privately to the editor of *la Revista Universale*, of Genoa, accompanying a religious discourse, designed for the columns of the Review. The *Revista Universale* is a liberal Catholic periodical, monthly, we believe, belonging to the same order, doctrinally speaking, as the *Correspondant* of Paris. It is edited by a personal friend of Father Hyacinthe, the Marquis Salvago, who is also a Member of the Chamber of Deputies; and it numbers among its contributors such men as Cæsar Cantu, the historian, Audisio, a learned professor at Rome, and other equally renowned and equally unsuspected Catholics. The Marquis wrote for permission to publish the private note with the discourse. Permission was given. The letter in question had been written just at the breaking out of the recent Spanish revolution, and when all the ultramontane press were firing the hearts of the faithful to rally them to the rescue of the Church, imperilled in the sacred person of the most Catholic Queen Isabella. In this note he said:

"The old political organization of Catholicism in Europe is tumbling over on all sides in blood, or, what is worse, into the mire, and it is to these crumbling and shameful fragments that they would bind the future of the Church."

Ill-disposed persons persuaded the Pope that this was an allusion to the declining fortunes of his temporal power, and Monsignor Nardi, *Uditore di Rota*, had given the letter that interpretation, in a communication to the *Osservatore Cattolico* of Milan.

His Holiness accepted the interpretation without hesitation or inquiry. "He says we are fallen into the

---

* Allusion to this is made by the General, in his letter of September 26, threatening Father Hyacinthe with excommunication in case he did not return to his convent within ten days.

mire, '*nella fanga*,'" cried out the Pope, to one of his court. He was excessively irritated, and directed orders to be sent at once through the State Department to Father Hyacinthe, to explain his letter in the next number of the *Revista*. "The soul of the Holy Father," they wrote to him from Rome, "is filled with bitterness."

Father Hyacinthe had no difficulty in washing his hands of whatever was offensive in the letter which had so disturbed the peace of his ecclesiastical sovereign, and showed, in a brief communication to the *Revista*, that his previous note had no reference whatever to the temporal power of the Pope. But while vindicating himself from this gratuitous accusation, he took occasion to remind the Pope of his fallibility in a way to leave a far more grievous wound than the imaginary attack upon his temporal authority had occasioned. He said that Austria *Concorditaire* had fallen in blood at Sadowa, and that absolutist and intolerant Spain had fallen into the mire with the government of Isabella II.; that to bind the interests of the Church to any of these expiring régimes was to bind them to impotent and dishonored ruins. He then dwelt upon the liberal and reforming spirit of the first years of Pius IX., and cited the following striking passage from the letter of the Pope himself in 1848 to the Emperor of Austria, to persuade him to yield to the Italian aspirations for national unity.

"Let it not be disagreeable to the generous German nation that we invite it to lay aside all hatred, and to convert into useful relations of friendly neighborhood a domination which would be neither noble nor prosperous if it rested solely upon the sword.

"So have we confidence that the nation justly proud of its own nationality will not commit its honor to bloody attempts against the Italian nation, but will rather make it a point to recognize her nobly for a sister,—since both are daughters very near to our heart,—each content to dwell within her natural frontiers with honorable treaties, and the Lord's blessing."

This letter committed the unpardonable fault of reproducing an epoch and acts which the Holy Father wished consigned to oblivion. It irritated him beyond measure. When, soon after this letter appeared, the General of the Carmelites at Rome asked the Papal blessing for his order, the Pope is said to have replied, "Yes, for all your order, but not for Father Hyacinthe."

It was in this frame of mind that the letter was conceived which summoned Father Hyacinthe to Rome in January, 1869.

Father Hyacinthe did not choose to comply with this summons at once. He assigned as reasons for deferring his visit, that he was fatigued with the conferences which he had just concluded, that his health had suffered from the rigors and privations of conventual life,* that he had certain engagements in France to fulfil, that the season was unfavorable to travelling, etc. With one or another of these reasons he excused himself from going to Rome, though repeatedly urged to come, and even threatened, if he longer delayed, with expulsion from his order, and prohibition from preaching or saying the mass. Independent of the reasons he assigned for this delay, there were others which it requires no very lively imagination to suppose were operating upon his mind. He was doubtless unwilling to reveal to the public the full force of the indignity put upon him by the Papal summons, as he would have done by obeying it promptly.

---

* He did not taste meat for the ten years he was attached to the convent, except when discharging duties outside. Then he had the privilege of living as others lived.

The effect would have been in every way as prejudicial to the Church as to himself. It might be, too, that the insensibility exhibited by the Pope for his feelings and position in the Church, might extend to his person, for in Rome prisons and graves as well as the churches yawn at the behest of his Holiness.

In the course of his journey to Rome, Father Hyacinthe passed through Florence. There he saw some of the Italian deputies, and especially M. Massari, the friend and posthumous editor of Gioberti. He also attended the session of the Chamber, always, of course, in his monkish dress, when the new Menabrea ministry was installed. A Carmelite monk fellowshipping with Italian liberals at Florence was not an event to escape notice or animadversion. He was rated for it very severely by *l'Unita Cattolica* and other ultramontane organs. He reached Rome at the Feast of Pentecost, and on the very day that the papers arrived announcing and denouncing his visit to the Italian Chamber of Deputies. Though sensible that his visit to Florence was not likely to increase the cordiality of his reception at the Vatican, he lost no time in applying for an audience. It was granted without delay, which, for a person under discipline, was unusual. This was his first surprise. On entering the papal presence, his countenance wore a respectful but sad expression, as became a man who had been treated with injustice and was conscious of the rectitude of his motives. The Pope extended his hand to him. As the Apostle refused to profit by the open doors to escape from the prison to which he had been unjustly condemned, so the Father declined the extended hand until he had kneeled and kissed the foot of the Pope, after the usual custom of the faithful. He then rose, and with his hands folded beneath his scapulary, stood silent. After a moment's stillness on both sides, the Pope asked why he had come to Rome. Father Hyacinthe made no reply, for he knew that his questioner had no more need than he of the information. The Pope resumed, "I told your General that I wished to speak to you, but you were occupied and unable to come."

Father H. "Very Holy Father, I was not only occupied, but suffering in health."

The Pope. "You have written some things lacking prudence and good sense, but I forget now what they are."

Father H. "Very Holy Father, it is very possible that I have written things wanting in prudence and good sense, but if I have, it has not been my intention to do so."

The Pope. "It was in an Italian journal; one of those journals which are striving to reconcile Jesus Christ with Belial."

Father H. "I have never written but for one Italian Review, *La Revista Universale,* of Genoa, but it is my duty to say to your Holiness, in reference to my letters in that print, that my enemies have attributed to me not only the opposite of my thoughts, but the opposite of my language. Monsignor Nardi has calumniated me."

The last words were repeated in Italian and emphasized with respectful firmness. The Pope resumed with affability, "Then why did you not set yourself right in the same Review?"

Father H. "I did so, and in the same Review."

The Pope. "Ah! yes, but you have reproduced a letter of the Pope to the Emperor of Austria. That was ill-timed."

Father H. "Very Holy Father, I believed I was doing honor to your Holiness. It is often affirmed that the Pope is the enemy of Italy; I have wished to show by his own words that while he condemns its faults, he loves the nation."

His Holiness was not insensible to the compliment latent in this reply, and appeared perfectly satisfied with the Father's explanation. He detained him in conversation for a full half-hour longer, and with a degree of affability and freedom which Father Hyacinthe had never experienced at any previous interview. They talked of the religious and political situation, of the approaching Council, of the temporal power, and especially of the Emperor and of the Archbishop of Paris, both of whom, though in different ways, have contrived to give the Holy Father not a little concern of mind.

The Pope gave Father Hyacinthe some prudential counsel in the most general terms, and having special reference to the gravity of the situation of the Church, but uttered not a syllable of censure upon his preaching or conduct. He did not ask him to withdraw a word he had spoken, or to undo anything he had done, nor did he impose upon him any sort of prohibition whatsoever.

While speaking of the temporal power, his Holiness observed that he only insisted upon it as a principle of justice, and added: "Ambition is not a motive with Popes."

Father Hyacinthe profited by this remark to bring back the conversation, become too general, to his own affairs, and said:

"If the Holy Father will excuse my referring to however remote a resemblance between us, I may say also that ambition is not the motive which inspires me. I became priest and recluse only to serve God and His Church, and to save souls; now they are trying to destroy my usefulness by poisoning the ears of your Holiness and of the Catholics in France with calumnies. I have for enemies, very Holy Father, the friends of M. Veuillot and the enemies of the Archbishop of Paris."

To this the Pope oddly enough answered: "If the Archbishop finds his position so delicate, and thinks it necessary to show so much caution in his relations with the Government, why do you not take counsel from some of the other bishops of France?"

The Father made no reply: there was but one thing to say, but that was unnecessary and would have been direspectful: "Why did you name him Archbishop of Paris?"

The Pope then blessed the Father very affectionately, saying: "I bless you, dear Hyacinthe, that you may never say what they accuse you of having said, and which you affirm that you never said."

Thus terminated the Father's third and last visit to the great Catholic metropolis. Each time he had gone there as an offender under discipline, and each time he left without a word of censure for the past or of instruction for the future. The cordiality and homage which awaited him from the court when the character of his reception had transpired, was proportioned to the coldness and reserve with which he had been received on his arrival. He was congratulated upon the great victory he had achieved, and the triumph that awaited him. Ambitious prelates flocked around him to testify their gratification with his success, and for the moment he was the lion of Rome. He did not, however, tarry long to enjoy his victory—for to him it was no victory.

It was an elaborate outrage. He was summoned to Rome in a way which only the gravest offence could justify; his usefulness in the Church and his standing with the world were gravely compromised. He reached Rome under the condemnation of his brethren, and though confident in his innocence, he naturally expected a serious investigation of charges plausible as well as serious in their character. He waits upon the Pope, who has or pretends to have forgotten what he came for; who accepts unhesitatingly an explanation of the offending letter, which a simple perusal would have rendered superfluous; he utters no word of rebuke; he asks him to retract nothing he has ever written or said; he prescribes no restrictions upon his future conduct, and closes with a peculiarly disingenuous effort to sow dissension between him and his Archbishop.

Father Hyacinthe set out for home, scarcely conscious himself, probably, of the change which the third visit to Rome had wrought in him. He had begun to learn with how little wisdom his Church was governed, and to ask himself if this is the sort of men whom it is proposed by a Universal Council to proclaim infallible? Is this the sort of statesmen whose temporal power and sovereignty are essential to the independence of the Church and to the protection of the holy Catholic religion?

A few days after the Father's return to Paris, M. Veuillot, in the *Univers*, pretended to give an account of what had passed between him and the Pope, presenting it, of course, in a point of view anything but advantageous to the monk. His article provoked the following reply from Father Hyacinthe, bearing date the 8th of June last:

"Sir: Too faithful to the practices of a certain press calling itself Catholic, you presume to divine what passed between the Holy Father and myself, on ground where neither delicacy nor self-respect permit me to follow you.

"It is very true that in consequence of attacks from a religious party which I am honored in having for adversaries, I have been summoned to Rome by the Holy Father; but it is no less true, that I was received by him with a goodness altogether paternal, and that I have not been required to retract a single word of what I have either written or spoken.

"This reply once made, whatever insinuations my public speech or private conduct may expose me to in the future, you will permit me to consult as well my taste as my dignity by maintaining silence.

"Receive, Sir, the assurance of such sentiments as I owe you, in the charity of our Lord Jesus Christ."

A few days after this note appeared in Paris, the following note appeared in the form of a communication in *l'Osservatore Romano*, an "officious" print, published in Rome.

Let us premise that the Convent of which Father Hyacinthe was Superior is situated at Passy, formerly a suburb, but now a part of the city of Paris, and also the site of a renowned asylum for the insane.

"From Passy, a place near Paris, renowned for its hospitals, and where mental diseases are healed with success, a French barefooted Carmelite writes to a Catholic journal a letter, the contents of which are not entirely in conformity with the truth."

This offensive paragraph was attributed to the Pope himself, both in the office of the *Univers*, and at the papal legation at Paris, and was the theme of a triumphant article in the ultramontane organ. The editor did not scruple to apply to it the words of St. Augustin:

"*Roma loouta est, causa finita est.*" Rome has spoken; the case is finished.

On the 10th of July, Father Hyacinthe was invited to address the Peace Society of Paris, and accepted the invitation. In his discourse were two paragraphs conceived in that large and comprehensive Christian charity which had already so often provoked the secret or open censures of the Jesuits and ultramontane Catholics.

"For my part," he said, "I bring to the Peace movement *the gospel;* not that gospel dreamed of by sectaries of every age—as narrow as their own hearts and minds—but my own gospel, received by me from the Church and from Jesus Christ; a gospel which claims authority over everything and excludes nothing—[*sensation*]—which reiterates and fulfils the word of the Master, 'he that is not against us is for us,' and which, instead of rejecting the hand stretched out to it, marches forward to the van of all just ideas and all honest souls." [*Applause.*]

Farther on, he made the concession which brought upon him the formal censure of his General, and may, therefore, be regarded as the proximate cause of his quitting his Convent. He said:

"To banish war, to say to it what the Lord says to death—'O death, I will be thy death'—we must make exterminating war on sin—sin of society as well as of the individual—sin of peoples as well as of kings. We must record and expound to the world, which does not understand them as yet, those two great books of public and private morality, the book of the synagogue, written by Moses with the fires of Sinai, and transmitted by the prophets to the Christian Church; and our own book, the book of grace, which upholds and fulfils the law, the gospel of the Son of God. The decalogue of Moses, and the gospel of Jesus Christ!—the decalogue, which speaks of righteousness, while showing at the height of righteousness the fruit of charity; the gospel, which speaks of charity, while showing in the roots of charity the sap of righteousness. This is what we need to affirm by word and by example, what we need to glorify before peoples and kings alike! [*Prolonged applause.*]

"Thank you for this applause! It comes from your hearts, and it is intended for these divine books! In the name of these two books, I accept it. I accept it also in the name of those sincere men who group themselves about these books, in Europe and America. It is a most palpable fact that there is no room in the daylight of the civilized world except for these three religious communions—Catholicism, Protestantism, and Judaism!" [*Renewed applause.*]

The concession of the privileges of salvation and grace to the Jews, not to speak of Protestants, was the *coup de grâce* to ultramontane forbearance.

The phrase in reference to the three religions, which was vehemently applauded, was immediately perverted by the *Univers,* and made the pretext for violent and prolonged attacks. They represented the preacher as saying that there were three religions equally acceptable in the sight of God, or at least three religions equally entitled to be taught to men; whereas, he had simply announced the fact, so honorable to the Bible, that the three religious societies which recognized its authority, the Jewish, the Catholic, and the Protestant, are the only ones upon which the sun of civilization shines.

This discourse produced a profound sensation at Rome, and brought promptly from the General of his order the following letter, dated July 22, 1869, not only reflecting upon the tendency of his past teachings, but strictly prohibiting him from meddling with any of the questions agitated among Catholics:

THE SUPERIOR-GENERAL TO THE MONK.

"Rome, July 22, 1869.

"My Very Rev. Father Hyacinthe: I have received your letter of the 9th inst., and in a short time after the speech which you delivered at the Peace League. I have not, happily, found in that speech the heterodox phrase attributed to you. It must be said, however, that it contains some vague propositions, admitting of unfortunate interpretations, and that such a speech does not come well from a monk. The habit of the Carmelite was certainly there no longer in its place. My reverend father and dear friend, you know the great interest I have always taken in you. From the commencement of your sermons at Notre-Dame de Paris, I have earnestly exhorted you not to identify yourself with questions in dispute among Catholics, and on which all were not agreed; because, from the moment you attach yourself ostensibly to one side, your ministry becomes more or less unfruitful with the other. Now, it is patent that you have made no account of the intimation of your father and superior, as last year you wrote a letter to a Club in Paris, in which you freely disclosed your opinions in favor of a party, having little wisdom, and in opposition with the sentiments of the Holy Father, the episcopacy, and the clergy in general. I was alarmed, as were also the French clergy. I wrote to you immediately, to enable you to see the false path you had entered on, in order to stop you. But in vain, for some months after you authorized from yourself a periodical review in Genoa to publish another letter, that has been the cause of so much vexation to you and me. Lastly, during your last sojourn at Rome I made you serious observations and even rather strong reproaches on the false position you were placed in, on account of your imprudence; but you had scarcely arrived in Paris when you published, under your own signature, a letter deplored by all, even by your friends.

"Lately, your presence and speech at the Peace League have caused as great scandal in Catholic Europe as happened about six years ago on the occasion of your speech at a meeting in Paris. You have, beyond doubt, given some reason for such recriminations by some bold, obscure, and imprudent phrases.

"I have done all that I could up to the present to defend and save you. To-day I must think of the interests and honor of our holy order, which, unknown to yourself, you compromise.

"You write me from Paris, November 19, 1868: 'I avoid mixing the Paris Convent and the Order of Mount Carmel with these matters.' Let me say to you, my dear father, that this is an illusion. You are a monk, and bound to your superiors by solemn vows. We have to answer for you before God and man, and consequently have to take the same measures in your regard as in that of other monks, when your conduct is prejudicial to your soul and our Order.

"Already, in France, Belgium, and even here, some of the bishops, clergy, and faithful are blaming the superiors of our Order for not taking certain measures in your regard, and it is concluded that there is no authority in our congregation, or that it shares in your opinions and course of action. I do not certainly regret the course I have followed, up to the present, in regard to you; but matters are arrived at such a point that I would compromise my conscience and the entire Order if I do not take more efficacious measures in this matter than I have done in the past. Consider, therefore, dear and reverend father, that you are a monk, that you have made solemn vows, and that by the vow of obedience you are bound to your superiors by a lien as strong as that which binds the ordinary priest to his bishop. I can, therefore, no longer tolerate your continuing to compromise the entire Order by your speeches or writings, no more than I can tolerate our holy habit appearing at meetings that are not in harmony with our profession as Barefooted Carmelites. Therefore, in the interest of your soul and of our holy Order, I order you formally, by this present, not in the future to print any letters or speech; to speak outside the churches; to be present at the Chambers; to take no part in the Peace League, or any other meeting which has not an exclusively Catholic and religious object. I hope you will obey with docility, and even with love.

"Now let me speak to you with an open heart, as a father to his son. I see you entered on an extremely dangerous path, which, despite your present intentions, may conduct you where to-day you may deplore to arrive. Arrest yourself, then, my dear son; hear the voice of your father and friend, who speaks to you with a heart broken with sorrow. With this view, you would do well to retire to one of the convents in the Province of Avignon, there to repose yourself, and perform the retreat which I dispensed you from last year on account of your duties. Meditate in solitude on the great truths of religion—not to preach them, but for the profit of your soul. Ask light from heaven, with a contrite and humble heart. Address yourself to the Holy Virgin, to our father Saint Joseph, and to our seraphic mother

St. Theresa. A father can well address these words to his son, although he be a great orator. It is a very serious question for you, and for us all. I pray to the Saviour that He may deign to accord you his light and grace. I recommend myself to your prayers, and give you my benediction, and I am your very humble servant,

"Fr. Dominique de Saint Joseph,
"*Superior-General.*"

This letter, in its tone and purpose, was so entirely at variance with the sentiments of almost paternal benevolence theretofore uniformly manifested by the General to Father Hyacinthe, that it was obvious that he was acting under a pressure which he could not resist. Hence the curious inconsistencies of it as a measure of discipline. Though forbidden to print any letters or speeches; to speak outside the churches; to be present at the deliberations of the Legislative Chambers; or to take part in any public meeting except for some exclusively Catholic object, he was privileged to retain his high rank in his Order; to hold on to his position as superior of the Convent at Paris; to remain one of the four Members of the Council of the Province; and to continue to preach, as usual, at Notre-Dame. Of these privileges, however, Father Hyacinthe did not think it his duty to avail himself. The letter he had received was, as he believed, a blow aimed by the Jesuits, through him, at the vitals of the Christian Church. It proved to him that in the present state of the Catholic Church, and especially under the rule of monastic discipline, the Evangelical Word was not free. It gave him an occasion, by which he deemed it his duty to profit, "to protest as a Christian and a priest against those doctrines and practices which call themselves Roman but are not Christian."

On the 20th of September, Father Hyacinthe addressed the following reply to his General at Rome; and on the same day he abandoned his Convent and the garb of his Order, thereby protesting, by act as well as by speech, against the abuse of ecclesiastical power, of which he felt that he was the victim.

To the Reverend the General of the Order of Barefooted Carmelites, Rome.

Very Reverend Father: During the five years of my ministry at Notre-Dame, Paris, notwithstanding the open attacks and secret misrepresentations of which I have been the object, your confidence and esteem have never for a moment failed me. I retain numerous testimonials of this, written by your own hand, and which relate as well to my preaching as to myself. Whatever may occur, I shall keep this in grateful remembrance.

To-day, however, by a sudden shift, the cause of which I do not look for in your heart, but in the intrigues of a party omnipotent at Rome, you find fault with what you have encouraged, blame what you have approved, and demand that I shall make use of such language, or preserve such a silence, as would no longer be the entire and loyal expression of my conscience.

I do not hesitate a moment. With speech falsified by an order from my superior, or mutilated by enforced utterances, I could not again enter the pulpit of Notre-Dame. I express my regrets for this to the intelligent and courageous bishop, who placed me and has maintained me in it against the ill-will of the men of whom I have just been speaking. I express my regrets for it to the imposing audience which there surrounded me with its attention, its sympathies—I had almost said, with its friendship. I should be worthy neither of the audience, nor of the bishop, nor of my conscience, nor of God, if I could consent to play such a part in their presence.

I withdraw at the same time from the convent in which I dwell, and which, in the new circumstances which have befallen me, has become to me a prison of the soul. In acting thus I am not unfaithful to my vows. I have promised monastic obedience—but within the limits of an honest conscience, and of the dignity of my person and ministry. I have promised it under favor of that higher law of justice, the "royal law of liberty," which is, according to the apostle James, the proper law of the Christian.

It was the most untrammelled enjoyment of this holy liberty that I came to seek in the cloister, now more than ten years ago, under the impulse of an enthusiasm pure from all worldly calculation—I dare not add, free from all youthful illusion. If, in return for my sacrifices, I to-day am offered chains, it is not merely my right, it is my duty to reject them.

This is a solemn hour. The Church is passing through one of the most violent crises—one of the darkest and most decisive—of its earthly existence. For the first time in three hundred years, an Œcumenical Council is not only summoned, but declared necessary. These are the expressions of the Holy Father. It is not at such a moment that a preacher of the gospel, were he the least of all, can consent to hold his peace, like the "dumb dogs" of Israel—treacherous guardians, whom the prophet reproaches because they could not bark. *Canes muti, non valentes latrare.*

The saints are never dumb. I am not one of them, but I nevertheless know that I am come of that stock—*filii sanctorum sumus*—and it has ever been my ambition to place my steps, my tears, and, if need were, my blood, in the footprints where they have left theirs.

I lift up, then, before the Holy Father and before the Council, my protest as a Christian and a priest against those doctrines and practices which call themselves Roman, but are not Christian, and which, making encroachments ever bolder and more deadly, tend to change the constitution of the Church, the substance as well as the form of its teaching, and even the spirit of its piety. I protest against the divorce, not less impious than mad, which men are struggling to accomplish between the Church, which is our mother for eternity, and the society of the nineteenth century, whose sons we are for time, and toward which we have also both duties and affections. I protest against that opposition, more radical and frightful yet, which sets itself against human nature, attacked and revolted by these false teachers in its most indestructible and holiest aspirations. I protest above all against the sacrilegious perversion of the Gospel of the Son of God himself, the spirit and the letter of which, alike, are trodden under foot by the Pharisaism of the new law.

It is my most profound conviction, that if France in particular, and the Latin races in general, are delivered over to anarchy, social, moral, and religious, the principal cause of it is to be found—not, certainly, in Catholicism itself—but in the way in which Catholicism has for a long time past been understood and practised.

I appeal to the Council now about to assemble, to seek remedies for our excessive evils, and to apply them alike with energy and gentleness. But if fears which I am loth to share, should come to be realized—if that august assembly should have no more of liberty in its deliberations than it has already in its preparation—if, in one word, it should be robbed of the characteristic essential to an Œcumenical Council—I would cry to God and men to demand another, really assembled in the Holy Spirit, not in the spirit of party—really representing the Church universal, not the silence of some and the constraint of others. "For the hurt of the daughter of my people am I hurt. I am black. Astonishment hath taken hold on me. Is there no balm in Gilead—is there no physician there? Why then is not the health of the daughter of my people recovered?"—*Jeremiah*, viii. 21, 22.

And, finally, I appeal to Thy tribunal, O Lord Jesus! *Ad tuum, Domine Jesu, tribunal appello.* It is in Thy presence that I write these lines; it is at Thy feet, after having prayed much, pondered much, suffered much, and waited long—it is at Thy feet that I subscribe them. I have this confidence concerning them, that, however men may condemn them upon earth, Thou wilt approve them in heaven. Living or dying, this is enough for me.

BROTHER HYACINTHE,
Superior of the Barefooted Carmelites of Paris, Second Definitor of the Order in the Province of Avignon.

Paris: Passy, September 20, 1869.

This thrilling protest was promptly followed by another letter from the General at Rome, threatening him, if he did not return to his convent in ten days, with a privation of all his dignities in the order of Carmelites; with the major excommunication, which, by the way, he had *ipso facto* incurred on quitting the convent without the authority of his superiors; and with the note of infamy, which is the severest penalty, we believe, that the Church has the power to inflict upon non-resident offenders. This letter ran as follows:

ROME, Sept. 26.

REVEREND FATHER: Your letter of the 20th only reached me yesterday. You will easily imagine how deeply it afflicted me, and with what bitterness it filled my soul. I was far from expecting you to fall to such a depth. Therefore my heart bleeds with grief, and is filled with an immense pity for you, and I raise my humble supplications to the God of all Mercies that he may enlighten you, pardon you, and lead you back from that deplorable and fatal path on which you have entered. It is very true, my reverend father, that during the last five years, in spite of my personal opinions, which are in general contrary to yours on many religious questions, as I have more than once expressed to you—in spite of the counsels I have given to you on several occasions relative to your preachings, and to which, excepting in the case of your Lent sermons at Rome, you paid but little attention, so long as you did not openly depart from the limits imposed by Christian prudence on a priest, and especially on a monk, I always manifested toward you sentiments of esteem and friendship, and encouraged you in your preachings. But if that is true, so also is it that from the moment in which I perceived that you were beginning to go beyond those limits, I was forced to begin on my side to express to you my fears, and to mark to you my dissatisfaction. You must remember, my reverend father, that I did so especially last year about the month of October, when passing through France, relative to a letter addressed by you to a Club in Paris. I then explained to you what annoyance that writing had caused me. Your letters published in Italy were also very painful to me, and also drew on you from me observations and reproaches when you last visited Rome. Lastly, your presence and speech at the *Ligue de la Paix* filled up the measure of my apprehensions and my grief, and forced me to write to you the letter of the 22d of July last, by which I formally ordered you in future not to print any letter or speech, to speak in public elsewhere than in the churches, to be present in the Chambers, or to take part in the *Ligue de la Paix* or any other meetings the object of which was not exclusively Catholic and religious. My prohibition, as you see, did not in the least refer to your sermons in the pulpit. On the contrary, I desired you in future to devote solely and entirely your talents and your eloquence to teachings in the Church. Consequently it was with painful surprise that I read in your letter that "you could not reascend the pulpit at Notre-Dame with language perverted by dictation or mutilated by reticence." You must be aware, reverend father, that I have never forbidden you to preach, that I have never given you any order or imposed any restriction on your teachings. I only took the liberty of giving to you some counsels, and of addressing to you some observations, especially on the subject of your last lectures, as in my quality of Superior it was my right and my duty to do. You were, consequently, as free to continue your preachings at Paris or elsewhere as in preceding years, before my letter of 22d July last, and if you have resolved not to reappear in the pulpit of Notre-Dame de Paris, it is voluntary and of your own free will, and not by virtue of measures adopted by me toward you. Your letter of the 20th announces to me that you are about to leave your monastery in Paris. I learn, indeed, by the journals and by private letters that you have cast off your gown without any ecclesiastical authorization. If the fact is unfortunately true, I would remark to you, my reverend father, that the monk who quits his monastery and the dress of his Order without the regular permission from the competent authority, is considered as a real apostate, and is consequently liable to the canonical penalties mentioned in Cap. *Periculoso*. The punishment is, as you are aware, the greater excommunication, *latæ sententiæ;* and, according to our rules, confirmed by the Holy See, part iii., chap. xxxv., No. 12, those who leave the community without authorization incur the greater excommunication *ipso facto* and the note of infamy. *Qui a congregatione recedunt præter apostasiam, ipso facto excommunicationem et infamiæ notam incurrunt.* As your Superior, and in accordance with the prescriptions of the Apostolic decrees, which order me to employ even censure to bring you back to the bosom of the Order you have so deplorably abandoned, I am under the necessity of calling on you to return to the monastery in Paris which you have quitted within ten days from the date of the present letter; observing to you that if you do not obey this order within the time stated, you will be deprived canonically of all the charges you hold in the Order of Barefooted Carmelite Monks, and will remain under the censure established by the common law and by our rules. May you, my reverend father, listen to our voice and to the cry of your conscience; may you promptly and seriously descend within yourself, see the depth of your fall, and by a heroic resolution manfully recover yourself, repair the great scandal you have caused, and by that means console the Church, your mother, you have so much afflicted. That is the most sincere and ardent desire of my heart; it is also that which your afflicted friends, and myself, your father, ask with all the fervor of our souls of God Almighty—of God, so full of mercy and goodness.

BROTHER DOMINIQUE,
of St. Joseph.

Of the same date with the preceding letter from the General of the Carmelites is the following letter addressed to Father Hyacinthe by Dupanloup, Bishop of Orleans, his friend and the friend of his friends in France:

"ORLEANS, Sept. 25, 1869.

"MY DEAR COLLEAGUE: The very moment I learnt from Paris what you were upon the point of doing, I endeavored, as you know, to save you at all costs from what could not but be for you a great fault and a great misfortune, as well as a profound sorrow for the Church; that very moment, at night, I sent your old schoolfellow and friend to stop you if possible. But it was too late; the scandal had been consummated, and henceforth you can measure by the grief of all the friends of the Church, and the joy of all her enemies, the evil you have done. I can only pray to God now, and implore you to stop upon the brink you have reached, which leads to abysses the troubled eye of your soul has not seen. You have suffered—I know it; but allow me to say it, Father Lacordaire and Father Ravignan suffered, I know, more than you, and they rose higher in patience and strength, through love of the Church and Jesus Christ. How was it you did not feel the wrong you were doing the Church, your mother, by these accusations, and the wrong you are doing Jesus Christ by placing yourself as you do alone before Him in contempt of His Church? But I would fain hope, and I do hope, that it will only be a momentary aberration. Return among us; after causing the Catholic world this sorrow, give it a great consolation and a great example. Go and throw yourself at the feet of the Holy Father. His arms will be open to you, and in clasping you to his paternal heart he will restore to you the peace of your conscience and the honor of your life. Accept from him who was your Bishop, and who will never cease to love you, this testimony and these counsels of a true and religious affection.

"FELIX, BISHOP OF ORLEANS."

To this letter Father Hyacinthe replied as follows:

"MONSEIGNEUR: I am much affected by the sentiment which has dictated the letter you have done me the honor to write, and I am very grateful for the prayers which you make on my behalf; but I can accept neither the reproaches nor the counsels which you address to me. That which you call the commission of a great fault, I regard as the fulfilment of a grand duty. Accept, Monseigneur, the most respectful sentiments, with which I remain, in Jesus Christ and in His Church, your very humble and obedient servant,

"FRÈRE HYACINTHE.

"*Paris*, Sept. 26, 1869."

The ten days' limit prescribed for his return to the convent expired on the 9th of October. On that day Father Hyacinthe embarked on board the steamer Pereire for New York.

On the 18th of that month the heads of the Order held a meeting at Rome, and pronounced the following sentence upon their insubordinate brother:

"The term fixed by the Rev. Father, the General in Chief of the Barefooted Carmelites, for Father Hyacinthe, of the Immaculate Conception, provincial definer, Superior of the House in Paris, to return to said convent, having expired—having examined the papers and authentic proofs that said Father Hyacinthe has not yet returned to his convent, the superior authority of the Order, by decree dated October 18, 1869, has deposed Father Hyacinthe of the Immaculate Conception from all the charges with which he was invested by the Order, declaring him besides attainted by his apostasy, and under the major excommunication, as well as all other censures and ecclesiastical penalties denounced by the common law and by the Constitution of the Order against apostates."

Such is an imperfect outline of the processes by which one of the most gifted and meritorious officers of the Latin Church has been provoked to revolt against his ecclesiastical superiors, and deliberately incur the severest penalties which are reserved for such insubordination. To us it seems incredible that any of the acts imputed to him by his enemies should have exposed him to the censure, still less to the persecutions, of any society of professing Christians. Let us recapitulate them:

1. In one of his discourses he treated the Revolution of 1789 as a political and social necessity.

2. In another he denounced Pharisaism as in the Church, as Jesus Christ had done before him.

3. In defending himself from an aspersion upon his charity toward persons having different religious views from his, he intimated that there were Catholics who mourned the disappearance of the Inquisition and the Dragonnades, a statement fully confirmed by the Encyclical letter of 1864.

4. In a private note to a friend, he stated that the Catholics who were trying to identify the fortunes of the Church with those of a disreputable woman who had been just expelled from the throne of Spain, were dragging the Church through blood and mire.

5. He quoted a letter written by the Pope in 1848 to the Emperor of Austria, which favored Italian unity.

6. He proclaimed that Jews and Protestants, as well as Catholics, came within the pale of an enlightened Christian charity.

7. He always preached a religion in sympathy with the progressive tendencies of modern civilization.

8. Finally, he persisted in being the friend of the Archbishop of Paris, and refused to place himself under the direction of any bishop of another diocese.

We make no account of his abandoning his convent and disobeying the order of his General to return, for those acts were the logical consequences of the prior offences, if the Church will persist in regarding as offences the acts which ultimated in the interdict from Rome of July 22. There is no doubt that he violated the laws of his Church in quitting his convent without permission, and that he exposed himself to the penalties which have been visited upon him by the executive officers of his Order. His Church provides a mode of procedure for the secularization of priests desiring to renounce their monastic vows, but Father Hyacinthe did not choose to avail himself of it. He declined to recognize an authority which, as he thought, had been abused in his person, which was degrading the priesthood, corrupting the hierarchy, and sapping the vital forces of the Church. He thought it his duty to stand to the faith he had conscientiously espoused, and which he believed Evangelical, rather than succumb to what he regarded as organized error and pharisaical oppression. It was the duty of some one to challenge the wolf which in sheep's clothing was devouring the faithful. He naturally enough concluded that there was no fitter person than himself to do it. Nor in this case was he mistaken. His piety; his well-known devotion to the Church; his eminent gifts of speech, which promised him every possible distinction that Rome can confer, and which therefore protect his motives from degrading suspicions, all seemed to conspire to make his the voice that should cry "in the wilderness, to prepare the way of the Lord and make his paths straight."

Since Luther, there has been no such signal revolt against the authority of the Romish Hierarchy. Fenelon professed doctrines which Louis XIV. compelled the Pope and his Cardinals to condemn. Though Fenelon defended his *Maximes* up to the last hour of the deliberations at Rome with unrelenting earnestness, the moment Rome spoke, though by a bare majority of the Cardinals, he succumbed and publicly denounced his book from the pulpit of his own cathedral. Lammenais revolted against the abuses of the Papal Government, but unhappily his religion had the Church, not the Bible, for its base, and he wandered away into rationalism and unbelief.

Lacordaire hovered all his life on the borders of the Church, forever preaching a broader Christianity than was tolerated at Rome, always tormented with the restraints imposed upon his tongue and conscience by his ecclesiastical Superior, and always in a state of mental and moral insubordination to the Papal hierarchy. But Lacordaire had not the physical health nor animal force necessary to brave the consequences of an open revolt. He was constitutionally timid; his monastic life had gradually incapacitated him for comprehending the vast resources for such a contest, which the living world around him, with the Divine blessing, would have supplied, and he succumbed to the rigors of ecclesiastical discipline and to disease, induced, no doubt, by his inability to live the complete life for which he had been created. He fell a prey to a sort of dry-rot, which fastens, sooner or later, upon all who commit their consciences to the keeping of fellow-sinners, who seek to escape sin by fleeing from temptation rather than by fighting and overcoming it, and who fancy that the best way of keeping the commandments is to spend all one's time in reciting them.

The eloquent Bishop of Orleans is also one of these representative men, too earnest and enlightened a Christian to accept the perverse follies of the Syllabus; but instead of taking his stand against it, he set himself to work, as soon as it appeared, to prove that it meant something very different from what it said, and that, instead of being in conflict, it was in harmony with the doctrines proclaimed at Malines. This disingenuous plea for the Papal Government was attributed by his partisans to his worthy desire to avoid dissensions in the Church. He preferred to see it a prey to error rather than to schism—to surrender the shepherd's crook to the wolf than to have the flock scattered by learning their peril.

The consequence is that this gifted and admirable prelate, instead of remaining what his genius designed him to be, a controlling power in the Church of Christ, has by degrees parted with his birthright, and is now the reluctant but unresisting instrument of a devastating Ultramontanism. Like Lammenais and Lacordaire and Fenelon, he has not proved equal to his opportunities. Like them, "he rejected the commandments of God that he might keep the traditions of the elders." Like them, too, he has always been toiling for reforms, but accomplishing none, because he had more faith in the Church than in Providence. "He made flesh his arm."

It was not so with Luther. Thus far it has not been so with Father Hyacinthe. Will he, too, fall by the way, or is he to share the reward reserved for those who endure unto the end?

—— Father Hyacinthe, it is believed, has thus far followed his convictions faithfully. When his conscience told him distinctly that Roman theology was not infallible theology, he refused to accept it as such; when his conscience told him that the temporal power of the Pope was maintained at the expense of his legitimate spiritual influence, that it was an element of weakness rather than of strength to the Church of Christ, he refused any longer to countenance or defend it. When he found pontifical allocutions and the canons of councils usurping the place and authority of the Bible in the Church, he chose to stay with the Bible rather than go with its papal substitute. In this firm faith in God and the right, in this bold rejection of all compromises with the priesthood of error, he alone of all the illustrious reformers of Catholicism since Luther holds an apostolic attitude. Will he maintain it?

To surrender deliberately and voluntarily the most cherished affections of one's heart is a fearful trial for any man. Few are equal to it. With Father Hyacinthe the Church of Rome had represented all that was most pure and lovely on earth. His life had been spent in decorating it with imaginary charms. To his youthful vision it was the New Jerusalem coming down from God out of heaven, with walls of jasper, gates of pearl, and streets of gold. He finally awoke from his illusion, and found that temptation and sin reap their harvests at Rome as regularly as elsewhere, and that "God alone is great."

Father Hyacinthe has no quarrel with the Catholic Church, but with its abuses. He wisely thinks that its maladies, like those of the human system, are to be cured from within and not from without; that the remedy must be applied to the heart, not to the skin. He does not, therefore, intend to abandon his Church, but to labor for it. He wisely declines to take refuge in any other religious organization, for he knows that the vices of which he complains in his Church belong to the universal human heart, and in one shape or another are likely to present themselves in all denominations. He has, therefore, given the world to understand that what capacities of usefulness remain to him, will be consecrated to the purification and edification of the Church in which he was reared, and which he thinks has enjoyed, and continues to enjoy, at least as much of God's favor as any other.

Naturalists tell us that the sparrow abandons eggs which she discovers have been handled, and refuses to give life to offspring which she feels herself too weak to protect. The eagle, on the other hand, confident in her strength, fights for her offspring; and if one is ravished from her nest, she cherishes the rest of her brood only the more tenderly. The *soi-disant* liberal Catholics of Europe since Luther, like the sparrow, take counsel of their weakness, and as reformers have begotten nothing; have abandoned their convictions, as it were, in the egg. On the other hand, Father Hyacinthe, like the eagle, confiding in that sort of strength which renders the feeblest arm invincible, is ready to fight in defence of his convictions, and, with the blessing of God, proposes to do what he can to deliver the Church from its enemies, and open its doors again, as in the beginning, to all who make the love of God and their neighbors the rule of their lives. Will he, in shooting the arrow of God's deliverance, "smite the ground five or six times," or like the King Joash, for want of faith, will he smite only three times, and stop?

Note by the Editor.—Since the foregoing was written, the Bishop of Orleans has thrown some doubt over the entire justice of placing him in the category of reformers who accomplish nothing, by a remarkable letter he has just addressed to the clergy of his diocese, in relation to the attempt making to have the infallibility of the Pope proclaimed by the approaching Council, as a dogma of the Church. It bears so directly upon, if it does not owe its existence to the exemplary revolt of Father Hyacinthe, that we have deemed it our duty to lay it before our readers in the Appendix.

The Encyclical of 1864, entitled "*Quanta Cura*," with its accompanying "Syllabus" of propositions denounced and condemned by the authority of the Pope, may be found in Appleton's Annual Cyclopædia for 1864

THE FAMILY.

THE NOTRE-DAME LECTURES.

ADVENT, 1866.

THE FAMILY.

LECTRUE FIRST.
December 2, 1866.

Domestic Society in the General Scheme of Human Society.

My Lord Archbishop and Gentlemen: It is characteristic of the questions of the present day, that they have a tendency to pass out of the domain of ideas into that of facts. Doubtless this has always been the instinct of the truth; but never has that instinct been so potent and so urgent as now. As we come down— or up, if you like it better—into the domain of facts (for I hardly know whether to speak of it as an ascent or as a descent when we pass from speculation to practice)—call it what you please, when we make our entrance into the realm of facts, the idea of modern days, be it true or false, is not limited, in its application, to the individual fact. It spreads out over the social fact

At the beginning of these Conferences, two years ago, I strove to bring to your notice, as the central point of the religious controversy of the hour, the question of the personality of God. It was not the infallibility of the Church, it was not the divinity of Christ, or, at least, it was not the Church, nor Christ, except as these may be considered as the affirmation or negation of the personality of God. That was the theoretical question; it occupied us for a year. But the theoretical question was followed by its practical corollary, and that corollary (which we studied last year) was morality, human or divine; morality, at the same time free and subject, or morality independent of God, and, therefore, fallen—"*independent morality*," a doctrine most weak in a scientific point of view and in the field of logical debate, but most potent in the domain of facts, because it is a radical doctrine, and because it is the only practical means of finally emancipating men's consciences, and of "exorcising," as some one calls it, "the ghost of the absolute."

Such, then, is the practical conclusion of the religious question as it affects the individual. But, as I have said, the affairs of the individual bring us to the affairs of society, and so in our last Conference we were led to remark, as the conclusion from the doctrine of the personality of God, and the doctrine of right and wrong, as founded upon God—the *Sovereignty of God over Society*.

This is the subject to which we come this year, the examination of which I propose to continue from year to year, unless something in outward circumstances or in the progress of my own thoughts (which I wish to preserve as free as your own) should occur to derange this plan, which I propose, but to which I do not bind myself.

This year, I intend to talk to you about the relations

between religion and *domestic society*—the first and most necessary of all forms of human society.

I should have to apologize for recurring, in this pulpit, to a subject which has been already treated here with a superiority and ardor which no one can have forgotten; but *the family* is one of those inexhaustible subjects on which there is always something left to glean, even after the best of harvesters.

I would only notify you, gentlemen, that the work which I mean to undertake is rather that of exposition than of controversy. I will not refute, point by point, everything that has been said against the Christian constitution of the family. I shall do this only as I may be brought to it by the current of my thought or speech. I prefer, in general, to set before you, in its completeness, its simplicity, its grandeur, what the family is when organized according to the Christian conception, under the sovereignty of the Father who is in Heaven and the father who is on the earth. This exposition, of itself—if I am not too far below my task—will be the best of refutations.

At this very moment all eyes are turned toward that centre of the kingdom and visible sovereignty of God upon earth—Rome! If I were undertaking a controversy against those who are talking so bravely every day of how religious questions have lost their power of interesting and exciting the men of our time, I should ask the secret of this grand and solemn expectation, and the reason why so much terror is prevailing alongside of so much hope—why there is so much bitterness and so much love at once. But it is not controversy that I have undertaken. I do not wish to put to the question either men or things. I would only collect my thoughts and compose my heart, before commencing, in that sense of responsibility which weighs upon the preacher of the gospel at this hour. And I would stay myself, by this thought and this heart, on that everlasting throne which is all the more immovable by so much as it is the more assailed, and all the nearer to its triumph by so much as it seems nearer its ruin.

My lord archbishop, there come to my mind the simple and noble words which you once said to me: "The Episcopacy is a chain which winds round the globe." That which I now salute, in your own beloved and honored person, is the whole episcopate—it is its chief, the bishop of bishops, and the father of fathers. Therefore it was, that, just now, as I bowed my head for that benediction which is no vain ceremony (there are no vain ceremonies in God's church)—the benediction of light, wisdom, and power—I was thrilled with a twofold reverence and tenderness; first because it is from yourself, my lord, and because, at the same time, it is from him.

PART FIRST.—*The Bonds of Society.*

I approach then, gentlemen, the religious side of social questions. But before treating of any particular form of society, I must define the meaning of *society* in general. It is not precisely the family, neither is it the nation, it is not even the church—it is simply society! I find myself in the presence of a great idea; one of those ideas which carry the greatest power and fascination in this century, and, since I belong in this century myself, I must needs add, one of those ideas which have been the passion of my youth, and which are to be the passion of my riper years. It is the idea of humanity, the fellowship of all men with all men, of all nations with all nations, of mankind with itself. I salute, then, universal society, I salute humanity—not only in my own behalf, but in behalf of every one of you.

[The speaker, considering this natural and universal society of the human race, to which every man belongs by the law of his existence, and apart from any consent or refusal of his will, first propounds this question: "What is it which thus unites man to his kind?" His answer to this question is briefly summed up as follows:]

It is a triple bond—a physical bond, an intellectual bond, and a moral bond—blood, reason, virtue.

1st. Individual men are joined together in a natural and universal society by the bond of a common origin—blood.

Human personality has its seat in the soul, but its base in the body; and in the view of science, as well as of revelation, "the life is in the blood."*

If we believed in the materialistic school, the blood, in man, would be a matter of purely physical transmission, as in the brute, in whose exalted image they are disposed to make us, since they will no longer allow that we are the image of God. But it is not so: there is a certain moral quality in the blood of man, and when it has passed into our veins from two hearts joined together in love, it has created the bonds of society.

It has created the *family*, that holy thing unknown to the inferior races.

It has created the *country*, the nation—in the normal constitution of which it fulfils so great a part.

And above the family and the country, including both the one and the other, as the genus contains the species, blood has created *humanity;* for in spite of that science which calls itself humanitarian and positive, but is nei-

---
* Leviticus, xvii. 14.

ther, it is by a common blood that humanity comes to be one single race. "God hath made of one blood all nations of men, to dwell on all the face of the earth."*

2. Individual men are joined together in natural and universal society by the bond of common *reason*.

If there is a physical bond between all men, there is also a metaphysical one. If it is one and the same blood of Adam that courses in the veins of our body, so it is one and the same ray of light, one and the same reason that irradiates our soul. Doubtless reason is an individual matter, as regards our possession of it: it is individual as regards the good or bad use which we make of it; but it is impersonal in the object it reveals to us—truth—and in the laws it imposes on us. Now, this impersonal reason, the reflection in each individual intellect of God's own word, is invariable. "Truth this side of the Pyrenees, error the other side," said Pascal. Doubtless there are varying forms of the one invariable truth, which change on one side of the mountains or the other. There are garments of truth that grow old and are laid aside, and must be renewed with the generations and the ages. But the body of the truth remains always the same, ever fresh and pure and beautiful. Invariable, the reason which enlightens me is also universal. Your axiom is my axiom, my law your law. I know, in advance of all experience, that man, wherever I may meet him, will have the same first principles as myself, because he is illumined with the same light: "The Word was the true Light, which lighteth every man that cometh into the world."† By reason, then, as well as by blood, there exists a natural and universal fellowship which we call humanity.

3. Individual men, finally, are united in a natural and

---

* Acts, xvii. 26   † John, i. 9.

universal fellowship by the bond of one and the same *virtue*.

No little reproach has been cast upon Christianity for practising personal virtue, and neglecting social virtue—of seeking the salvation of individuals, and not concerning itself with the salvation of humanity. It is true, we are the party of the personal idea, of individual virtue, of individual salvation. We claim that man is responsible before everything, for good or for evil, to his own conscience. We say that he ought to do the good and shun the evil, apart from the advantage which will accrue from it to humanity. "Seek first the kingdom of God, the personal God, and His righteousness;" and then the good of the country, the good of the human race, "will be added unto you;" yes, *added,* as a clear gratuity, but it is a gift which does not come in any other way, and which springs necessarily from the personal idea itself.

What is it, in fact, that is necessary in order that I may practise individual virtue and achieve my individual salvation? I must obey two great commandments—justice and love. Now these two laws, which maintain the distinction of persons, create at the same time between them a tie more near and sacred than those of reason and blood. In fact, what is justice, if not a mutual care and fulfilment, among men, of their rights and duties? What is love, if it is not the gift of more than another's due, the claiming of less than one's own right; a gift not only outward but inward; a gift from the very person itself; the gift of each to all; the love of the human race?

Men, then, are bound to men by a threefold cord that cannot be broken—blood, reason, virtue.

The social state is not, then, a state of degeneracy, as

Rousseau had dreamed.... and so above the society of home, above civil society, above religious society, there is universal society—the human race.

And here, for one moment, on these heights I pause. It is good for us to be here. O sublime, O radiant heights! Heathen antiquity had caught a glimpse of you in its dawning twilight; but it was for Christianity alone to reveal you, and if the philosophy of this age has followed in her train, it may try in vain to banish her and cast her down from thence. It can only sit at her feet as her disciple.

One glance more, Gentlemen, at these heights, before we leave them. These are true Christian heights—these summits to which the idea of humanity has attained—Christian in the original light which lightens them: "he hath made of one blood all nations," to populate this orb of earth—Christian in the last light on which they look, and which is none other than God himself.

"Father," said the true Redeemer of the human race, and, therefore, its sole effectual organizer, the Lord Jesus Christ, "Father, grant that they may be one, even as we are one."* This is our title to the possession of these mountain heights:—Adam, at the beginning, with the fountain-head of his blood; God at the end, with the splendor of his glory; and in the midst humanity. "All ye are brethren," said Christ, "for one is your Father, which is in heaven."†

O that with one bound I might rise to loftier summits still! Is there not, far away in those higher regions, whither some of the men of this generation refuse to look—is there not a reasonable nature, a nature wholly one, wholly indivisible, and yet manifold in per-

---

* John, xvii. 22.   † Matthew, xxiii. 8, 9.

sonality, fellowship of God with God, of Father with Son, of Father and Son with Holy Spirit? O holy commonwealth of eternity, mysterious state wherein the three Persons dwell in equal majesty, in complete distinctness, in perfect unity! O God! Thou art the prototype of men, and therefore it is that Thou hast made us at the same time one in our nature and manifold in our persons; profoundly distinct and yet profoundly one; by nature free, by nature equal; obedient to no commands but such as have their origin in Thee, and venerating, under these borrowed earthly majesties of the Family, the State, and the Church, naught but that sole and supreme majesty which is in Thee.

PART SECOND.—*The Forms of Society.*

[Having considered human society in its general aspects, and the bonds by which men are joined together in a natural and universal solidarity, the speaker proceeds to examine the principal forms which society assumes, which are three in number: the *family*, or domestic society; the *nation*, or civil society; the *church*, or religious society.]

1. The *Family*.

This is the first form of society in order of time, and I might almost say—for in one sense it is true—in order of importance. Domestic society, the natural fellowship of man with man, is at the root of the two other forms of society, which could not exist without this, and for which, for a long time at least, it was a substitute.

Man, on coming into the world, is confronted by two most mysterious and mighty laws—the law of the sexes and the law of death; the one divides him in his own nature, the other limits him in his brief career. See, now, how man, in the progress of the sublime and sacred drama of the family, shall get the victory over this twofold enemy.

In the married life, man finds in his companion that complement of himself—that better part of his thought and of his love which had been wanting to him. "It is not good for man to be alone;—the twain shall be one flesh."* In the relation of father, he outlives himself in the offspring of his body and his heart, in the heir of his blood and his traditions; and through his children he enjoys a sort of earnest of immortality in this world. Thus human life finds itself to be organized in domestic society.

For ages, man knew no other society than this. The father was at once king and priest; civil society and religious society were absorbed in the family. I open humanity's grand book, the Bible: it commences with the history of the family, from the cradles of Eden to the tents of Abraham, Isaac, and Jacob; and of all the pages of human records, this is without controversy the sweetest and most sublime.

Even at the present day, if we listen to the charming tales of travellers, we learn that it is still the family that reigns on the lofty table-lands of Asia, among those vast steppes which have been most fitly called "the hive of nations." When the civilized nations have found themselves, by the very excess of civilization, carried down into incurable decline and barbarism, God sounds toward the desert that hiss of which the prophet speaks;† and forthwith from the depths of those solitudes, behold, there troop forth upon their fiery steeds young populations, strong and proud, grown lusty with the milk of their wild herds, and

---

* Genesis, ii. 18, 24. † Isaiah, vii. 18.

bearing behind them, on the croups of their horses, their faithful families, their roving homes. Whatever their names—Huns, Tartars, or Mongolians—it matters not. They are coming to bask in that immortal sunlight of Christianity which awaits them, and to create new civilizations on the ruined fragments of the old. Now these people, as travellers who have visited them attest, have no civil organization, and only a rude sort of religion: but they have the family; and far away in those providential climes, the family preserves a stock, full of youthful vigor and of the promise of the future.

2. The *Nation*.

The second form of society, not natural, but artificial, since it is man's own creation, is civil society.

When families become multiplied, there arise various and opposing interests, manifold and conflicting rights. As in the case of the herdsmen of Abraham and Lot, when there was a strife between them,* it becomes necessary to separate on the face of the earth, or else to establish a common and permanent arbitration. Whatever may have been the historical origin of civil society—an origin which must have varied more or less with circumstances of place and time—this is the philosophical notion of them, and the idea which constitutes and characterizes them: it is an understanding among the heads of families, representing the domestic societies over which they preside, to establish a common government, under some form or other—a government which is doubtless their own creation, but which is consecrated by the fact that God is the father of all order and all power. The object of this government is not to suppress or to create individual or family rights, but to regulate the *manner* of exercising all rights; to extend

* Genesis, xiii.

over them the protection of justice, and if necessary, the protection of the sword, against all attack, whether from without or from within.

3. The *Church.*

When the human race had attained that culminating point of the ages which St. Paul has called "*the fulness of time,*"* religious society in its perfect form was organized.

Domestic among the patriarchs, *national* among the Jews, the Church was extended over the whole human race by Christ, and became *Catholic.* By *right* all nations belong to this Church; and it is our right to hope that after many struggles, after centuries, perhaps, the *fact* will fully correspond to the *right.* "For there is neither Jew nor Gentile," says St. Paul, "neither Greek nor Barbarian, neither bond nor free; but ye are all one in Christ Jesus."†

Such are the three principal forms of human society.

PART THIRD.—*Relative Importance of Domestic Society.*

[Under this third head, in concluding the Lecture, the speaker considered domestic society in its relation to civil and religious society. He insisted especially upon this subject as one of immediate importance at the present time.

1. As respects civil and political society, what is the great question of the day? I hesitate to pronounce in this pulpit a word exposed to so many perils and perversions; but I must deal sincerely with language as well as with ideas, and I cannot but reply, Democracy. The great question of the time which affects all noble minds and generous hearts, is democracy, that is, in the

---

* Galatians, iv. 4; Ephesians, i. 10.   † Romans, x. 12; Galatians, iii. 28.

honest, liberal, legitimate meaning of the word, the extension of civil and political liberties, the fullest participation of all citizens in the management of public affairs, and, as far as possible in this poor land and this unhappy planet, the government of the country by the country. This is the worthy meaning of the word democracy. Now I ask myself, why does democracy remain so often a dream that will not be realized—why? It is because men do not remember to establish it on the foundation of the family.

There are two formidable shoals, on the right and the left, which must be avoided if we would settle the constitution of liberty in order, and of order in liberty. These two shoals are individualism and centralization.

Individualism—it is a good thing and a holy! It is the origin of personality—that which makes me free, which makes me worthy and noble, if I will but show myself a man. Centralization—this, too, is a good thing—a necessary thing, always, because it is the creator and conserver of nations; but especially necessary in our grand modern unities, which need, in order to save them from dissolution, a mighty central power. But there is an excess of individualism, which we call anarchy, and there is an excess of centralization, which we call despotism. And whenever the constitution of liberty does not rest upon the family, it goes driving upon anarchy, and then, falling back from Charybdis upon Scylla, it is dashed to pieces against despotism. Yes, you shall have individualism—a fine sight, indeed! a nation ground to atoms, without cohesion, without settled authority, without the family; nothing but individuals unattached, the fine dust of a social desert; incapable, henceforth, of being built into anything; capable only of being caught up and whirled aloft in some whirlwind, to be let fall, anon, in pools of mire, or in clots of gore. Such is anarchy.

And when society, frightened at such a work as this, shrinks backward, it comes upon absolute centralization —whether it be vested in the hands of one man or of many; whether it be a republic or a monarchy—that, after all, is of little consequence—it is only a question of form and words; in either case, society will inevitably come out, if it proceeds in this direction, on the absorption of all the living forces of a nation in one abnormal centre, the establishment of the most terrible despotism our race has known! These are the two shoals!

Show me families worthy the name—true domestic commonwealths, father and mother, king and minister, enthroned together in the midst of the circle of their children, talking to them of ancestors, of honor, of duty, and being hearkened to—commanding in respect, and still more in love, and being obeyed; show me a father, king in his own house, and so much the more free in the world without, as he is authoritative in the world within; show me homes like these, and I will show you republics! The genuine free citizen is the father, respected and obeyed at home. It is out of such sturdy materials as this that lasting social order can be built.

2. In *religious* society, what is the pending question which is now disturbing and dividing us? It is the question how best to repress the two most terrible scourges of our time—skepticism and immorality. What can we do in France and in the greater part of Europe? what can we do in the nineteenth century—I do not say to refute and confound theoretically, but practically and efficiently to repress these two enemies of God and man—skepticism and immorality?

There are two schools of opinion amongst us Catholics. One, very liberal, comes forward and says: "No compulsion! absolute liberty! The Church is mighty, because it is truth and love. Let it speak and act, let it teach and suffer, let it pour forth the sweet savor of its prayers toward heaven and the sweet savor of its sacraments toward the earth, and it will triumph without the aid of any secular arm!" This school, as I was saying, is very liberal; but when it pushes things to these extremes, it becomes chimerical.

The other school—whose language and attitude, I am sorry to say, too often repel those who feel as I do, but which nevertheless plants itself on great truths—tells us: "Truth, charity, these are all very well, but you are in a fallen world. Man is evil through the inheritance of original sin. In the faculties of the individual, and even in the forces of society that are engrafted on the individual man, there is a chronic rebellion against the reign of truth, justice, and charity. Alongside the force of moral suasion we need a force of coercion—we need the sword; and as the hand of the Church cannot bear the sword, it must needs lean upon the secular arm!"

Such are these two schools, in the plainness of their language, and the inmost depth of their thoughts. Each of them has a certain share of truth, and each its share of error.

[Father Hyacinthe proceeds to demonstrate with the second of these schools the abiding consequences of original sin in the man and in humanity, and concludes upon the necessity of severe discipline, and of a power of education and coercion to struggle effectively against these rebellions of the instinct of evil.

Then he remarks, with the former, that through the combination of a multitude of facts and laws, which have forever outgrown the control of man, and which would seem to have been arranged by a providential plan, the modern conscience in the sphere of religion has been emancipated from the tutelage of civil authority.

In the lands and ages when such a state of things prevails in the conscience and in society, what is to be the secular arm of the Church? What power shall wield the coercive force which henceforth the State is neither willing nor able to exercise? It is to be the authority of the parent.]

In every household strongly, Christianly organized, the father is, in some sense, the secular arm of Christianity. He exercises the educational and restraining power. For he believes not only, like the free-thinker, in the right of advising his child, but in the duty of enforcing morality, and since morality is inseparable from religion, in the duty of enforcing religion. He it is, the father of the family, who having had the power of bequeathing to his son his blood, and with his blood the traditions of his family, has also the power of bequeathing to him the inheritance of his soul, and of constituting him a believer like himself. It is on him that the duty devolves of putting out of the way skeptical or immoral books; of excluding from the family corrupting conversations; of moulding by precept, and, when necessary, by punishment, the young barbarian, the little savage bequeathed to him by original sin, who can become a civilized being and a Christian, only by undergoing this troublous baptism.

The whole world, at this moment, is anxiously questioning the future. The old Europe is falling to pieces. What is it that shall constitute the new? I answer, The Family.

Surely, in a country like this, that has been a warlike country from the days of Clovis down, and which never can be otherwise, I cannot at this hour disregard the importance of armies. And albeit the principal force of armies, however men may forget it, is a moral and spiritual force—the soldier's patriotism, his bravery, discipline, devotion, everything which goes to make the hero; yet I am far from denying the might of modern inventions applied to war—and, nevertheless, I say that the ultimate future of the world does not belong to armies! The lasting, acceptable, fruitful victories are not those of the needle-gun and the rifled cannon! The future of Europe and the world belongs to those nations which best learn to practise the principles of right, the nations least infested with sophists and harlots, and most enriched with numerous, industrious, and Christian families.

LECTURE SECOND.

December 9, 1866.

CONJUGAL SOCIETY THE FOUNDATION OF DOMESTIC SOCIETY.

Gentlemen: Having to speak this year on *domestic society*, we have enlarged our scope and included the whole scheme of human society. The family has appeared to us under a double aspect. First, in its general and primitive sense, this word has revealed to us the tie of blood which unites all mankind: in this view, the *family* is nothing less than the universal form of human society. According to the Catholic doctrine, in fact, human society, the great total of humanity, constitutes one family of brethren, having a Father in heaven, even God, and a father on earth, the man, Adam. Then, restricting this appellation of family to that group of human beings which is properly so called, that sacred group living under the same roof, sitting at the same table, receiving light and warmth at the same fireside, we said: "The family, in this second point of view, is one of the three forms in which mankind is organized in this world—domestic society, civil society, and religious society. And it is in the family, in domestic society, that at all times, and especially in our own times, the solution of the great questions of civil and religious society is contained."

Such is a brief abstract of our last lecture.

The subject to which we come to-day, is the first element of domestic society, in other words, conjugal society.

Domestic society is the basis of the human race, but it is itself based on conjugal society. And because conjugal society is not only an idea, one of the grandest of the thoughts of God, but a fact, one of the grandest facts of humanity, we will examine it in the order of time and in the light of the two great acts which make and divide the centuries—the act of creation and the act of redemption. Conjugal society, then, in the light of *creation*, and of *redemption*, as related to the Creator and to the Renewer, is the subject which is to engage our attention.

It is a great, a difficult, a delicate subject, I know; I do not approach it without fear; but I am to speak in your presence, Gentlemen, and I count in advance upon the inspiration that is to come to me from you. And then, if I must needs tell all my thoughts, I am to speak in the solemnity of the Immaculate Conception of the Virgin Mary; under the light of that dogma, the foundations of which are as old as Christianity itself, but its formula young as our own generation. Thence I await that pure and steadfast light which shall give me the wisdom and the courage to speak with freedom, and at the same time with reserve.

PART FIRST.—*Conjugal Society in the Light of Creation, or as related to God the Creator.*

1st. [Father Hyacinthe begins by seeking in the *law of sex* the first principles of conjugal society.]

God, we are told in the book of Genesis, "created man in his own image."* And then follows this astounding expression, "male and female created he them."†

"In the likeness of God!" But for my part I see in

---

* Genesis, i. 27. † Ibid.

this, at first glance, only the likeness of an inferior life; for this mysterious law of sex does not, after all, belong exclusively to humanity; it reigns throughout animated nature in its whole extent; it reigns there, but does not create the family. In the physical system, in which I shall first consider it—since, as St. Paul says, "that is first which is natural, and afterward that which is spiritual"*—in the physical system, even among men, this law is powerless to create conjugal society in its grandeur and tenderness, in its purity and dignity. Its legitimate and necessary object is the reproduction of the individual, the propagation of the species. But look closely! In this point of view the two partners, in relation to each other, are two *means* of parentage, they are not two *ends*. Now the requirement of the law of personal life—the dignity of a human being—is this: that in relation to his fellow-beings he should be an end, and not a means—that he should be esteemed, desired, loved, for his own sake.

Ah! do you know, Gentlemen, do you know why, in every land and every age, the harlot has been the object of such profound contempt? It is because she is a human being who has forgotten her human dignity; it is because she has scorned, outraged in herself the grand majesty of the human person; and because, discrowned of the glory of being an end, she has consented to the shame of being a means, the toy of caprice and the instrument of lust! For that cause there has fallen upon her a mantle of shame, a garment of ignominy which can never be removed.

Suffer me now to say, that if the Christian woman were nothing but a means of the propagation of mankind

---

* 1 Corinthians, xv. 46.

—if she were only a mother, not a wife, she would be a right noble instrument, an instrument consecrated to parentage, but, after all, nothing but the means to an end. That must not be! That might do for heathens, who saw in woman nothing but a necessary evil of the state! And this is what the boasted marriage of Greece and Rome amounted to, a marriage which, in the better days, was chaste indeed, but never noble and holy. The woman was loved for her children's sake, never for her own.

[Father Hyacinthe shows then how the *law of sex*, brought into relation with the moral system, and transformed into a *law of souls*, is the starting-point of conjugal society.]

Love! this is the word which we must have courage to pronounce, if we would express the essence of the conjugal relation, its inmost principle and law. I know well that this word is exposed to the sneers of skepticism, which knows no greater chimera—next to God—than love. I know, too—O wretched, miserable fact!—that it wakens involuntarily in the mind the recollection of numberless abuses and unequalled desecrations. But what matter the abuses! What matters the shame of the sinner! Thank God, my heart has remained pure, my reason has continued sound, and, preacher of the Gospel as I am, teacher of the understanding and heart of man, it is my right, my duty, to speak of love. Yes, love. And if our morals are going to ruin, if the basis of the family is undermined, if domestic society leans and totters like a ruined edifice, it is because men have forgotten to put love at the foundation of the house, the love of two beings who love each other in honor, in respect, in holiness.

Let me open my old Bible. I am a Bible man, and I

do not blush to declare it before this generation. I open the book at the first page. It is an unstained page, for sin had not yet existed—a page all filled with love and conjugal society. I have led you, Gentlemen, before now, to this cradle of our race, called Eden; I am going to take you back to it to-day. It is not, believe me, a caprice of my imagination, or a captivation of my heart, but a sober, serious conviction, that therein lie the secrets of humanity. I believe that the final solutions of things have been set by God in their primordial principles. I turn again, as I have said, to Eden: I turn to it again, on that first day of the world, when God founded the marriage state. It is the first day of the world of mankind. There had been other days, ages perhaps, the cycles of geology; but now, at last, the world of human life begins, in all the freshness of its dawn. O how fresh the breezes that breathe over every thing!. how pure and glorious the light that shines upon this paradise of earth, this abiding-place of holy pleasures! Lo, man comes forth the latest born of this long series of beings, which is summed up in himself, and over whom he holds imperial sway! Hail, man, thou king of the creation! Hail, great Adam, father of the human race!

He looks through all the infinite scale of nature, through all the gradations of being; his gaze penetrates their inmost parts, and his speech expresses their qualities, for "he calls them all by their own names."* His language is rich, his mind luminous, but his heart was unawakened; "there was not found an help-meet for him."† I know not whether upon that serene majestic brow of Adam there came the

---

* Genesis, ii. 20. "Appellavit nominibus suis." † Ibid.

shadow of a cloud; or whether, from some inner recess of his heart, unknown even to himself, there was breathed a complaint. I know only that God spake these words in a mystery: "It is not good that the man should be alone."* A strange thing! God, so well-pleased hitherto; God, who had gloried in each of his works, and had said: "It is good."† God, who had gloried in the completed whole, and had said: "Behold it is very good."‡ Now, in the presence of his masterpiece, like an artist who has failed to reproduce his ideal, turns away, and says: "It is not good!—It is not good that man should be alone!"

To the work then, great Artist! For thy image, thy likeness upon earth must not remain unfinished. It is God made visible in the world: endow it with all his beauty and majesty! And the Artist takes up again his brush to retouch the canvas; he seizes his chisel to shape again the marble. Bending over the form of Adam, the Lord pierces his side. Adam had fallen into a sleep—into no common sleep, but into a trance, the first and sublimest of prophetic trances. He was to be not merely passive, but conscious and active, consenting inwardly, in the light of prophecy, to that which was wrought upon him from without. Adam slept in ecstasy, he waked in prophecy; he saw the wound that had been opened in his flesh—this rib that had been separated from next his heart, all warm and pure from contact with that abode of love and innocence—and in that rib the marvellous structure of woman. "God builded the rib into a woman."§ A biblical expression, full of marvels, and full also of instruction—marking the structure on which the master architect had exhausted his art—the visible structure of

* Genesis, ii. 18. † Ib. i. 10. ‡ Ib. i. 31. § Ib. ii. 22 (margin).

that body in which shines the highest beauty, the invisible structure of that soul in which the highest goodness breathes, the complete structure of that person in which the highest dignity resides! All honor, all honor to the highest work of God, O all ye whosoever have not forgotten what it is to honor any thing here in this world.

And when Adam awoke, he no longer spoke, he sang! his lips unclosed in grace and sanctity, and from his heart came forth these words:

> "Now is this bone of my bones,
> And flesh of my flesh.
> And Woman shall she be called,
> For she was taken out of man.
> Therefore shall man leave father and mother,
> And cleave unto his wife,
> And they twain shall be one flesh."*

Thus speaks the Bible; that ancient book of ancient wisdom, that virgin page, which tells me nothing of *mother*, everything of *wife!* Man is suffering, or about to suffer, from loneliness: God creates for him society, and, best of all, conjugal society. There is no reference to anything else in the sacred narrative. It is not till after the fall that the woman receives a distinctive name:—"Eve, the mother of all living."† Hitherto she was called by the one name common to the pair, which indicated the perfect unity which love creates between a true husband and true wife. "He called their name *Adam*, in the day when they were created."‡

Thus, then, Gentlemen, in the view of the Bible, and in the view of the reason and heart which speak to

---

* Genesis, ii. 23, 24. † Ib. iii. 20. ‡ Ib. v. 2.

us in the Bible, conjugal society is a society of perfect love; and if I were called upon to define it, I should not define it by its *extrinsic* end, important as it is—the procreation of offspring—but by its *intrinsic* and essential end, which consists in perfect union. I should define it: "the fullest, closest, holiest union that can exist between two human beings." Such is marriage. As such Tertullian and St. Augustine understood it. As such the Roman law itself defined it, far in advance, in this respect, of the ideas and morals of the time:—*Conjunctio maris et feminæ, consortium omnis vitæ, divini et humani juris communicatio:* "the union of male and female, the partnership of the whole life, the fellowship of rights divine and human." Admirable definition to address to all our skeptics, and even to many Christians! Marriage is not only the mere union of man and wife, but a partnership of the entire life; it is not only a fellowship in human things, but also in divine—*divini et humani juris.*

It is enough to say that marriage presupposes and includes, by the fact that it exceeds them, all other unions that can exist between two human creatures. Start with that simple good-will which the countenance of man can kindle in the eye of his fellow-man, and ascend the long chain of hearts' affections up to the closest friendship, that friendship which has been tested in turn by happiness and misfortune, and which neither life nor death can sunder, and I will tell you: "These are but steps that lead to conjugal love; these are but strands of that cord which shall bind two persons into one single life: *Consortium omnis vitæ.* The love of husband and wife, such as God would have it, is the grand perfection of friendship. It is the latest flower, the most exquisite, most brilliant, and most fragrant flower in the paradise of the heart; it is the consummate fruit, the richest and sweetest fruit of that great faculty of love—the most vast, the deepest, the most inexhaustible of all the faculties of our soul; a real tree of life or of death, according to the use we make of it. It is the highest expression of love in this world!"

How many points, alas! I must pass by, with a mere glance! If time, if your strength and my own would permit, how many things would I have to say here!

3d. [Father Hyacinthe indicates *harmony* and *subordination* as the two conditions of perfect love—conditions which are so rarely found in mere friendship.]

When man associates with man, Gentlemen, he brings to him what he had already—not what he lacked. But man and woman are two halves of the same soul, which mutually complement each other. Man is reason, energy of thought and will. Has not my master, St. Paul, said, "the husband is the head of the wife?" "As God is the head of the man," says the energetic apostle, "so is man the head of the woman,"* and woman should think in that head, and be inspired with that manly and kingly wisdom. In like manner, we are told in the book of Genesis, that woman is the heart of man. Look into your rent heart, O son of Adam! it lacks in tenderness, it lacks in a certain delicacy and depth, which you will never find, except in Eve, in your mother, your sister, or your wife. Man is the head of the woman—woman is the heart of man; this is *harmony*, the first moral requisite of their perfect love.

This is the proper place to remark, that there ought to

---

* Ephesians, v. 23.

be, between husband and wife truly worthy the names in their best meaning, a community of moral and religious conscience. The disregard of this cardinal point is one of the greatest mistakes in marriage at the present time. A celebrated statesman of the last century, Turgot, used to say: "We need to have marriage preached to us—and true marriage." Now, true marriage cannot be that superficial union of two existences, which do not touch each other by their deepest sides—by the moral and religious life. In this grave question, Gentlemen, the truth lies in extremes. Either it is in the believer, who says to his wife, "Together let us trust and love and worship the God of our fathers and our children, the God of Bethlehem and Calvary;" or else it must be in the logical and consistent skeptic, the hard-headed political economist, who says to his partner, "I will have only one conscience between thee and me; no priest to bless our couch, no priest to consecrate our child, no priest to pray and weep over our grave!" There is a genuine marriage, Gentlemen; faith, or its negation, in one and the same morality and religion! *Harmony* is the head thinking in the heart, the heart inspired from the head!

But, alas! this great division of the family has entered into society as well. We are two Frances in France, and I might almost say, two Europes in Europe,—a manly but skeptical France, which does not think with its heart, which clings to an abstract and unbelieving science, which woman—and rightly enough—will have none of: and then a feminine and believing France, the better France, the France that is our salvation, but which has no longer a higher thought with which to stay and illuminate its love. Here you see our social evil, and at the same time our domestic evil.

So much for *Harmony* in the marriage relation. I have spoken also of *Subordination*. Friendship implies equality; it makes equals even when it does not find them: *Amicitia pares invenit aut facit*. But this is not true of that grand friendship which we call love. Love demands subordination—it implies, even in the moral system, an active principle and a passive principle. Of two beings loving each other, one will love the more in the way of sacrifice—will give up more largely and more freely, or at least in another form—will become thus the joy and glory of the being beloved.

Now this affectionate surrender of self, which cannot be realized from man to man, is naturally realized from woman to man. Woman, indeed, the complete equal of man in her soul, and all that pertains to her personal rights and dignity, is not his equal in sex and in the position assigned to her in civil and domestic society. "The man was not created for the woman, but the woman for the man," * says St. Paul. Man was alone, and he was sad; God gave to him this mysterious and sublime counterpart, which is for him, which belongs to him, and I had almost said, which is himself: "She shall be called woman, because she was taken out of man."† And St. Paul says again, "the woman is the glory of the man:"‡ man has radiated this glory from himself, and looks upon and loves himself in this sweet and luminous atmosphere.

I know that sophists are preaching the equality of the sexes. But the heart of woman cries out as loudly as the reason of man against an error destructive of the family. What woman wants, what Christianity wants, is the equality of souls, the equality of persons, in the same rights and the same duties, equality in chastity,

---

* 1 Corinthians, xi. 9.   † Genesis, ii. 23.   ‡ 1 Corinthians, xi. 7.

equality in fidelity and love. "The laws of Cæsar are one thing," exclaimed St. Jerome in his sharp and energetic language, "the laws of Christ are another thing!" Amongst us, Christians, what we forbid to women, we do not allow to men. As respects any one and the same duty, obedience is of equal obligation upon both.

4th. [Having pointed out these two conditions of perfect love, *harmony* and *subordination*, which render conjugal society so intimate, the speaker recognizes the final seal of its union in the child, that third person in the terrestrial trinity. He concludes as follows:]

O Lord, my God! it is but just now I proclaimed Thee, in the exaltation of my thought and of my heart, the type of human society—as one in thy nature, and manifold in thy persons; we ourselves, also, manifold in in our persons, and one in our blood, in our reason and in our moral unity. I proclaimed Thee, O my God! as the type of the great fellowship of mankind! I hail Thee now, I venerate and I adore Thee as the especial type of the society of home.

Yes, the Lord is God, he is the Father, and within himself is his own glory; for "the Word is the glory of God." He thinks of his glorious Word, in substance and in person, his beautiful and living Reason, his Son. He contemplates his Word, and in this meditation, from the two, the Father and the Word, proceedeth the Holy Spirit—that is, love—love in substance and in person. And the Father and the Word abide in it! The cycle of divine life is consummated. God is complete, God is blessed. And there are three that bear witness in heaven, the Father, the Word, and the Spirit; and these three are one!

Now there are three also that bear witness on earth. Man is not satisfied with his own solitary personality; he also must have his glory; and, like God, he must have his word, his beautiful reason made visible, his sweet and strong conscience to surround him with its clear, pure light. And with this blessed image, called, like the Word, "the express image of his person," the stainless mirror of his beauty; with her he begets his son, a third self—a third term common to the husband and the wife, in which their love becomes incarnate, and fixes itself, and abides. The cycle of human life is accomplished. Like God in heaven, so man is complete and blessed on the earth, and there are three that bear witness—the father, and the wife, and the child; and these three agree in one.

PART SECOND.—*Conjugal Society in the Light of Redemption, or before God the Renewer.*

But over the splendors of Eden sin has cast its baleful shadow. Woman has fallen, love is profaned, marriage is debased! And when the Redeemer had descended into this world that the Creator had made—one day, Jesus was in the Temple at Jerusalem, and the Pharisees of the old law brought unto him a blushing, trembling woman, a woman taken in adultery: "Master," said they, "Moses in the law commanded us, that such should be stoned; but what sayest thou?"* This woman was not only *a* woman; but woman, man, all conjugal society, degenerate, guilty, corrupt! There she was, upon her knees, veiled with her hair and bathed in tears—on her knees in misery. And Jesus spake not, but "stooped down and with his finger

* John, viii. 4, 5.

wrote upon the ground, as though he heard them not." He wrote the gospel of mercy and regeneration; and to those Pharisees, those scribes, who were clamoring for punishment—stoning—execution—" Jesus lifted himself up, and said, 'He that is without sin among you, let him first cast a stone at her!' And again he stooped down and wrote upon the ground." And when all had gone out, says the Evangelist St. John, beginning at the eldest, the bald heads and white hairs—when the men without mercy or pity had gone out, there were none left but these two, face to face; Jesus, writing upon the ground, and the woman in her blushes and her tears—the Son of the Virgin and the adulteress: "Jesus was left alone, and the woman standing in the midst;" or to use the words of St. Augustine, "Great misery and great mercy:" *magna miseria, et magna misericordia.*

1st. Jesus has rebuked the corruptions of love, but he has not rebuked love; he has not despaired of love, nor of conjugal society. Far from that, he has looked into the face of love with that eye, at once Virgin and Divine; he has taken it into those hands of his that were lacerated on the cross and bathed with the blood of redemption; and of that love so long desecrated he has constituted one of the sacraments of the Church, one of the seven columns which bear up the spiritual world. "This is a great sacrament," says St. Paul; "but I speak concerning Christ and the Church."* And the Council of Trent assures us that it is this natural and human love—*naturalem illum amorem*—which Jesus has purified and consecrated in the sacrament of marriage. How great the work! in which Jesus has not only followed the counsels of his mercy: he was the

---

* Ephesians, v. 32. "Sacramentum hoc magnum est."—*Vulgate.*

Word, and he has followed the counsels of eternal reason.

In fact, if we consider love as it is in nature, we discern in it a profoundly *religious* side. If we observe love as it is in a state of sin, we discern in it a side profoundly *idolatrous;* and it is because of these two sides, the religious and idolatrous, the side of nature and of sin, that it was just, or at least it was meet for the Divine Word to rescue natural love, and make of it that holy and thrice sacred thing, a sacrament.

Love is *religious* in its nature; our ancestors understood it better than we—those haughty Germans—beneath the immemorial forests that sheltered their valor and their virtues. Tacitus, who found consolation in them for the hopeless degeneracy of Rome under the Cæsars, remarked: "The Germans believe there is something divine in woman:" *inesse quid divinum.* The Germans were right. There is in woman, as we have said, the reflection of God; and consequently, in the love she inspires, when it is the outgoing of a heart profound by nature and pure of life, there is something that is religious.

Yes, love is naturally a religious sentiment, and I shall need nothing but this argument—this fact—for it *is* a fact—to confound all the positivists and materialists of our generation. What! you say that man cannot get free from the finite through his reason? I tell you that he escapes from it not only through his reason, but also through his heart! What! you say that man is nothing but matter, that his life is bounded by a cradle full of tears and a grave full of worms, and that pent up in this brief and sad existence, he is only capable of thinking of matter and loving matter? I tell you, Nay; ye blasphemers of human nature! Nay, ye sophists of the nineteenth century! Nay, ye corrupters of my noble France, my grand human society, my glorious modern civilization! Nay, it is not true! Man goes forth from the finite, he emerges from matter through his reason, because he thinks of God; and through his heart, because he loves his mother, because he loves his sister, and because he cherishes his wife!

There is, then, something divine in woman, something sacred in love; and for that reason I add, something idolatrous in its profanations.

It is these perversions of the sentiment of love that have given rise to one of the least studied and yet most notable facts of the ancient religions—the idolatry of woman, or idolatry through woman. I do not dwell upon it, but there are great revelations to be found here for one who studies the human heart. As to the modern paganism which tends to grow up among us, it feels too powerfully the influence of Christianity, even while combating it, to reach that excess of positive and avowed idolatry. But the passion of which I speak assumes each day, in ideas as well as in facts, the characteristics of a moral idolatry. I might cite a certain book written with unquestionable talent and with no less unquestionable conviction, in my opinion, in which the worship of *woman* and the religion of *love* are substituted for the worship of the true God and the religion of Christ. But what am I saying! I might recall an odious but needful recollection, a recent infamous page of our history, which meets, now-a-days, with apologists, hardly with imitators. Remember the time when the French people repudiated the God of France, the God of Clotilde and of Clovis—the time when the worship of Reason was preached to a nation that had broken loose from faith! Well, reason was too cold and abstract, and in its place there was set up upon this altar the spectacle of a live woman! The professed idolatry of the ancient world and the practical idolatry of the modern world have both exalted love and woman; and have both debased, humiliated, almost annihilated them. Love is no longer love, but lust; and woman is the idol or the priestess of this hideous worship!

[The naturally *religious* tendency of love uncorrupted and the *idolatrous* tendency of corrupt love are, according to Father Hyacinthe, two distant and obscure preparations for the elevation of conjugal love to the rank of a sacrament. Love was a vague *religion* of the heart; it was good to exalt it and to formulate it. Love was an *idolatry*, and an unclean idolatry at that; it was good to enlighten and purify it. Christ has constituted the union of two Christian lives into a sacrament.]

2d. But what is a sacrament?

The catechism, that book which is too little known, but which contains the solutions of all our moral and religious questions, tells us that a sacrament is a sign which expresses and a force which operates the grace of God. The union of husband and wife is then a sign and a force in the sacrament of Christ; a sign which expresses and a force which operates the supernatural grace of Christian love.

I am in haste to close; but what wonders might we yet discover in this new *significance* which Jesus has given to love! The love of husband and wife, in itself so great and holy, has become the symbol and the image of the love of Christ and his Church! Jesus has loved the race of man; the Word of God drew near to us, not as father to child, not as friend to friend, but as husband to wife. The Lord, so say our sacred books, has loved the souls of men; the Lord, continue their inspired pages, has loved the nations;—he has loved souls and united them to himself in the invisible unity of his Church; he loved the nations and united them in the visible structure, in the corporate unity of this same Church. The oneness of God's love with our souls; the oneness of God's love with the nations—with all humanity,—God descending to the bosom of the immaculate Virgin, and there espousing human nature, my blood and my flesh;—God, the immolated and glorious spouse, lifted up upon the bloody and fruit-bearing branches of the cross, and there espousing all generations regenerated by him in his sacrifice; this is the *type* of Christian marriage! The love of God and man is the marvellous theme of the Song of Songs. All the ancient East—the monuments of India, in particular, attest it—all the ancient East has recognized in the union of man and wife a poetic and religious image of the union of God with the soul. . . . . . .

Such are the lofty thoughts which should reign in the hearts of Christians when they are joined together in the sacrament of holy wedlock. This man is a Christ upon the earth! that woman is a daughter of God, a sister of Jesus Christ! Both of them were ransomed on Calvary, baptized in the sacred water, fed with angels' food, refreshed from the altar-cups. They are worthy to love God each in the other—they are worthy, in that communion of souls which is accomplished in the sacrament of marriage, to give their God to one another, when they give their hearts!

To enjoy a soul, in the ordinary human way, is of itself sublime! to enjoy an immortal thought, to enjoy a heart tender and strong, a heart loving and chaste, is almost divine! What, then, must it be to enjoy a soul in a way that is really divine? to possess in common with that soul all the most marvellous, the deepest and most exquisite things that the grace of Christ has wrought upon its thought and affections; if so be this mystery, of God received and held within that soul, is delivered by it to that beloved one from whom it has henceforth no secret? Such, nevertheless, is Christian marriage! "Husbands," exclaims St. Paul, "love your wives, even as Christ also loved the Church; wives, love your husbands as the Church loved Jesus.* Marriage," continues he, "shall be an honorable and glorious thing, and the marriage-bed undefiled." †

Now this is no dream. I have said, a sacrament is a *sign*, and it expresses. I add, it is a *force*, and it works. It contains a grace which lifts man's heart to the height of such exalted virtue. Man, in the plane of nature, is ever dreaming, down to the very frosts of old age, even when he comes under the very sneers of skepticism and immorality—dreaming a long, long dream that never comes true. He would fain love forever, and he loves but for an hour; he would fain love in the depth of his soul, and he loves but in the senses; he would fain love the ideal, and again he finds himself always confronted with the fallen reality! But lo! the Christians whose hearts have been touched with the grace of God through Christ! and these have loved in truth, in unity, and for eternity! "This is a great sacrament," I say, in Jesus and the Church..... Question our old Gallic firesides, question our European homes wherever the sap of Christianity has conserved its vital power, and they will answer you with the grand echo, so grave and tender, of conjugal love.

[In the peroration of this conference, the speaker shows the superiority of virginity to marriage which he has so extolled.]

* Ephesians, v. 25.   † Hebrews, xiii. 4.

A young Christian married pair were one day sailing over the Adriatic, reading in the pages of a pure book, and, deeper yet, in the pages of their own pure hearts. The words which they read from without, and to which they harkened from within, were these: "Is it not misery to love for this life only? Have you no longing for eternal love?"* Ah! it is the misery, the longing of us all: the misery of transient love and the longing for eternal love! I know, indeed, that the love of husband and wife shall continue in another form in future ages, and it is from some delicate, subtle apprehension of this that the Church has derived the repugnance it feels for second nuptials, to which it refuses the solemn benediction of the priest. There is a love and fidelity beyond the tomb, a love for eternity. But, after all, this love is no longer conjugal; for in conjugal love, exalted as I have deemed it, there are two profound infirmities. It is too earthly, the senses have a share in it, and the senses are always fallen; it is too exclusive, and in the heart itself, elevated as it is above the senses, it too much absorbs two individual beings each in the other, at the expense of great loves and sacrifices for humanity. Therefore it is that Jesus Christ, when questioned by the Jews on the mystery of the life to come, answered, "In the resurrection they neither marry nor are given in marriage, but are as the angels of God."†

No more marrying and giving in marriage, in the earthly sense; and yet there is a grand continuance of love; there is the latest bloom of what I have called the tree of life, the consummate flower of love, *virginity*. O, vainly have men sought to make virginity the foe of love; it is the sister, the continuator, the perfecter of

---

* "A Sister's Story," by Madame Craven. † Matthew, xxii. 30.

love; it is the reproach that men cast upon my Roman Catholic Church, and it is its glory. For me, this alone would be its demonstration, a demonstration that needs no further proof:—the Catholic Church has always accepted, affirmed, and practised voluntary celibacy; and highly as it has extolled conjugal love, higher still has it exalted Christian virginity.

Ah! virginity is that craving for love in another life; it is the exclusive longing after love eternal, infinite; for "the marriage of the Lamb,"* of which St. John speaks in the Revelation; when one shall no more love one single person; when one shall no more be absorbed in a single created mind and heart; when the veil being rent (for love in this world is a veil—as it were a bridal veil that is spread over the wedded pair—a transparent veil, which reveals the mystery of God, but hides it even more), as in the temple of Jerusalem, when the hour of types and figures had passed away and the Jewish people was making way for the Christian. .... O let me, let me rend away the veil! I long to love God, no more through a heart finite and fallen, like mine, however pure and tender it may be—I long to love God, face to face, heart to heart, and to clasp him in the exclusive embrace of my love!

David has sung of these things of old. He has spoken of the lonely bed where by night the tears flow, drop by drop like the dew, or in torrents like a storm of rain. I long for these drops—these streams; I long to groan and cry out in my heart, in solitude: "I have roared by reason of the disquietness of my heart."† O God, thou art my God, early will I seek thee!"‡ "My heart and my flesh crieth out for the living God."§ As the hart in the sultry days of summer, I am athirst—

---
* Rev., xix. 7. † Ps. xxxviii. 8. ‡ Ib. lxiii. 1. § Ib. lxxxiv. 2.

athirst for the infinite beauty! O eternal love, ever old, and ever young, without spot or wrinkle! O rapture of the heart! O calmness of the reason! My bones are fevered and again are chilled, and "all my bones murmur: 'Lord, who is like unto thee?'"*

This is the utmost expression of love!

The day shall come when all Christian spouses, freed from the veil, relieved of the burden of the flesh, released from the prison of an exclusive, individual, selfish love, shall say these things! They say them already, in the types and shadows of all holy loves; and they see, afar off, those nuptials at which every spouse shall be a virgin, and every virgin a spouse, and when the one race of man ransomed by Christ shall perfect the bloom of conjugal love, in the bloom of eternal virginity!

* Psalm xxxv. 10.

LECTURE THIRD.

December 16, 1866.

THE CORRUPTION OF THE CONJUGAL RELATION BY THE IMMORALITY OF THE AGE.

[IN a rapid exordium, Father Hyacinthe showed the connection of this Lecture with the preceding. The latter had for its object to bring distinctly to view the ideal of the marriage relation as the Creator had realized it in the beginning, and as the Redeemer had restored it in the fulness of time. To-day the speaker proposes to study the corruption of this relation by immorality in general, and especially by the immorality of the present age.

The contest between good and evil belongs to all ages; but it has certain more dramatic situations—certain more solemn and startling crises. In Europe, and particularly in France, we have arrived at one of these conjunctures. The immorality of the age attacks the conjugal relation: 1. In its *essence;* 2. In its *legislation;* 3. In its *supernatural consecration by the sacrament.* Such are the three points of view taken by the speaker.]

PART FIRST.—*Corruption of the Marriage Relation in its Essence.*

[Father Hyacinthe shows, first, how the immorality of the age attacks the very *nature* of the conjugal relation, and disregards the *essence* of marriage in separating it from love.]

I believe I have proved, in the last Lecture, that the idea of marriage is love—love, in truth and in justice, love in all the demands of personal dignity. Marriage, I said, is the exclusive form of love among men, the only one which it can assume in order to be worthy of our grand personal nature.

Now, the tendency of society, in our day, is to separate marriage from love, and to put asunder what the law of God and the heart of man have made one. In marriage without love, and in love without marriage, there is a twofold immoral tendency—the expression is not too strong—and it is the fountain-head of a large part of our moral disorders.

1. I have said that marriage is the indissoluble partnership of two lives—that is, two souls, two persons, two existences, in which everything is shared, nothing divided: *consortium omnis vitæ.* It is the communion between husband and wife, in all things pertaining to heaven and earth, to man and God: *divini et humani juris communicatio.* This is true marriage, as the Romans defined it, and as Christians have practised it. Such marriage obviously implies love. It implies harmony of character and conformity of taste, agreement of temperament and age, community of moral habits and religious convictions. It supposes, in one word, in respect both to soul and to body, everything which can attract to each other two human beings who are some day to be united, never thenceforth to separate.

Now, is it not true, that generally, in the contracting of marriages amongst us, these personal considerations are almost wholly set aside, or at least subordinated to considerations of interest? Is it not true that, once sure of a certain fitness (which, by the way, is susceptible of a most elastic construction) in the position of the families, the question which is considered, the practical and decisive question, is the combination of fortunes? And between two beings who yesterday were unacquainted and to-day have hardly met, they make up a match (I am forced to say it) as they would drive a bargain! I am not talking about exceptional cases. I am speaking of the general law among the wealthy classes of our country, and even in the most honorable and Christian families. Now, Gentlemen, I make bold to say that in this way marriage is falsified, perverted by the very act with which it begins—the choice of the partners to it.

[2. After having shown in detail, how, in thus constituting marriage without love, the institution has been perverted, Father Hyacinthe proves, on the other hand, that love without marriage becomes the source of incurable corruption.]

What, then, is to be the result? Inevitably, I had almost said legitimately—I should have erred, I should have been false to the dignity of this pulpit—inevitably, fatally, love, banished from conjugal society, will establish itself separate from marriage, just as marriage has been established separate from love. Thus human nature takes its triumphant revenge against the falsehood and tyranny of social prejudice. Love, only, is overthrown in this seeming victory; it perishes in the act of avenging itself. There is no marriage worthy of the name without love! But then there is no love worthy of the name without marriage! The true seat of love, the seat of its repose and dignity, is the soul. But, exiled from marriage, love is by that very fact exiled from the soul. It ceases to be a virtuous sentiment, and becomes a distempered passion. Thenceforth it tears itself from the pure heights of our moral being, peopled with those joys which the conscience shares with the affections—*gaudium de veritate conceptum*—

and goes down, down to those troubled regions where the spirit is imprisoned within the senses, and sinking ever lower and lower along this swift declivity, and under this fatal weight, it finally deserts the soul and becomes the tenant of the body. Love then is no longer love—it is lust!

[3. Father Hyacinthe next considered the social result of this separation between marriage and love. Marriage without love tends to extinguish the true type of the *wife;* that type preëminently ennobling, radiant with a grace at once so alluring and so pure. *Gratia super gratiam, mulier sancta et pudorata.* "Grace upon grace, is a holy and modest woman."* Love outside of marriage tends to realize the type of the *harlot.*]

More than once I have had to speak the name of the harlot; to-day I am forced to stop and look her in the face. Shame on the over-nice and prudish surgeon who shrinks away from the wound which he ought to examine and touch and heal!

The Lord said of his chosen people: "There shall be no harlot of the daughters of Israel."† The word of the Lord was not obeyed; the harlot was in Israel, and everywhere. The Greeks knew her; they had seen her born of the foam of their azure waves and the rays of their fiery sun. But the Greeks were wrong. She is not the child of nature; she is the child of humanity. Ah! let me not brand her infamy upon her till I have first done her justice and showed her mercy! I am bound to say, even in the presence of this most corrupt and corrupting being, that in the ruin of woman, as a general rule, man is the great criminal. Woman is the victim—man, the murderer.

It is not prostitution that is a novelty in the world; it

---

* Ecclesiasticus, xxvi. 15.   † Deut. xxiii. 17.

is the position it occupies. Of old time, prostitution was almost exclusively an appendage of aristocracy or royalty. When it entered France, it was concealed at first; but afterward it came forward, unabashed, among those privileged ranks where men too often thought themselves above the laws—above morality itself; and there it sowed that seed of storms from which we have reaped a harvest of whirlwinds! But truce to these memories! Let the dead rest in peace! The wave of revolution has swept over the palaces and washed them with blood! To-day the reign of the harlot is more democratic. Without deserting, alas! the mighty of this world, she has constantly enlarged the circle of her empire. It is a strange application of the law—the just law—which governs modern society, and which tends, little by little, to make the privilege of the few the common property of all! She has extended her view; she has reached out her sceptre over the different grades of the social hierarchy. Formerly it was only a multitude, to-day it is a world;* and this world, the "half-world"—the *demi-monde*—as it is well named, attempts to give tone and fashion to the real world; must I say it, Gentlemen? in sight of their constantly growing success, the virtuous woman, unable to keep by her side her husband, her son, it may be her father, has more than once been driven, in her anguish, to ask the secret of this fascination: "What power has this strange woman, and why may I not have it?" She has watched that leering eye and marked the strange fire with which it glows; she has studied that smile, the inflexions of

---

* " Without collecting, as I have done for the past ten years, the grievances of families thwarted in their dearest interests, it would not be possible to suspect the social disorders produced in Paris by several thousands of women acting in open rebellion against the duties of their sex."—(" Social Reform in France," by M. Le Play, I., p. 277, second edition.)

that voice and the motions of that form;* she has searched into the mysteries of those toilets and that luxury; and too noble and too pure to acquire in reality the arts of vicious seduction, she has acquired, alas! too easily their outward appearance.

[Thus the first characteristic of this reign of corruption is, that it *is spreading* more and more amongst us; its second characteristic is, that it is becoming more degraded in proportion as it is extended; and in the sphere of morals, it is a reflex of the materialism of doctrine which has come in upon us like a flood.]

They tell us that philosophic doctrines have no influence on the morality of men. I reply, that they have an influence even on their immorality; that they fashion into their own image our vices almost as much as our virtues. Yes, in societies elevated by a spiritual philosophy, vice has different sentiments and a different language from what it has in communities debased by materialism, and which glory in coming from the monkey, to end in nothingness, or in worms! In the former, the influence of courtezans is derived sometimes—rarely, it is true—from their heart; very frequently, from their wit; always, in some degree, from their grace and their beauty. But in our day all these charms are supplied by a single one. "No, no," cries sensualism; "we don't want any supplementary attractions. No more distraction for the mind and heart; it is a bore to think, and an effort and a weariness to love! No more sentiment, but sensation! And if beauty or youth are any hindrance to this, what's the use of youth and beauty? O Circe, thou sorceress, give me thy cup, and let me wallow in sensuality."

---

* "Lust not after her beauty in thine heart; neither let her take thee with her eyelids."—*Proverbs*, vi. 25.

And now there are people that ask me not to be indignant! They would like me to stop coolly at the refutation of error, and choke down in my man's heart, my priest's heart, the cry of moral indignation! No! there is something more here than an error in logic: it is a shame upon our character and a peril to our social existence!

PART SECOND.— *Violation of the Legislation of Marriage by the Immorality of the Day.*

[In setting forth the *ideal* of the conjugal relation in the last lecture, Father Hyacinthe said nothing, strictly speaking, of its *legislation*. This was because the laws which govern it, in its moral and religious relations, are only a simple corollary from the proposition developed in that lecture—that marriage is love under the limitations of personal respect and personal dignity. These laws are chiefly two—*unity* and *indissolubility*. They form the *primitive* legislation of marriage, at once natural and divine, and they are *anterior to all the positive enactments of civil and religious powers*.]

I know well enough that at this point, too, I shall meet with gainsayers. The new schools affirm that man began with the savage state, with fetichism in relation to God, and with communism in relation to women. This is not the place to enter into an exhaustive discussion on these two points. Positivism, which forbids us all inquiries as to origin and end, is forever stumbling into such inquiries itself without thinking of it; and whatever it may say for itself, it is by the merest hypotheses that it pretends to throw light upon the past or the future of mankind—hypotheses unsupported by facts, or rather contradicted by all the data of experience. For these savages, from whom they say that we have descended, are not only to be found in remote centuries. We have no need, in order to find them, to grope our way backward into the darkness of the stone age, and to penetrate into the mysterious caverns that have been excavated by our geologists. Africa and America, on their scorching sands or in their icy forests, have preserved for us the living representatives of these tribes; we know the savages—we have seen them—we have spoken with them, and we have recognized in their moral and physical type, not the germ, but the decadence of humanity. They are fallen, or rather degraded races, which we must take care not to confound with simple barbarians. Barbarians can rise from their fall—if not of themselves, at least by contact with a foreign civilization; but savage races are so crushed under the sway of the senses, that hitherto not a single one—history makes affidavit to it—has been found susceptible of civilization. They are to-day what they were thousands of years ago; asleep on the confines of brute life, they do not even dream of reascending the frightful declivity down which they have fallen. Ah! if savages were the primitive race that you pretend, and if on the other side, as you also assert, progress was the destined law of humanity, there would be no more savages, no more barbarians, the entire world would be civilized! How then, and by what hand, so often continued from age to age, has this mighty spring of progress been relaxed among some races and broken among others?

[Here Father Hyacinthe, having re-established the *facts* that had been denied by *hypotheses*, shows man beginning with *monotheism* and *monogamy*—that is, with the two great principles of natural *religion* and natural *morality*. These principles were afterward obscured, in consequence of original sin, but they never totally perished from among men. The sacred deposit of the monotheistic traditions was intrusted to Shem, and especially to the race of Abraham. The chain of monogamist traditions was continued through the pure and vigorous races that sprung from Japhet; through the Greeks and Romans in their best days; through the Celts, the Germans, and the Scandinavians. But *polytheism* held sway among them, while *polygamy* was tolerated among the Jews; and in this way, the two civilizing principles were isolated from each other.]

The children of Abraham, especially the Jews, worshipped one God, alone, solitary, and majestic as that desert in which he had appeared to them, lofty and stern as the sky of brass above their heads. They were *monotheists*, like their father, but like their father, also, they were *polygamists*. Through motives of profound wisdom, which it is not my present duty to unfold, God had blessed in chastity and fecundity the limited polygamy that had prevailed under the tents of Abraham and Jacob; and afterward, by a concession needful to the training of this rude people, Moses had, I do not say approved, but tolerated and regulated divorce on the part of the husband. "From the beginning it was not so; but Moses, because of the hardness of your hearts, suffered you to put away your wives;"*—because they had not yet hearts pure enough and tender enough to love with constancy the same wife, and to sacrifice everything to this one love.

Polygamy and *polytheism* divided the world between them. There was one God under the tents of Shem, the *polygamist;* one wife at the fireside of Japhet, the *polytheist.* But, lo! the hour is at hand for universal reconciliation: Japhet shall sit down under the tents of Shem, and dwell with him, in brotherly love: "God shall enlarge Japhet, and he shall dwell in the tents of Shem."† The reconciler and organizer of our race appears: Christ sends his apostles to proclaim through-

---

* Matthew, xix. 8. † Genesis, ix. 27.

out the entire world the doctrine of one God, and the duty of having but one wife! Then, during a succession of terrible but most fruitful centuries, Jews, Romans, barbarians, blended, intermixed, by the overturnings of history and under the influence of the Church, there is seen rounding into form this unique civilization, to which there is no parallel in the past and can be no successor in the future, the grand modern and Christian civilization, whose children we are. Yesterday it was called *Europe*, to-day, *The West*, for America joins hands with Europe across the ocean; to-morrow it will be called *The World*, and it will be for this to unite at last in one resplendent halo on the brow of mankind, those two rays of Eden for so long separated, so long a time obscured, *monotheism* and *monogamy*, the worship of one God in heaven and the love of one woman on earth!

[As a matter of *right*, monogamy belongs to *natural* morality, as monotheism to natural religion. As a matter of *fact*, however (although it has been too little noticed), Christianity alone has had the power to establish their reign and maintain it and make it universal in the world. The speaker called attention to the efforts of the immorality of the age in comparison with the efforts of the unbelief of the age; the one striving to abolish from our morals the practice of *monogamy;* the other striving to wrest from our minds the belief in *monotheism*. Their triumph would be the advent of barbarism to Christendom.

We are still too French and too Catholic to have the unity and indissolubility of marriage effaced from our codes. But the immorality of the age tends to reduce them to the state of legal fictions. It multiplies the violation of them in common life with a frequency and publicity which our fathers never witnessed, and against which public opinion has ceased to protest. It parades them as a spectacle, amid the applauses of the theatres; it demands the justification of them at the hands of a lying philosophy, and their glorification at the hands of a corrupt literature.

The land is swarming with adulteries, adulteries of old so rare, of old so severely branded by public opinion, so severely punished by the law of the land; adulteries—the violation of the most sacred rights of the human person! The scourge of the harlot *without* the walls of home; that of the adulterous wife is *within*.]

PART THIRD.—*Violation of the Conjugal Relation in its Supernatural Consecration by the Sacrament.*

[Father Hyacinthe had already shown, in the last lecture, how marriage has been elevated by Christ to the dignity of a sacrament.

Now, from this new consecration, the two great laws of *unity* and *indissolubility* have derived at once a more absolute rigor and more sacred significance. The union of husband and wife in one love and one flesh, should be the living image of the union of the Word with human nature and with his Church in the mystery of the incarnation. Now Jesus Christ is the spouse of but one: He has espoused one Church, and cannot be divorced from it. "Lo, I am with you alway, even unto the end of the world."*

But how is it possible to elevate and maintain at such heights so earthly and inconstant a thing as the human heart? Christ has placed in the sacrament of Christian marriage not only the *sign* which enlightens, but the *force* which sustains.]

He has said to the husband and the wife, "Come to my altar—come, and kindle there the flame of a pure and immortal love." And we see the two young Christians coming forward amidst flowers and incense, and the sweet and thrilling harmonies of the organ—they are no longer bridegroom and bride, but two priests; for Christian love is not only a religion but a priesthood! They come to the steps of the altar of the spotless Lamb; they look at the sacred tabernacle, and they blush not, neither do they tremble! The invisible angels of the

---

* Matthew, xxviii. 20.

sanctuary are there, and we hear the beat and rustle of their wings, and the sweet savor of the love of heaven is shed down upon the love of earth. The Catholic priest is there, but, O strange sight! he seems despoiled (as it were) of the omnipotence of his priesthood. He is there, delegated by the Church as intercessor and necessary witness—as intercessor, to pray and bless, as witness to see and hear; but by an exception unparalleled in the economy of divine things, he, the dispenser of all the sacraments, from baptism to extreme unction, is not suffered to be the minister of this amazing sacrament. The ministers are these wedded ones themselves; their hearts are stirred with the purest and deepest influences alike of grace and of nature; their voices tremble, but do not hesitate, and while their hands are joined in a holy clasp, two words fall from their lips and are blended in one harmony: "I take thee for my wedded husband"—"I take thee for my wedded wife." Enough. By one act, in the presence of the witnessing priest, and angels, and God, they have sealed the compact of their natural love, and the sacrament of their supernatural union.

This is marriage as our fathers understood it. It is the fashion, now-a-days, to say that all this is a very fine theory!

In this decay of faith of which we are witnesses, the sacrament of marriage becomes for many Christians a *religious fiction*, as the text of our codes has become a *legal fiction*. Its forms are observed from considerations of propriety and conventionality, but the *sign* that enlightens and the *force* that sustains are things which are not remembered as they ought to be.

And yet is it not here that we must seek the true source of those nobler inspirations and those more generous deeds, which the steadfastness of married life demands? For in marriage there is something more than a mere compact.

"The chief thing in marriage" (so says a noble Christian writer of our own day, with admirable felicity of expression), "the chief thing in marriage is a sacrifice, or rather two sacrifices. The sacrificing priest and priestess bear in their hands two cups; and these two cups must needs be alike filled to the brim, in order that the union may be holy and be blessed of heaven."* These two cups, my friends, are filled with tears as well as joys.

True love is more than a passion; it is a virtue. Therefore it should stand in no fear of the disappointments and the bitterness the future cannot but have in store for it. But how could love be a virtue, but that it rests on God?

[The Lecture concluded as follows:]

Our trouble at the present day comes from these two causes: we have separated love from marriage, and we have separated marriage from God. It is time for a reaction against these two errors. Let us have a *moral* marriage, which shall unite two persons with the bond of personal love, the only bond worthy of them; let us have a *Christian* marriage, which shall cement this union with the indestructible power of God! Then we shall have restored from its ruins conjugal society. Then we shall be able to face Europe with confidence, and say, "We are the same old France still, ever in the van of all your forward movements, the van of the progress of thought and character! Europe cannot

---

* Ozanam, "Civilization in the Fifth Century." Lecture on The Christian Women.

perish. She is like that bark that was bearing Cæsar through the storm. "Fear not," said the dictator, "you are bearing Cæsar and his fortune!" We too may say to Europe, to America, to Christendom: "Fear not. The thunderbolt may rend the sky—the abyss may yawn beneath your feet—fear not, you are bearing Christ and his Church." Western Christendom cannot perish.

But one thing is not impossible—God forbid that it should ever come to pass!—that France should descend to an inferior rank in Christendom. Ah! if to those great Christian countries—that Germany that fasts upon the eve of battle, and carries the New Testament in the shako of her soldiers; that England that offers her common prayer on the days of public humiliation, and keeps her Sabbath rest, the glory of her industry and civilization; that America which, at every crisis of her national life, proclaims her faith in God as the foundation of her safety and her greatness;—if, I say, we have nothing left to send to these countries but the echo of an abject—yes, abject skepticism, and an immorality more abject still—great God, what is to become of France? O call no longer upon liberty and democracy! Prate no more of a just balance of power! The direct, legitimate heir—it is a law of Providence in heaven, and it is a law of human nature on the earth—the direct, legitimate heir of all skepticism and corruption, is not freedom; it is slavery!

LECTURE FOURTH.

December 23, 1866.

FATHERHOOD.

GENTLEMEN: I have finished what I had to say upon the conjugal relation; and in spite of the fatigue which I had to struggle against last Sunday, thanks to God, and thanks to you, I was able fairly to reach the end of this important subject. We looked at it, you will remember, under the two aspects which all topics relating to humanity present—the *positive* aspect, and the *negative* aspect—the aspect of light and the aspect of darkness. In the light of God the *Creator* and of God the *Redeemer*, we saw this conjugal relation to be founded in love—love on its earthly side, and love on its heavenly side—*natural* love, perfect, tender, chaste, between man and wife—*supernatural* love, which is at once a reflection and a portion of that which subsists between Christ and his Church. From these two forms of love, blended into one, we easily deduced the two principal laws of the conjugal relation—*unity* and *indissolubility*. Passing then to the negative element, as it has been brought into existence during the course of ages, by the weakness and perversity of mankind, we observed that the evils of the conjugal relation, the violation of its laws and the perversion of its idea, arise from the fact that it has been separated both from affection and from religion. Men have wanted marriage without love, and without God!

I have now to complete the idea of the conjugal relation by speaking to you of *fatherhood*.

Gentlemen, the primary object of the conjugal relation is to be found in the relation itself. This object, which in the first Lecture I called *intrinsic*, is the personal and Christian love of the married pair—the perfect union that is set up between them. When love is real, when it is pure and deep, it has no other object than itself; we love for the sake of loving, and that is all. But there is an *extrinsic* purpose in the conjugal relation, not less important, not less essential than the former—the reproduction of the individual, and the propagation of the species. These two terms, harmoniously blended, consecrate paternity as the highest act of human life in the plane of nature. We will consider them one by one.

But before beginning, let us pause for a moment of religious recollection. Let me, for my part, a son of the apostles and an ambassador of Jesus Christ, remember those great words that were breathed from the lips of the apostle Paul over the cradle of Christianity: "I bow my knees unto the Father of our Lord Jesus Christ, from whom every fatherhood in heaven and earth is named."[*] Yes, and I too bow my knees, bend my intellect, and prostrate my soul before this Fatherhood, which is at once the origin and end of that human fatherhood, whose obligations, whose glory, whose felicity, my stammering tongue would strive to utter forth!

[*] Ephesians, iii. 14, 15. The Vulgate translation (constantly cited in the Roman Catholic pulpit) has *ex quo omnis paternitas ... nominatur*, which is much nearer to the original than the common English version. "Every lineage" would be, perhaps, the most nearly equivalent phrase.—TR.

PART FIRST.—*Fatherhood considered as the Means of Reproduction of the Individual.*

I was saying, Gentlemen, that man, at his entrance into the world, finds himself confronted by two mysterious laws, which dominate all his future—the law of *sex* and the law of *death*.

We have seen how man triumphs over the law of sex, and makes it a law of honor and happiness, in the conjugal relation. But the law of sex is a law of nature; the law of death is a result of sin. Therefore, against death the whole nature and person of man rebels. Ah! for my part, I know that there are no minds, save those that have been spoiled by long indulgence in sophistry, or, perhaps, in immorality, that can look on death and annihilation with indifference. The unperverted man hungers and thirsts for immortality! God promises him an immortality beyond the grave, in the eternal world: first, the immortality of his soul; afterward, "in the last day," the immortality of his body, which is also to come forth from the darkness of the grave. But this is not enough. Man is not content to become immortal in the future world; he would be immortal in the present world. And so, indeed, he becomes, through fatherhood. In the fulness of his life and strength, in the maturity of his reason and affections, man has measured himself, in spirit, against death, and has said, "Good! I can master him! I shall open in my blood a fountain-head of life, and with my blood I shall impart my soul, and with my soul I shall bequeath my works. I shall still act among men, I shall dwell forever in the land of the living!"

It is the triple victory of fatherhood over death—by its *blood*, by its *soul*, by its *work*.

1. And first, the father gives his *blood,* and with it that physical life of which the blood is the principal and the base.

Have you seen, Gentlemen, in our ancient forests, an old oak bending under the weight of centuries, and almost ready to crumble into dust? Before the catastrophe, it has foreseen it, we might say, by the sure instinct of nature, and has sown around itself young and vigorous offshoots, full of its sap, and lusty with its life. Man, also, is to die. The tree bends beneath the weight of its peaceful centuries; man, less happy, beneath the burden of his few and evil years. But he, also, has made of himself twain: one he leaves to fade away in death and wither in the tomb; he sees the other springing into life, and shooting out into the future. It is his own flesh that buds and flowers again in this other flesh; it is his own bones that, renewing their youth, are the framework that supports it; it is his blood which flows and throbs in these veins, and his heart which lives again in this heart. Carve thy wrinkles on my brow, Old Age! Whiten my head with the chill and dreary blast that breathes from out the place of tombs! thrust me, bowed and unresisting, down that steep decline which no one reascends! I have vanquished death by fatherhood! His dart is broken by the hands of my children! "O Grave, where is thy victory? O Death, where is thy sting?"*

2. But it is not only the body of the father, in some sense, it is his *soul,* that lives again in his children.

Of all the mysteries which we carry within us, the one least understood by science, least explained by revelation itself, is that of human generation. A sacred

---

* 1 Cor. xv. 55.

veil covers the cradle of life. I will imitate the reserve of the Church upon these problems, before which the genius of her illustrious doctors has paused in hesitation, and leaving the secret things to God, will content myself by asserting the mystery. The fact, which may be proved but cannot be explained, is this: the son bears the impress of the moral nature of his father; he is not only the offspring of his flesh and his bones, he is also the offspring of his soul.

It seems to me that we get here a glimpse of light on the mystery. St. Thomas Aquinas tells us somewhere that the son is borne into existence by the soul of the father.* The principle of life in man is but one; it is the soul itself: according to the elegant formula of the schoolmen, the soul is *the formal cause of the body*. The act of fatherhood, then, is an act of the soul. The whole soul is concerned in it; it goes forth therein in love, from husband to wife, from wife to husband, and descending, through the parental relation, this glorious scale, goes forth from parent to child. The parents, so to speak, have shaped by their souls the body of their child; and when, from the bosom of God, at the summons of the father, there comes down a soul into this sacred mould, it finds there fold upon fold prepared to receive it, and I know not what circumvolutions of matter, in which are traced already, to a certain extent, the lineaments of the mind. Away, then, with the materialism which denies the action of the soul, and even its very existence! but away, also, with the exclusive and senseless spiritualism, which denies the close alliance of the two substances, and the legitimate influence of the body upon the soul! "And Adam begat a

---

* Est quædam motio ab anima patris.—(*De Malo*, quæstio iv. Art. 6.)

son in his own likeness, after his image."* The parents transmit to their children, with a resemblance in feature, something of a resemblance in soul; with their physical temperament, something of their moral temperament; and the work of assimilation which education is to carry out, begins with the very fact of parentage.

Here, then, we have a man who lives again, both in his body and in his soul, and who can go on with his own work.

[Here, before showing how the father hands down his *work* to his son, the speaker drew from the idea of paternity this first lesson of duty—the law of *worthiness*.]

Every sound moral is derived from a doctrine. I have set forth the doctrine of fatherhood, and you see how this first law of duty springs from it at once—to be a father one must be worthy of the office. To us, fathers of souls, priests in the sphere of the supernatural and divine, there comes a command from heaven, "No man taketh this honor unto himself, but he that is called of God, as was Aaron."† And may I not bring home this stern command to you, priests of the family, fathers of the body, indeed, but also of the soul, in the sphere of the natural and human? May I not say to you: Take not this honor unto yourselves, unless ye be called; dare not usurp these lofty functions, if ye be not worthy?

Thou who art yet in the early spring of youth, some day you shall be worthy, but not yet. Do not think that fatherhood is some common thing—a means, and not an end; something to be thrown to a child as an outside defence against temptation—a borrowed shield against the dangers of youth! Learn to wait in the

---

* Genesis, v. 3.   † Hebrews, v. 4.

vigils of toil and chastity; and when you have fairly developed to its full maturity that grand human nature which you bear within you, you may begin to dream of transmitting it!

And you, young man, there was a time, perhaps, when you were worthy, but you are not now! What have you done with the integrity of human nature? what have you done with those two elements of paternity, a sound body and a sound mind?* Ah! as I was just saying, our blood is within us, but it is not ours: mine belongs to my ancestors in the past; yours, to your descendants in the future. It is a trust, a trust more sacred than deposits of gold. And yet you have not known how to keep this treasure of the blood, with which you have been put in trust for other generations. You dare not bequeath to your sons the poor, dwindled current, or the deadly poison which is flowing in your veins! There is such a thing as a blood of the soul, "*sanguis quidam animæ,*" as St. Augustine says, the blood of principles in the intellect, and the blood of virtues in the will. This blood of the soul you have squandered in the debauches of skepticism, as you have squandered the blood of the body in the debauches of immorality. You have lost the energy of truth, you have not even the energy of falsehood. Impotent to deny Christianity as you are to affirm it, exhausting yourself in the sterile luxury of doubt, you poor, pitiful eunuch in matters of intellect and conscience—what! you would be a father! when there does not lie in you the divine seed that men are made of? No! no! it is not for you.

3d. [After having thus deduced from the first two characteristics of fatherhood the law of *worthiness*, the speaker proceeds to consider the third characteristic, immortality in *works*.]

* "Mens sana in corpore sano."

Every man has a work to do in the world, a work of the intellect, or a work of the hands; and there is intellect even in the work of the hands—" by the intelligence of his hands," as the Scripture says.* And when man once understands this profound and noble law of work, he no longer submits to it as a necessity, no longer regards it as a retribution, or as a mere means of acquiring ease or wealth; all these ideas, no doubt, have their legitimate and powerful influence in his purposes, but the charm of work is quite another thing. I was just saying that love, in one sense, is the end of love. I may say the same of work. Man loves labor for the labor's sake; he devotes himself to his particular work for the sake of that work, and for the direct and immediate results which are to proceed from it.

It is the husbandman, the first of human workmen, who has best preserved the inheritance and work of Adam upon the earth. *"I am a husbandman; and Adam is my example from my youth."*† He looks at earth, through all her thorns and briers, in her seeming ugliness, but hidden beauty, and says: "I love thee! be my bride: I will give thee the sweat of my brow, and thou shalt give me thy fruit; and thou shalt be a fertile mother of mankind!" He loves the earth, then, both for herself and for her fruits; he loves the fields for themselves, and for the splendor of the golden harvest which covers them in summer; he loves the vines for the abundant and fruitful branches of autumn, and for the new wine which rejoices the heart of man. These trees which he plants, and under whose shade he shall never sit, he loves them for themselves, and for the sake of his children and his children's children, who are to sit beneath the shadow of their spreading boughs.

* Psalm lxxviii. 72.   † Zechariah, xiii. 5. (Vulgate.)

The merchant and the mechanic devote themselves to their handicraft and their commerce, as the laborer to the soil; they pride themselves upon the wonderful things which they produce or exchange. They love their work, down to the very tools they handle; they love the labors of their days and the watches of their nights, the anxieties of their uncertain youth and the triumphs of their riper years.

In fact, it is the same with all work, under whatever form and in whatever sphere: the magistrate administers justice out of respect to justice; the philosopher searches for truth from love of truth; the artist gives expression to the beautiful, from his passion for the beautiful.

Thus it becomes the legitimate and profound desire of the father of a family to see the work to which he has devoted his life descend to his children, and be continued by them; and such is in fact the custom of well-established society, which is at once traditional and progressive—either before it enters into the great crisis through which we are now passing, or after it has emerged therefrom.

If, then, we do not find it always thus amongst us, it must be attributed to circumstances. Human nature has not changed, and when the father cannot bequeath his work in its exact form, he strives at least to bequeath it in those grand traditions of probity and honor, of patriotism and religion, which are connected with his fortune and his name. When he has done that, a man can afford to die; for he has bound together in one firm association the two dearest creations of his life—his work and his son; he has won for himself a real immortality upon the earth; and from that other immortality which he shall enjoy in heaven among the chosen ones, in the bosom of God, he shall smile upon his race with a sweet and holy pride, and shall bless them, like Jehovah, to the third, the fourth, the thousandth generation.

[In concluding, as follows, what he had to say of fatherhood in its relation to the *individual*, the preacher showed from the foregoing considerations the origin of the *perpetual authority* of the father over his children.]

An illustrious thinker has said: "The child is always a minor before Nature, even when he is of age before the State. The paternal authority is essentially perpetual." In a certain sense, the child comes to his majority the day that he fairly attains the age of reason; he has from that time a sense of justice and injustice, he is free and responsible, he holds directly from his own conscience and from God. But if man is essentially free by virtue of his personality and his manhood, he is essentially subject, as a derived being, and as a son. And as the statue, the picture, the melody, the inspired book, if they had souls, would constantly refer their existence to the creative soul from which, in some hour of genius, of anguish, of rapture, they had sprung, just so the son of man, if he have the spirit of a son, even though his brow be bald, and his hair be white, will bow his white hair and his bald forehead in respect, in love, and in obedience before the ever venerable head of him to whom he owes his being and his life!

PART SECOND.—*Fatherhood considered as the Means of Reproduction of the Human Race.*

[In leaving the sphere of the *individual*, wide as it is, to pass to the *social* sphere, which is still wider, Father Hyacinthe spoke of paternity as laying aside all that it has of narrow and almost selfish. The father, in this view, is no longer the creator of his son, but the creator of the *humanity*.]

1st. We are asked every day by false science: "But what is your God busy about? Nowhere, in nature, can we find his personal action, but only laws, calm, solemn, immutable as fate itself." Well, it is true! Since he placed man as his vicegerent upon earth, God has retired from the field of direct and personal action. He reposes, as on a throne, upon the majesty and immutability of these laws, which hide him so well from the proud, and reveal him so clearly, so divinely to true thinkers and true believers; "he rests from all his work that he has made."* God created man, but he left to man the glory of finishing the greatest of his works, and creating the human race. "Male and female created he them," says the sacred historian; "and God blessed them, and God said unto them: Be fruitful, and multiply, and replenish the earth, and subdue it; and have dominion over the fish of the sea, and over the fowl of the air, and over every living thing that moveth upon the earth."†

"Be fruitful, and multiply, and replenish the earth!" It is this great command that the married pair still hear resounding through the depths of their love, if so be they are intelligent enough and pure enough to penetrate the secret of that love. It is no longer an individual love; it is a humanitarian love. It is no longer the home, that sweet and cherished home, that is to be peopled; it is the world. "Replenish *the earth!*" It is no longer a particular family which they dream of creating; it is the entire human race!

* Genesis, ii. 2. † Genesis, i. 27, 28.

They hear this voice in the understanding, and they catch the echo of it in their hearts; they are rapt in a sacred ecstasy; they feel themselves, in some sort, the priests of humanity! I have said that marriage was a priesthood, and I have no thought of retracting it. It is the true priesthood of natural religion. I even suspect that had it not been for the sin of our first father, it would have been the only priesthood. They feel themselves priests. They are priests; they look upward like the priest at the altar—upward to Jehovah, the father of all creatures; upward, in the clear light of faith, and the light of reason also. For man's reason, whatever may be said of it, is the direct and living reflection of God's reason. For the ideas by which it is filled and illuminated are, as St. Augustine has so well said, principal forms and radiations of the things which exist in the eternal intelligence: *idæ sunt formæ quædam principales et radiationes rerum quæ in intelligentia divina continentur.* Well, then, in their human reason and in their Christian faith, in these royal forms and in these divine illuminations, the married pair behold one of the most sublime and glorious of conceptions, the conception of human nature, and they cry: O God, send to us this marvellous gift! And like Tobias and Sara, in the twilight of their chaste nuptials, kneeling before the marriage bed, breathing forth that song which the Holy Scriptures have preserved for us,* so the bride and bridegroom of humanity, the wedded ones of the new Israel, breathe the like aspiration—" Blessed art thou, O God of our fathers; let the heavens and the earth bless thee, and the sea, and the rivers, and the fountains abounding with water! Let everything that liveth and moveth in the creation show forth thy praise,

* Tobit, viii. 5.

O Father! Author of life! And from us grant that a holy posterity may proceed, that shall sing thy holy name from generation to generation!"

2d. [The speaker next proceeds to follow out this idea of the office of fatherhood in the propagation of the human race, into the special form in which it appears in the reproduction of a nation.]

The vast body of humanity has members and organs: these are races and nations. The races and nationalities of humanity are of divine institution. I know that human law came afterward; and because it is law I honor it,—law of nations—law of war—law of treaties; but behind all these laws there is another, the law of God!—the law of the same blood flowing in the same veins, the law of the same tongue speaking through the same lips, the law of the same ideas and the same character, the law of the same loves, and, if need be, the same hatreds. There has been a typical race through which God has spoken to all nations, a race old as the world, and which still endures, strong and rugged as the rock of Sinai, where it was born, as the loins of the old nonagenarian patriarch, in which it was borne. And what is said to this race? "Remember the days of old, when the Most High divided to the nations their inheritance; when he separated the sons of Adam; when he set the bounds of the people according to the number of the children of Israel. For the Lord's portion is his people; Jacob is the lot of his inheritance."*

Away, then, without ceremony, with the patriotism which cuts itself off from humanity—which is anti-humanitarian! Away with that humanitarianism, too, which cuts itself off from country, and is anti-patriotic!

* Deut. xxxii. 7-9.

It is in our own race, above all, in our own blood and speech, that we ought to love the whole race of man!

O husband and wife, grand, ideal, Christian husband and wife, it is not alone at the altar of your kind that you minister, but at the altar of your country! The question is, shall our country be preserved? I am speaking as a Frenchman, to Frenchmen! The question is, shall France, our great and beloved France, be expanded, elevated if possible, but at least saved from humiliation and decay?

Ah! Gentlemen, I see a new law emerging here, the law of *fecundity*.

I hear it said that there are races that increase, and others that decrease, or at least remain stationary. I hear this said in the most eloquent of all languages in the way of demonstration, the language of statistics; and it is a most heart-moving language on this point, because the race that is decreasing is said to be our own—it is said to be France. I am not one of those who would estimate the strength of a country by the weakness of its neighbors: this is an old heathen notion which all Christian statesmen must repudiate. But I do not wish my country to sink while others rise. I do wish that in time of peace, as she stands looking at her wealth-producing plough, France might not have far to seek for hands to grasp it and to spread fertility through all her fields. I do wish that in that terrible and glorious hour when war breaks out, without quitting the plough, without suffering those peaceful wounds upon her sides to close, that flow with life and abundance, France might find other hands to seize her valiant sword, and wield it right bravely and proudly to strike down her enemies. I do wish, when I look abroad .... of Germany I shall say no more, I have already spoken of it; neither shall I speak of Russia, which is in a fair way to conquer Northern Asia, and which will soon, perhaps, rule China, to the furthest East; but on the other side of the Channel, I see the noble Anglo-Saxon race, one of the noblest in the world, and when I look at it I do wish not to be compelled to blush. I do not count its provinces and its colonies, I do not stop for the details; but a vast empire in the Indies, a flourishing and gigantic republic in the United States, and a new continent emerging from mid-ocean, Australia, which is soon to rival Europe and America! Pardon me, O my country! forgive one who loves you well for addressing you with such respectful but most painful frankness! but I do wish that I need not hear this reproach, without having one word to utter in reply: "And you, sons of France, there are not enough of you to colonize and people Algeria!"

Gentlemen, in this pulpit, which is God's pulpit, and before this audience, so well fitted to inspire one with the truth, and then to give ear to it, I shall not spare all my resources of sincerity. It is not pleasant to reflect indirectly upon men whose talents and convictions I respect, even in the midst of their monstrous errors; but I am bound to hold up to view certain doctrines that have something to do with a state of things that has already become inveterate. Now this is the doctrine of *positivism*, or at least of one of the most eminent representatives of that school. In a remarkable book which I glanced over yesterday on your account, this author proposes as the supreme remedy for the sufferings of the people, and especially for the decline in wages, "the limitation of the size of families in the laboring classes."* I quote word for word, and it is not an accidental page, a chance

---

* John Stuart Mill, "Principles of Political Economy." Vol. I.

phrase; it is an idea repeatedly expressed in this work, and which pervades it all, as the translator himself acknowledges. This author "expects little improvement in morality, until the producing large families is regarded with the same feelings as drunkenness, or any other physical excess."* He comforts himself, however, with the hope that the time is approaching when "we shall be able to convert the moral obligation," not to have too many children, "into a legal one," and when the law will "end by enforcing" this obligation upon "the recalcitrant minority."† This is the sort of stuff that is called, now-a-days, science, progress, the future! And yet there are those who would call me to account for having spoken of the approach of European barbarism, and for having given warning of the danger of such a despotism as the human race has never known!

[But fatherhood ought to obey not alone the law of *fecundity;* it should follow one law more—the law of *morality*. Father Hyacinthe developed this cardinal law. He showed the resemblance of every father of a family to Abraham, when God showed him in the stars of heaven the symbol of his race: it was not only his sons who are to go forth from him, nor his sons' sons, but, in the course of centuries, whole nations.‡ Now these generations are, so to speak, contained in him, living one and the same life with him; and, according to the energetic language of the Scriptures, he carries them already in his loins.§ In this way it is, that by the good or evil use which a man makes of his liberty, by the wounds which, in his own person, he inflicts upon human nature, or by the respect with which he surrounds it, a single man can exert an influence either happy or fatal, salutary or corrupting, upon countless generations. Original sin cannot otherwise be explained; it is a consequence of the exceptional dependence of all men upon him in whom fatherhood was impersonated in all its plenitude and its energy. The races peculiarly cursed, of

---

* *Ibid.* page 459, *note.*   † *Ibid.* page 464.
‡ Gen. xvii. 4.   § Heb. vii. 10.

which the Scripture tells us, have this origin only: in cursing the son of Ham, Noah simply expressed the law by which the depravity of the father passes to the children.—It is not invariable: there are on the one hand the fatalities of nature, on the other the liberty of the individual, which may free the son, whether for good or evil, from the influence of the parent. But with these exceptions, the law none the less remains such as experience and common sense have proved it to be—"like father, like son;"—such as the Holy Book has expressed it, in showing the Lord as visiting the sins of the fathers upon the third and fourth generation, and remembering mercy to the thousandth.—It depends, then, at the last resort, upon fatherhood to raise or lower the physical and moral level of humanity.]

I hear it said by sophistical science, that in an approaching cataclysm of the globe there is to rise a new race superior to our own, just as we ourselves arose in the last of the transformations of the earth. We should be destined, then, to be to this race of the future what the brute races are now to us; but science consoles itself for this in its pantheistic indifference. Gentlemen, there is a truth beneath these dismal fantasies;—it is, that it depends upon fathers, not to create a race superior to man—man is the last expression of creative wisdom—but to raise the human race above its present position. It depends on them, first by fatherhood, and then by education, to elevate, from generation to generation, the physical and moral level of our great and progressive humankind; as it depends upon them also to depress, to impoverish, to corrupt it in everything—in blood, in ideas, in morals! Humanity is in their power; they may, at their pleasure, raise it up to God, or depress it to a level with the brutes.

[In conclusion, the speaker insisted upon the *religious character* of paternity.]

And yet it is not glory enough for Fatherhood to add something to human nature day by day; it must also, if I may venture to say it, add somewhat to the divine nature. Doubtless, God is perfect and unchangeable in himself; but he needs to grow in us. He has bidden us, through Christianity, to be "partakers of his own nature,"* and his desire is to impart that nature ever more and more to the bosom of humanity. Such is the sublime goal of Christian fatherhood. It prepares new subjects for that divine "adoption of sons" of which the evangelist St. John has said: "As many as received him, to them gave he power to become the sons of God, even to them that believe on his name, which were born not of blood, nor of the will of the flesh, nor of the will of man, but of God."† Christian fatherhood brings forth children for baptism, for the holy supper, for all the real and secret marvels of grace, for all the wonderful intercourse of the personal and living God with man.

In their ardent longing for the Messiah, the Jews watched unceasingly for his appearance among the children of their fruitful marriages; every faithful father hoped that some day, while embracing one of these sweet creatures, lost in joy and adoration, he should recognize beneath the features of his child the ambassador of Heaven. The dream of the Hebrew family is the reality of the Christian family. Christian father, put back those fair locks, look at that pure forehead from which the water of holy baptism has hardly dried away, look at that clear and limpid eye, wherein is mirrored the blue of heaven, and with it, the smile of God! This child, so lovely and so innocent, this angel that comes to you from heaven and leads you back thither, is

---

* 2 Peter, 1. 4.   † John, 1. 12, 13.

the Messiah. The redemption of Christ is upon him, the grace and the virtues of Christ dwell within the soul, and the Christ himself lives again in your son!"*

Fatherhood, then, is an eminently religious thing. Like all that is truly great, it pertains to God, and partakes of him. It proceeds from him, for he is at once its origin and its law; it returns to him, because it brings into existence not for this human life alone, but has its final purpose in the formation of a divine being. How overwhelming the thought! Once more I utter from my heart that cry of wonder and of prayer: "I bow my knees before the Father of our Lord Jesus Christ, from whom all fatherhood in heaven and earth is named!"†

* See Gal. ii. 20; Phil. i. 21; Eph. iii. 17. † Eph. iii. 14, 15.

LECTURE FIFTH.

December 30, 1866.

EDUCATION IN THE FAMILY.

Gentlemen: We now understand fatherhood. It has appeared to us as a very simple thing, seated by every fireside in the world; and at the same time as a very grand thing, superior, in a sense, to all royalties, associated with all priesthoods, receiving directly from God this wonderful power of vanquishing death by reproducing the individual, and enlarging the creation by propagating the kind.

A reproduction of the individual in his *blood*, in his *soul* (in that orthodox sense in which I have explained it), and finally, in his *works*, paternity creates for man a primary immortality upon the earth, that immortality of race which the divine promise has never separated from the immortality of the person, and of which we have an illustrious example in the posterity of the holy patriarchs, Abraham, Isaac, and Jacob. Contemporary rationalism is right in asserting this immortality of the present life; but it is wrong, while asserting this, in denying the immortality of the life to come.

It is in the right, also, when with us it honors in paternity the noble instrument of the propagation of our kind, in the first place, under that grand *humanitarian* form, which our age seems to be called, more than its predecessors, to know, to love, to serve; and secondly, in those more particular and determinate forms which are called *races* and *nations*. But it ought better to understand and better to practise those two holy laws of *fecundity* and *morality* which expand mankind and the nations in point of number, at the same time that they elevate and ennoble them by virtue.

It should, above all, recognize that human fatherhood finds its end, as its origin, in God himself, seeing that it has for its supreme mission to prepare new subjects of participation in the divine life in the bosom of Christianity. Arrived at this climax, we have learned, Gentlemen, to honor the name of *father* as that august title for the glory of which one might almost say that God and man are rival claimants.

Well, then, great as it is in its *first act*, which is *generation*, fatherhood is greater still in its *second act*, which is *education*, that gradual and glorious moral generation.

[It is upon this subject of education in the family that Father Hyacinthe proposes now to speak. He will consider successively the *agents* and the *laws* of education.]

PART FIRST.—*Of the Agents of Education.*

1. [At the outset, by way of preliminary, he proceeds to define education, and determine its precise object.]

The deeper meaning of words is generally found in their etymology. According to the Latin root, *education* means a *drawing-out*, from the Latin *educere*. Education is not, then, the creation of life, but the development of the life already created. To *bring up* is another word which carries a similar idea—to convey from a lower to a higher plane; it is to carry a being from the state in which he exists now to a state in which he does not yet exist. Education supposes, on the part of God, creation—on the part of man, fatherhood; and it rests upon another law, universal in this world, the *law of the germ.*

In whatever sphere I contemplate life, outside of the bosom of God—in the animal as in the vegetable kingdom, in the world of souls as well as of bodies—everywhere I find it beginning in a germ, where it lies latent, and as if wrapped, up in a mysterious sleep. And, as I am speaking of man, there are in him two germs, folded one within the other—the soul and the body. The body is formed with all its organs; all its functions are there in a rudimentary state; and yet it is obvious that thus far it is nothing more than a marvellous epitome of man. The soul is constituted with all its faculties, and even with the direct and involuntary exercise of them. To speak only of the understanding, which is the root of all, it bears already within itself one pre-existent idea, the most simple and the most fruitful of all ideas, the idea of *being*, a dawning light, which by and by shall illuminate everything, but which now falls upon no definite object, and in which the gaze of the infant is lost without consciousness either of it or of itself.

Now, it is when subjected to this educational force, that the germ begins to open, unfold, and to exhibit outwardly, by their motion and outburst, the elements infolded in its bosom. The educational force, for the plant, is the soil in which it is rooted, the sunbeams and the dew-drops; for man, it is a cause as personal as himself. Upon this education, so different from all others, the seal of individuality is set, with an unparalleled dignity. Reason and liberty are essential to its ministers; and for its subjects, passive obedience is not sufficient, we must have besides an intelligent and free response. Education is not a thing imposed; it is a free gift, freely accepted; it is to-day from father to son, what it was originally from God to man—a work of reverence: "with great reverence thou dealest toward us."*

[Education in general, then, is the development of a *pre-existent germ;* and the education of man in particular is the development of a *personal germ* by the action of a free and intelligent agent without, by the free and intelligent co-operation of the subject within.

2d. This idea explained, Father Hyacinthe comes to the question proposed in this first part of his discourse—who are the true and legitimate agents of the work of education? It must be observed that this question is answered by the very idea of education, which is only the complement of generation. The agents of education can only be the authors of the life itself—the parents.]

I well understand that we must recognize three forms of human society. I said so at the commencement of these studies, and I still purpose to explain, in turn, their rights and their dignities. There is *domestic society*, as we have seen; but there is, besides, *civil society* and *religious society*. This child belongs to the family, but he also belongs to his country, which is temporal, and to the Church, which is eternal. Thus I am very far from denying the necessary and legitimate intervention of Church and State in his education. I am not of the mind of those who say, pretending to speak in the name of Catholicism, "The State is a policeman;" and I am not of their mind who say, in the name of rationalism, "The State is an insurance company." The State is neither a policeman nor an insurance company, but the

---

* Wisdom, xii. 18.

highest organ of civil society, in the moral as well as the material system. It has, then, a power over the things of the soul, in relation to those matters which do not pertain to the sphere of the supernatural; and the most sacred of its rights, as of its duties, is to watch over the education of youth. As to the Church, I should not be its minister, if I had forgotten the words of Jesus Christ to his apostles: "Go ye, therefore, and teach all nations."* Depositary of the religious instruction, and, by an inevitable consequence, of the moral instruction, which are the salvation of families and empires as well as of the individual, the Church is, by the nature of things, the great instructress of the generations of man. I fully recognize, then, under different titles, and in different degrees, the authority of the Church and of the State, in education; but I nevertheless vindicate the *priority*, and in a sense the *superiority* of the family; I assert anew, that the father and mother are, by *natural* and by *divine* right, the proper educators of the children whom heaven and their love have given them.

[The father and the mother are the agents of education. They fill each a separate function, and yet they carry on the work *in common*. Father Hyacinthe remarks that in the first place the father has the supreme authority in all domestic education. It belongs to him of right, as the head of the family. This supreme authority is delegated to the mother, but its source and royal seat is always in the father; for, as it has been already said, "the man is the head of the woman." As for the *more special* share of the husband and wife in this complex work, it is determined by the same principles which settle the harmony of the conjugal relation: man is especially the representative of reason, woman of the affections.]

I return, Gentlemen, to the premises which I have laid down on the subject of love. I said, in speaking of con-

* Matt. xxviii. 19.

jugal love, of rational, personal, and Christian love—the only kind of which I spoke—that it presupposes an intimate harmony between the two halves of human nature: the one, the head which thinks and governs; the other, the heart which loves and inspires. That which is necessary, then, in the love of husband and wife, is necessary in the education of children—we must have the presence and the combination of these two powers. The man, representative of sovereign reason, to utter those lofty teachings of intelligence and faith, of which the woman shall become the interpreter; to inculcate those rules to which all owe obedience, not merely the children, but the wife herself; to punish when punishment is necessary, and " to drive foolishness from the heart of his child by the rod of correction."* But the woman, the wife, the mother, has a function which is the complement of the first, and which surpasses it in gentleness, often in efficacy—the function of imparting inspirations, and those tendernesses which enfeeble not, but rather strengthen;—that office of the heart which pours itself into the heart, and which, by a sublime reaction, develops the reason on the one hand, while it strengthens the conscience on the other!

To form a man, we must have these two forces, not isolated, but associated in a *common action*. And this, Gentlemen, allow me to say it in passing, is one of the strongest arguments against the sophistry of *divorce*. Ah! love, of itself, can triumph over divorce; but if it should fail of its influence over hearts that had lost their sweetness or their tone, I should appeal to parentage,—I should appeal to its work, left such a hopeless abortion, if the parents separate before they have completed it. Ah! if you can no longer love each other

* Proverbs, xxii. 15.

for each other's sake, love at least for the sake of your child! O father's reason, turn not away from the mother's heart! O heart of mother, do not revolt against the father's reason! but like the two halves of a single shield joined into one complete and necessary defence, surround this cradle and protect it.

[After these general considerations on the separate work of the parents, the preacher entered into certain details to establish the *special* importance of the maternal education.]

I said a great deal about the father, last Sunday: I did so with a purpose. I fear that sometimes, in the Christian pulpit, the part of the father is too much sacrificed to that of the mother. But now I need to render to the mother the homage which is due to her. In this education of the child, which commences with birth, or rather with conception, the influence of the mother is the first in order of time, the most intimate in the order of depth and penetration. The old Arabian prophet was right when he said, "Man that is born of a woman."* We have not thought of this enough: the most decisive education of man, for body and for soul, is given in the cradle. Now the real cradle of man is the womb and the arms of the mother. The long repose of nine months, that chaste and close embrace, where the child is one flesh with its mother, and I might almost say, one soul! And when it is torn from this first caress, it is to find others, no less close and fruitful, in the arms which await it! "What, my son!" cries the mother, "what, the son of my womb! and what, the son of my vows!"† Leave the infant in its mother's arms! Who can fill the place of

* Job, xiv. 1. † Prov. xxxi. 2.

the mother with the child, of the dearly loving with the dearly beloved?

Recall that charming type of Christian art, that from the Catacombs to the Renaissance is so often modified, but which is never changed—that type of the Virgin Mother, the pure and tender mother carrying in her arms the Divine Child! Ah! I know that it is a reality; I know that there was at Nazareth a daughter of royal stock, a mechanic's wife, ever virgin, yet the mother of Jesus Christ; but I know also that this woman has become, in the glory of Christianity, the supreme type of motherhood! O Christian mother!— or, rather, whoever thou art, daughter of humanity, created by the Almighty, redeemed by Christ—O human mother, if only thou have a mother's heart and sympathies, look at the woman of our sculpture and our painting, the mysterious and radiant image of our cathedrals! it is thy sister, thy model, and thy law—it is thyself, if thou canst understand it! Be thou the stem rising from the earth, and never separating from its flower, so full of tender beauty and sweet perfume; be the blooming "branch that groweth out of his root."* Be the mother that holds her infant, night and day, cradled in the caresses of her arms—cradled in her own purity and love. Like her, nourish it on thine own substance; it is God who has filled thy breast; *ubere de cœlo pleno*, as the Church sings. Lavish upon it that divine food, the best of all for its physical and its moral life. This substance is living with the life of thy own soul, which penetrates and quickens it; with every wave of this sweet draught, with every gush of this chaste intoxication, something of thy heart and thy thoughts is passing into thy son!

* Isaiah, xi. 1.

It is, then, in the arms and from the heart of its mother that the child receives its primary education. It is there that it receives those first cares for the body, which are at the same time the first things to waken and stir the heart. The infant is sensible only of that which touches its body; it is upon that that its entire attention is concentrated; consequently, the mother herself should hold this body, this little sacred body, in her arms, not only because she has for the task inimitable hands, hands instinct with intelligence and delicacy,* such as other men and women have not, but also because in touching the body she shall reach the heart, and awaken its life in a smile. O Gentlemen, this is not poetry; or, if it be poetry, it springs from the very bosom of fact. What, then, is the meaning of a child's smile? Look at the animal, and on its inert lips and in its eye, deep as it often is when nature is dreaming there, you will never catch a smile. The smile is the first gleam of intelligence, the dawning twilight of reason and affection: that is the reason why it belongs only to man. So long as no distinct thought has lighted up the baby's mind, it does not smile. But, some day, among the chaos of forms that flit before the dim gaze of its bodily eye, and the still more uncertain gaze of its mental eye, one form is perceived more distinctly defined; the child has seen its mother, the first individuality that has been revealed to it, the first thought which has enlightened its mind, the first affection which has throbbed in its heart. The human world opens before it, the clouds of native ignorance are riven asunder, and like a rainbow, his radiant smile lights up his cradle.

It is at the age of six weeks that the child first smiles

* Ps. lxxviii. 72. "In intellectibus mannum suarum."—*Vulgate.*

upon its mother; it is not till after a year that it speaks its first word—an event in the domestic history which always makes a family-festival, and which really marks an important epoch of life. The smile marks the beginning of thought in the child; but this thought is of an inferior order, it cannot abstract itself from the external objects with which it is connected, and come back freely upon itself, and hold self-consciousness and self-control. To deliver it from this tyranny of individual forms which fix and absorb it, it must have a sensible sign—for human thought cannot separate itself completely from the senses,—a sensible, but arbitrary sign upon which it may depend in its abstraction. This sign is speech; speech, which is not only the expression, but the liberator of thought. The father of the human race received it from God, and every son of Adam receives it from his mother. As the mother's gaze has revealed to him the world of visible realities, even so it is the mother's tongue which opens to him the world of invisible realities, and the most august of all, God! It is a tradition of Christian firesides, that the first intelligent word addressed by the mother to her child should be this great name of God. Sublime prerogative, which elevates the priesthood of the mother, in this, at least, above that of the father, even above our own. O lips of woman, ye beguiled us in Adam, and behold how God has counted you worthy to teach us his truth, and to reveal to us his nature!

Ah! I cannot but remember that prophecy of Genesis, when the old serpent of error and evil deemed himself the conqueror of our race forever. The Lord God said unto him: "On thy belly shalt thou go, and dust shalt thou eat all the days of thy life: and I will put enmity between thee and the woman, and between thy seed and her seed; she shall bruise thy head, and thou shalt bruise her heel."*

I do not wish to hurt any one's feelings, but I must speak the truth; those doctrines, those crawling doctrines that cannot rise from the ground, but which make it their business to lie in ambush for men's heels—for all these infirmities of ours which bind us in thought or feeling to material things—materialist, skeptical, atheist doctrines, which sometimes lift their heads a moment, but can never do more than crawl, even while they are giving such a magnificent hiss—I tell them: You appeal to science; but science does not know you, and the real struggle is not between her and you! Take care, you have a more dangerous enemy than she can be: "*I will put enmity between thee and the woman!*" Your enemy is the woman, with that innate tenderness and purity which makes mental corruption as repugnant to her as physical; the woman, with that supernatural power with which Christianity has endued her! Between us and you, there stands the woman! Between your sophistries and our reason, there is our mother! After twenty, thirty years, and more, we still keep within our souls the echo of her words and the impress of her embraces! The warmth of her caresses is still glowing; the sting which her lips have made still bleeds; and we carry in that mother's kiss—that divine salutation—a permanent and infallible revelation of all that is highest in heaven, of all that is deepest in the soul! No, until you have closed the lips of the Christian mother, you have not succeeded in extinguishing the Kingdom of God upon the earth!

* Genesis, iii. 14, 15. (See the Roman Catholic versions.)

PART SECOND.—*The Laws of Education.*

[After observing that education is not left to the caprice of parents, but should be carried on according to those higher *laws* which spring from the very nature of things, Father Hyacinthe reduces these laws to three principal ones. The first relates to the surroundings in the midst of which our life is developed; the second, to its starting-point; the third, to its point of destination. The direction given to education should be in conformity to the actual facts concerning these three principal elements of human existence.]

First Law.—*True education is that which is intended to prepare man for actual life.*

I do not know, Gentlemen, if there exists an error more common, and at the same time more fatal to the happiness of the individual and the progress of the race, than that which bears upon the real elements and the practical direction of human life. The father who does not desire to bring up his children to barren reveries and cruel disappointments, will carefully avoid this error.

The two principal spheres of our existence, are our *family* and our *work*.

It is for *family* life, above all, that man is to be fitted: for its interests, which are to be the great object of his solicitude, and for its virtues, which are the great object of his aspiration; for its affections and its griefs, which will always be the supreme delight and the supreme bitterness of the human heart—that double cup of which I have spoken, full of joys and full of tears; but whose joys have something of grave and holy, and whose tears, however bitter they may be, do yet borrow something of the sweetness of the joys. Public life itself is subordinate to private life. What is a country, but an association of homes? What is public life itself, if not the resultant of all the forces which act in all the homes? The existence and prosperity of nations consists entirely in the existence and prosperity of its homes; and this is why the two fundamental laws of civil society have always been the law of property and the law of marriage.

After education for the family, nothing is more important than education for *work*, that other substantial and constituent form of our existence. The child may choose between mental and manual labor, and in each of these great divisions will find many varieties answering to all individual aptitudes as well as to all social needs; but his choice once made, he must apply himself with love and constancy, and remember that work is not only a means, but, in a very true and noble sense, an end. The work for which men, taken generally, are to be fitted, is manual—agriculture, mechanic art, commerce; and it is one of the distinguishing characteristics of modern progress, that it elevates in importance and dignity these common occupations, which Christianity has always honored, but which the prejudices of the world have too often sacrificed to the liberal professions. These great things, sciences, letters, arts, politics, with wars and treaties of peace, have not, however, the exclusive or even the primary importance that has too often been given them in our education. All this movement of human things is more on their surface than in their substance. It is limited in its nature, often very brilliant, but often, also, very corrupt; and it is not, I venture to say, the true movement of humanity. The history of our race, as it is to be written in the future, will be, more than anything else, the history of these two elements of genuine life, these two foci of all sound and lasting civilization—the family and the workshop.

I have named the two main foci of civilization, which is equivalent to naming the two main schools of popular education—the *family*, where we are practically trained for life, and the *workshop*, where we are practically trained for work.

Popular education is deservedly one of the most living interests of our time; and the way which appears to many as the only efficacious way of reaching this noble end, is the creation of schools, properly so called, distinct from the home and the workshop. For my part, I agree that the importance of the school had not been sufficiently understood down to these later days; it is a fruitful truth which it is well to bring into the light, but which, nevertheless, must not be exaggerated. Everywhere, but above all, in France, there is nothing more to be dreaded than exaggerated truths. Even in the region of the higher education, it is not the school which gives thorough knowledge of ideas and things, experience of life, of men, of facts; how much less, then, can it do so in the more modest and practical sphere of popular education! That which the child of the people wants of the school more than anything else, is the actual mechanical details of reading, writing, and arithmetic, and a certain general culture, in which, some day, I hope, no French citizen will be wanting. But as for that luxury of learning, reserved for an intellectual aristocracy, which must not be too much enlarged lest it be too much lowered, the workman has nothing to do with it; and as for the more profound knowledge of his own art, he will prefer to obtain it by practice in the workshop, rather than theoretically in the school. The practice of good workshops has frequently been in advance of the theory of the schools; and this theory, moreover, remains barren and uncomprehended until applied, and sometimes rectified, by the rude hands of the workman. However important the school may be, it does not contain the great solution of education for the masses; this solution must be sought, first of all, from the family and the workshop. Give the people uncorrupted and well-ordered workshops—there are too few now-a-days; give them back their homes—there are none of them left in our great cities; and you will have done more even than by multiplying our glorious schools! The educators of real life are the parents, in that sanctuary of the family which we call the *home;* and the masters, the true and worthy masters, in that sanctuary of labor called the *workshop.*

Second Law.—*Education must not mistake about the real starting-point of human life.*

[The preacher here reproaches the new schools of opinion with solving two questions of origin by two chimerical hypotheses: the origin of the species by the hypothesis of the monkey, or at least of the savage; and the origin of the individual by the hypothesis of an unfallen nature.]

I would answer with the poet:

"Give me nor insult nor excess of praise."

The human race did not commence with the savage, and the individual is not born perfect; he is born in original sin. He who conducts the work of education with no reference to this starting-point, will make a bad and false thing of it.

I have to thank the eminent author of that very fine and excellent book, *Social Reform in France,* a book of *really* positive philosophy—a book that deals with facts without falsifying them, and which looks at them with the reason of an observer and the heart of a good man. In this book, one of the things which affected me most, is the noble courage with which the author has laid down as the basis of education and all social progress, the dogma of original sin. I call it a *dogma*, because I am a priest, and am speaking in the name of the Church; he calls it a *fact*, because he is a man and is speaking in the name of experience. Well, it is a dogma, and it is a fact,—a dogma, because God has revealed it; a fact, because experience proves it. There is not a father of a family, not a serious and thoughtful teacher, who has not seen with his eyes and touched with his hands the reality of original sin.

Man is born in a fallen state; with tendencies toward truth, I admit—with aspirations after good, I claim. For man is great even in his fall, like a palace tumbling in upon itself, like a temple which even in its ruins keeps something of the majesty of the god which dwelt in it! Man is great even in his ruins; but he is in ruins!

It is not a perfect being that we have to work upon, but a fallen being. It is not alone the good tendencies in him which must be developed, but the depraved instincts which must be repressed. It is not a rough sketch of civilization, which we have to complete, to develop, and to perfect, it is an incursion of barbarism which we must conquer and subdue. Yes, in every century, in every generation, we are witnesses, in the bosom of our great civilization, of a veritable invasion of barbarians: they do not come now from the forests of Germany, the deserts of Scandinavia or Scythia, they come from the depths of original sin. Your children, as nature gives them to you, are barbarians, and it is for you to civilize them! This is the great work of fathers—the work which gives such dignity to domestic society, as compared with civil or religious society. The civilizers of the human race! say no longer that they are the princes and the magistrates, the thinkers and the orators. All these, no doubt, are ambassadors of God, and benefactors of man, but theirs is necessarily a secondary part. The true civilizers—the creators of France and of Europe, the legislators of modern society—are fathers!

Original sin, being the starting-point, necessitates a coercive force in education. All society worthy of the name contains within itself a coercive force—the Church as well as the State, and domestic society as well as both the others. I recognize the usefulness and the necessity, according to the circumstances of time and place, of a more or less considerable exercise of this power. I simply add that it is itself subordinate to a superior power, that of persuasion, of moral improvement through reason and love. The principal instrument of the Church is not coercive power. Do we make sincere believers, virtuous Christians, solely or chiefly by repression? No, we make only rebels or hypocrites! Neither is the supreme force of the State its material force. Can we make citizens, and above all, French citizens, by repression and force? Well, it is the same thing in the family: and the father who wields only the rod of discipline, is as guilty and as powerless as he who rejects it in over-indulgence, and never knows how to command or punish! There is a medium—the great and wise medium which avoids both extremes—persuasion, by reason and by love! Speak, teach, by precept and by example. Bring down from those heights on which the father and mother dwell, and toward which the child is constantly looking upward—bring down that power of truth and virtue which takes hold of the free faculties of the mind and heart, and you will have healed in your child the wounds left by the original evil!

Above all, have God with you. I cannot conceive of the repression of sin without the divine action! God must interfere in all the acts of the family, and must himself be, so to speak, an inmate of the home. This is the grand tradition of all free and prosperous peoples in Europe or America, and it is not for our France, with all respect to the sophists, to repudiate it! The presence of God in the majesty of the paternal brow, in the authority of the sovereign reason—the presence of God in the depths of the maternal heart, in the tenderness of the love which freely gives itself as God has freely given himself to it—this is, as we shall shortly see, the third element necessary to education, the most efficacious of the laws which govern it.

Third Law.—*Education must not mistake about the destination of human life.*

[The end to which education, as well as life, should tend, is God. Father Hyacinthe here shows that the presence of God is necessary, not only to the repression of evil, but to the development of good. There are faculties in human nature which cannot be brought into exercise, except by religious training.]

I would not have morals independent of religion; neither, on the other hand, would I have religion independent of morals! If religion find no place in education; if the religious sentiment be not cultivated in the child's heart; if the child be not led, in his will and understanding, step by step toward God, religion will not be destroyed, but it will be made independent of morals and education.

It will not be destroyed, because we cannot suppress facts by denying them. It is a very fine thing to deny the existence of the religious faculty in man, amid the applause of some feeble creatures in whom this faculty has become atrophied; but for all that, the religious faculty will continue to exist in human nature. And if we refuse it all culture and all direction, it will break out in some form savage and barbaric as original sin. Ah! you did not wish to bring God into the training of your child's soul? you did not wish to train up your child for God? Well, then, beware of terrible retribution from God and from the child!

Let me cite a recent, but historical example. The founder of Positivism in France, the man who passed his whole life in denying religion in all forms, and even in its very essence, ended his career in a state of profound mysticism, and by a strange but sincere attempt at a new religion. His favorite book was the *Imitation of Christ*, and he recommended it to his disciples as a manual of humanitarian piety. He composed a Positivist calendar, in which Christian saints go hand in hand with pagan heroes; and, finally, he left to the executors of his will the care of his room, as the cradle of the worship of humanity, of which he believed himself the first high-priest.*—This was the way in which the religious faculty, so long despised, avenged itself. God was driven out by the gate of reason, and God came back again by the gate of madness!

[In the presence of such facts among cultivated minds, the preacher asks, what would become of the masses if Christian education no longer gave to the religious sentiment in them its legitimate direction. It is safe to assert, that after a few generations, we should see the formation of a new paganism, and perhaps even the reproduction of the most monstrous extravagances of the old paganism—religious prostitutions and human sacrifices.]

Leave us then our Jesus! I end with him what I had to say of education, because my theme has not changed,

* Auguste Comte et la Philosophie Positive, by M. Littré, p. 643, et *passim.*

my tone is as unvarying as truth; I can only begin and end with God. "I am Alpha and Omega," says he, "the Beginning and the End."* And again: "I am the First and the Last; I am he that liveth, and was dead; and behold, I am alive for evermore."†

Leave us, leave us our Jesus Christ; he is better than all your inventions! Leave us that old Bible, that we may teach our children to spell in it,—the Bible which has created printing, the Bible which has civilized Europe! It is from the Bible that the little Germans and Scandinavians are taught their language, and to love at the same time their religion and their native land! Leave us our Bible—us Frenchmen and Catholics; and above all, our Bible expounded by the Church! In that Bible my young kindred and your children may spell out softly and solemnly the name of Jehovah in heaven, and the name of Jesus in the manger and on Calvary.—What, Jehovah, Jesus, that boundless ocean—wouldst hold it in that little hollow in the beach which we call the heart and mind of a child? Yea! Behold the miracle! That which distracted and skeptical sages find it impossible to comprehend, the child accepts without difficulty, like the light of day, like the words and caresses of his mother. He believes in the eternal God, who loves, creates, and redeems him. He believes in Him, he loves Him in return, and tells Him so in prayer. The Bible and the Church for his understanding, prayer and the sacraments for his affections. This is what will give to France and to the world that grand future of which I shall never despair

---

* Rev. 1. 8. † Rev. _. 17. 18.

LECTURE SIXTH.
January 6, 1867.

HOME.

My Lord Archbishop and Gentlemen: In order to live in this world, things invisible—ideas, souls—must take to themselves a body and a local habitation. Royalty has its palaces, religion its temples; the family should have its home. The family and the home imply each other, and prepare each other like soul and body in the person of man. According to our point of view, we may say with almost equal truth, that the soul forms the body, and that the body forms the soul; just so we may assert alternately that the family establishes and preserves the home, and that the home moulds and keeps the family.

"I said: I shall die in my nest; I shall multiply my days as the sand."* Who has not repeated these words of Job in his heart? Who has not loved thee, possessed thee, or dreamed of thee, thou dearest abode of man, sacred nest of our loves and our griefs, where it is so sweet to live, and almost as sweet to die!

On this threshold, Gentlemen, let us pause.

We are about to part to-day for another year, and we can nowhere better take leave of each other than here. You are going back to this abode of earthly happiness; I am going to seclude myself in that abode of self-denial

* Job, xxix. 18.

and heavenly happiness, the cloister! The cloister and the family are not foes—they are not even strangers. Awaiting the time when Providence shall bring us together again, we shall work, I hope, for the triumph of the same cause; we shall serve together the personal and living God, Christ, the Organizer and Redeemer of our race, and the Church, the supreme union of family, and country, and of all mankind!

[Father Hyacinthe proposed, in this Lecture, to study the home in its three phases: 1. Ownership; 2. Transmission; 3. Occupation.]

FIRST PART.—*Ownership of the Home.*

There is no need of doing for Home what I have done for Education. In naming it, I have already *defined* it. The Home is the dwelling-place of the family.

A human family must have a dwelling-place; it needs, by all means, to own a home. As for us who belong to the Catholic celibacy, we may do without! Jesus Christ, bidding us count the cost in advance, has told us: "The foxes have holes, and the birds of the air have nests; but the Son of man hath not where to lay his head."* He alone, then, who feels himself called to follow him afar off along these heroic paths, may taste their austere delights; he cannot enter into voluntary poverty but by the gate of absolute continence. But the man of family, the man who is not one but many, is not free to divorce himself from the earth: it would be folly; and if this folly were possible, it would be a crime! He must have in this world—on this soil on which we tread—some sacred corner where he may

* Matthew, viii. 20.

place the bed of his wife and the cradle of his children. But this transient and make-shift possession of a home —a home that is occupied, but not owned—does not suffice to realize the ideal of the home. That ideal is absolute ownership, conferring not only the right to use for the time being, but the simple and permanent fee. This is the sort of ownership which becomes to the family a principle of *liberty,* of *order,* and of *happiness.*

The ownership of the home is a principle of *liberty.* Yes, indeed! we are not really our own, as a general thing, unless we are completely in our own house. This is a great principle in the legislation of all civilized nations—the inviolability of the citizen's domicile: and this inviolability covers another—it is the safeguard, the affirmation of the inviolability of the person. I venture to assert that the inviolability of the man and the citizen is never more strongly affirmed and more effectively secured than in the ownership of the dwelling, the absolute and complete ownership of the house in which he dwells. And if this be true of the man—if it is the right of property which makes him free and sovereign at home, which draws around him those lines that no one in the world dares cross without his leave, how much more is it true of the family, of that collective person which has many lives to defend, and which is attached to life by many and varied ties! Ah, the family—it is like those giants, sons of Earth, who when they fell, plucked up strength again as soon as they touched the ground; and even in the bosom of poverty, it will live on, full of energy, full of faith in itself and its future, if it can rest secure in the possession of its little cot and its little field! "Better," says the inspired book, "better the meal of the poor under a thatched roof, than splendid banquets in a strange house!"

But ownership is not only a principle of independence for the family, it is also a principle of *order*. It is thus that God has arranged the laws of the moral world; he has joined together things which at first sight seemed incompatible. The family must be free, but the family must also be conservative. For ownership is not only a fact, it is a fact glorified by an idea; it is not only an interest, the first of all interests, containing the germ of all the rest, it is an interest consecrated by the holiness and majesty of right! Touch not this patch of ground! it is guarded, not by one feeble individual only; it is defended by the solidarity and confederation of all rights! All rights are interdependent in this world: the rights of the weak cling to those of the strong; and the rights of the strong, when their hour of peril comes, are fain to fall back upon those of the weak. Property, then, is conservative; it breathes a certain inspiration of equity which affects the poor man, the laborer, the peasant, which renders them deaf to the perfidious whispers of revolution, and leads them to hope, not in catastrophes, but in progress—normal and harmonious progress. Consequently, the possession of property by the people is the solution of the most difficult questions of the time in which we live, this age of mingled industry and democracy. Let it be brought about little by little, in our great cities, in our manufacturing centres, that the workman shall be no longer the tenant of some damp cellar, or some freezing garret, but the owner of his home, and I repeat it, he himself, henceforth both liberal and conservative, will set the seal of reconciliation and peace upon those cruel antagonisms which divide and destroy us.

The ownership of a home is not only a principle of liberty and a principle of order, it is also a principle of *happiness*. The proud sentiment of liberty is one of the inmost sentiments in the mind of man. Another of these inmost sentiments is the calm and sober sentiment of order! But there is something, in my opinion, deeper yet—the sentiment of domestic happiness! We cannot live always in the dreams of the imagination, the passions of the heart, or the intoxication of the senses. There comes an hour when man aspires, by all that is noblest and deepest in his nature, for something settled—something which will fix the movements of his life without confining them, which will settle and make them fruitful. Somewhere or other he seeks a corner of the earth for himself: there he builds his dwelling; and hollowing out a fireside in the thickness of the wall, he lays together bricks and stones in a cement which will defy the centuries! And then, his work finished, he seats himself beside it. He peoples it in imagination with a joyous group—the future companion of his life—his children that are to be. Looking silently into that sacred niche—mysterious centre of the human family—he listens to the distracting sounds without—the din of the city; the sounds of nature; the confused rumors of trouble; the uneasy tumult of the throng of yesterday; to the careerings and whistlings of the wind; to the rain, which beats against the windows, fierce but powerless; and the while, he, sitting there in honor and in peace, leaning his head and resting his heart by this warm and quiet fireside, murmurs in his soul, if not with his lips, "This is my rest forever; here will I dwell, for I have desired it."*

Stability in the happiness of domestic life—this is the

---

* Psalm cxxxii. 14.

idea which is connected with the possession of a home. It is a rude, but most delightful symbol, of the permanence which is promised to man after this life, and which dwells already in the depths of the Christian heart. "We have a building of God, a house not made with hands, eternal in the heavens."* We have a home and household joys with uncreated truth and justice; but, until the time when we shall take possession of our heritage in the infinite, when we shall inherit from God the home in eternity, we must needs be heirs of that sweet reflection from the heart and face of God, the family fireside. This is why the inspired books delight to unite these two things, religion and the family. It is to that roof, the guardian of good morals as well as of true joys, that they are continually sending their disciple. "Drink waters out of thine own cistern," cries the sage of Israel, in that Eastern style so full of boldness and purity: "drink running waters out of thine own well, and let them be only thine own, and not strangers' with thee! Rejoice with the wife of thy youth! Let her be as the loving hind and pleasant roe: let her breasts satisfy thee at all times, and be thou ravished always with her love."†

David has sung this domestic happiness on the harp of the God of Sinai: "Blessed is every one that feareth the Lord; that walketh in his ways. For thou shalt eat the labor of thine hands: happy shalt thou be, and it shall be well with thee. Thy wife shall be as a fruitful vine by the sides of thine house; thy children like olive plants round about thy table: Behold, thus shall the man be blessed that feareth the Lord. The Lord shall bless thee out of Zion; and thou shalt see the good of

---

* 2 Corinthians, v. 1. † Proverbs, v. 15-19.

Jerusalem all the days of thy life. Yea, thou shalt see thy children's children, and peace upon Israel!"*

You see, Gentlemen, how the prophets of God, the teachers of the Jews and of mankind, have celebrated the holiness and happiness of home. For in this law of happiness there is a law of holiness: man cannot be happy unless he finds something as great and pure as infinity, at the depth of his loves. Go to the broken cistern, go to that happiness which is only of the flesh, and you will find but a dribbling thread of water, a scanty and insipid draught, which can never quench the great, infinite thirst of the human heart! but go to the well of the family and of God, go to the well of Jacob, where the Lord sat and talked to the Samaritan woman; drink at those founts of joy which God himself has consecrated; you will drink in happiness with holiness, like a foretaste of that well of water that springeth up unto everlasting life.

PART SECOND.—*Transmission of the Home.*

[The preacher remarks, in the first place, that perfect ownership implies *transmission*, and that, in consequence, this second characteristic of the home grows out of the first.]

The home ought to be transmitted; but why?

First, because it is a *fact*. People insist on facts now-a-days, and with reason, for it is from facts that we derive ideas and laws. Now, it is a fact in the history of domestic life, among all races and in all ages, that the home has been handed down from father to son. It is enough for me that it is a fact, and I assert it on the testimony of all mankind.

* Psalm cxxviii.

For my part, I shall never be one of that sort of philanthropists who have no respect for humanity except where it is not to be found—that is to say, in the future: strange minds, who have nothing for its past but blasphemies, and nothing for its present but revolt; but who make amends for this by the adoration with which they honor it in some imaginary and impossible future!

Besides, this hereditary transmission of the home is not only a thing of the past, it is a thing of the present also. It exists throughout all Europe; and though France should seem to be an exception, I must nevertheless insist upon it as a law of the civilization of the present day.

France, Gentlemen, France is an exceptional country —exceptional in her glory, exceptional in her misfortunes. For eighty years France has been a devoted land. She has devoted herself as a victim, she has devoted herself as a martyr, to the pursuit of great ideas which it is her mission to popularize in the world, but of which she has not yet discovered the settled definition and the practical application. I admire France in her work—I admire her in her heroic sacrifice of herself in the pursuit of an unknown end; but I do not take her for a rule, in all the blind gropings to which her mission condemns her.

And after all, our country is not an exception in this respect. If we consider the real France, in the provinces as well as the capital, in the country as well as in manufacturing towns, the law of the transmission of the home is still the controlling law of our national usages. It is, then, an assertion based upon facts, in the present as well as the past, that the transmission of the ancestral home is not, to be sure, among the absolute necessities, but one of the normal and prosperous conditions of domestic society.

But I wish to find the *reason* of this law.

The family is not that ephemeral thing we sometimes see, which does not last even for a man's lifetime, and which, beginning with the marriage contract, ends with the coming of age and scattering of the children. The family is an institution which is all the stronger in the present as its roots are deeper in the past, and as it has a manlier ambition and more practical means of perpetuating itself in the future. The true father, when he bequeaths to his son the glory of his blood, the traditions of his mind and heart, the carrying forward of his work, sees other sons beyond this one—he beholds generation after generation; and getting the victory over death, he lays claim, not to an ephemeral immortality, but to an immortality for ages to come.

The family, then, is a permanent institution, and therefore implies, on the one hand, the transmission of material interests; on the other, the transmission of moral traditions. The family has these two bases: in its moral relations it rests upon love, honor, religion, virtue; in its material relations it is founded upon the soil, upon property, upon all the interests which attach thereto. I repeat, then, these moral and material traditions are not the things of a day nor the work of an individual; they are the work of generations, and they occupy the course of successive ages!

1st. Let us take, first, *material interests:* let us study them in these country-places of which I have spoken. Country life is the primitive life of man, as it was instituted by divine authority, in the person of our first parents.

"The Lord God placed man in the garden of Eden, to

dress it and to keep it."* This was our original vocation, and whatever we may do, we all preserve, in the depth of our nature, a sort of instinct for it, stronger than all our errors. Every year, as the Spring comes round, the wealthy resident of the city feels these memories revive within him; he exclaims, like Horace, weary of the court of Augustus: "Dear country, when shall I behold thee once again?" *O rus, quando te aspiciam?* and away he goes to seek health and happiness at his country-seat. Furthermore, besides these exceptional cases, there are an immense majority in every nation, who always live in the country; and theirs is the model and perfect home—the home not cramped up among streets and alleys, but surrounded by grounds, where the family, truly free and sovereign, without crossing the line of their own property, can get from their own land, by their own labor, all that is necessary or useful to the comfort and even the luxury of life. And here, again, I recall a verse out of our holy books—a very simple, but a very true and very original idea: "For the good, are good things created from the beginning. The principal things for the whole use of man's life are water, fire, iron, and salt, flour of wheat, honey, milk, and the blood of the grape, and oil and clothing."† Now all these things are found on the country homestead. There are the bees that give wax and honey; there are the flocks which yield wool and milk. The country homestead is ready to take part in every covenant between man and those living forces that have been intrusted to nature by the hand of God, for the service of human civilization.

But all this, I repeat, this creation of the country homestead, is not the affair of a single day, nor the work

---

* Genesis, ii. 15. † Ecclesiasticus, xxxix. 25, 26.

of a single man. The earth is like the child of whom I was speaking not long ago; it bears the marks of original sin. "Cursed is the ground for thy sake—thorns also and thistles shall it bring forth to thee!* It answers with barrenness and frowardness to thy sweat and thy labor. The earth itself is a rebel and a savage, and it is not till after long years of laborious education, that it yields at last to the hand of man, and advances from barbarism to civilization. But what thought and experience, what perseverance, have been demanded in the head that directed the progress of the improvement of the land! What energy and courage must equip the hands that have wrought out these plans into execution! It is not the work of a single man to make covenant with the vegetable kingdom, to plant trees and enjoy their shade and their fruits; neither is it the work of a single man to make covenant with those inferior races in which Providence has given us our lawful slaves, our indispensable allies, and (if I might so speak) our too much neglected benefactors—the domestic animals, who, as their name imports, are a part of the home, and to whom the Lord did not disdain to extend the covenant he made with Noah and his family: "Behold, I establish my covenant with you, and with your seed after you, and with every living creature that is with you."† To develop and improve these races, to associate them with the habits of the country family, and with the whole system of the cultivation of the soil, we still need traditions, years, generations!

Now, Gentlemen, if you refuse this element of time, if you will not inscribe over all property, and especially

* Genesis, iii. 17, 18.   † Genesis, ix. 9, 10.

over all country property, this great word, transmission, inheritance, what is to become of all this work? And when the man who shall have undertaken it, the father of the family, feels himself bending beneath its burden far more than beneath the burden of years; when he feels creeping upon his temples what they call, in the poetic language of the south of France, "*graveyard flowers*"—the first gray hairs—he will look mournfully at what he has begun, what he is never to finish; he will look at the possessions which are about to slip away from him, and be desecrated by uncaring hands; and then he will have no more courage to toil and labor as now, he will have courage only to weep; and property will receive a wound that all your Reports on Agriculture will never cure, to the end of time.

Our peasants understand this matter,—those practical philosophers, learned in the lore of experience and tradition. I say again, I am not speaking against my country, but with her and in her behalf. I could point out to you, in one of our provinces, among their rugged but fertile mountains, races true to their old proverb—"The hearth-fire must be kept a-light."* And that the sacred flame may be kept burning in the same dwelling and by the same hands, they make long migrations to the great cities, that they may bring back their savings, the honorable reward of toil, and find once more that fireside which their sacrifice has saved—that fireside, the sight of which cheers the heart as well as the body, as they say, "Aha! I am warm, I have seen the fire!"†

2d. I pass now to *moral interests*. It is not the accident of blood which attaches the child to the father. Paternity is pre-eminently a matter of liberty and fore-

---

* Proverb of Auvergne: "Il faut que la maison fume." † Is. xliv. 16.

thought, in its moral relations. Like God, whose image he is, the father has "created all things in number and measure and weight."* He has weighed everything in the balance of his reason and his heart, and has said: "I will have sons, I will raise up a race unto myself, and I will bequeath an uncorrupted blood, an honorable name; and with these, immortal traditions of honor, and patriotism, and religion! The things I learned on my mother's lap, and between my father's arms—the things I have loved, and for which I have toiled—shall never perish from beneath the sun!" What constitutes the family, then, in the moral system, is that combination of principles, sentiments, and operations, which our ancestors have wished to maintain after them; it is a life which is developed and perpetuated in a collective person.

But let us take care not to become too spiritual: mind does not cut loose from matter. Look at the grace of God, of all things in the world the most spiritual, for it is the communication of his own life to our souls—it has not disdained to connect itself with matter. It is joined to some little drop of water or oil, some particle of bread or wine! So the moral traditions of the family attach themselves to material things—to the portraits of ancestors—to family heir-looms—to the house, all impregnated, as one might say, with the spirit of the ancestors—to the blessed roof which has sheltered them—to the fireside that has been the confidant of their joys and of their griefs, that has shone upon so many a cradle and so many a coffin! All this speaks to the heart! Who can deny it? But lo! the mere hired apartment of our parents, the house where we were born, where we grew up, children of the fluctuating and tumultuous city! when we see it again after

* Wisdom, xi. 20.

a lapse of years, we feel a wound re-open in our hearts, our eyes fill with tears of inexpressible anguish and delight, and we cry with the poet:

> " O lifeless objects, have ye then a soul,
> That clings to ours, and forces it to love?"*

If a house in which we have lived for a few years, speaks so eloquent a language to our soul, what must be that of an old ancestral mansion, in which generations have followed generations, where honor has accumulated upon honor, where goodness and virtue have gathered, as it were, in layers upon the walls? The parental home is a sort of sacrament of the family, making the family visible and operative! A sacrament, as we have said, is both a sign and a power: the ancestral home is a sign which expresses the collective unity of a race, and a power which works the perpetuation of it from generation to generation.

PART THIRD.—*Occupation of the Home.*

[The preacher here puts the question why the home, as he has described it, is less and less understood and realized among us; why we do not feel more keenly the importance of its possession and its transmission? One of the principal causes is the violation of this third law: the family home should be *occupied*.]

Alas! of this poor broken-up and wandering hearth, even that which still remains to us is deserted! Sacred stone of the family, centre of the domestic group, like Jerusalem, thou art "left desolate!" Let us fix our eyes a while upon this picture of desolation. It is painful, but it must be done!

The children—where are they? They are but two or

---

* Objets inanimés, avez-vous donc une âme
Qui s'attache à notre âme, et la force d'aimer ?
Lamartine.

three in number, sometimes but one. A lonely plant, always sad, often puny, of selfish nature, without tenderness and without joy, finding nothing around it to love or to play with. This little solitary, a nuisance to itself, and a nuisance, or at least an embarrassment to others—they make haste to be rid of it out of the house; and a boarding-school education finishes the work of a barren wedlock.

But the father of the family? Ah! for the true father of a family, for the true head of a house, his home is the dream of all his day. For long, long hours, work and business keep him away from it. But in the evening? The day is for labor, the evening is for the family and for God! The star shines not in the sky so sweetly as the rays of the lamp or the reflection of the firelight in the window of that distant house, the place of his joys and his repose, toward which he wends his way, in meditation or in prayer. But no! what should he do there? Home has no charm for him: his children are no longer there; his wife is there, no doubt—yes, his wife!—but too often virtual divorce has divided them in heart and mind: they bear the same name, they live in the same house; but there is no near and high communion between the two. They have nothing to say to each other, because there is no love between them—no community of thought and feeling.

The wife without a husband, the mother without children—the woman doubly-widowed! Ah! I see her, wandering, like a piteous ghost, by certain hearthstones whose honor she cherishes amid their ruins, weeping over those cold ashes, the ashes of her own heart and life! "Call me not Naomi, call me Mara, for the Almighty hath dealt very bitterly with me!"* A

* Ruth, i. 20.

bitter lot, in truth, and few the heroines among those on whom it falls.

I look at the two extremes of society, and I see the ruin of the family completed through woman, both in the higher and in the poorer classes.

In the poorer classes, there was a time when woman was called wife, mother; they have baptized her, now-a-days, by a name that does not belong in our language—the *workwoman!* The workman I know and honor; but I do not know the workwoman. I am astounded, I am alarmed, whenever I hear this word. What? This young woman—is toil, unpitying, unintelligent toil, to come bursting in her door in the early morning, to seize her in its two iron fists, and drag her from what ought to be her home and sanctuary to the factory that is withering and consuming her day by day? What? Is toil—brutal, murderous toil—to kill her children, or at least to snatch them screaming from their cradles and give them over into stranger hands? And all the time a false philosophy will be lifting its head and shouting: "Equality! equality for man and woman! equality for the workwoman by the side of the workman!" Ah, yes, equality in slavery! or rather a profound inequality in slavery and martyrdom!

Ah! Gentlemen, I breathe again; for all these things are but the excesses of industrial enterprise. But there is something else than this amongst us—thank God, there is something else! Only the day before yesterday, to go no further back, I saw the proof of it. This Universal Exposition of industry, which promises us, instead of the horrors of war, the glories of peace, has understood that it is becoming more and more necessary to impress upon the work of material riches the seal of moral goodness. The Exposition has instituted a special jury to award prizes to social virtue, the virtue which contributes most directly to peace and public order. Well, the day before yesterday, in a meeting of that grave body, there was but one voice, one unanimous voice, to proclaim the keeping of the mother of the family at home as the remedy for our evils, and the stimulus to our progress. If we are compelled to open our eyes, then, to craving wants and profound miseries, we must also lift our heads hopefully, and struggle against them energetically.

And now what shall I say of the other extreme of society? The woman of the higher classes in our great cities is subject to another seduction—to a different tyranny: the seduction of the world, the tyranny of pleasure.

I would not drive our French ladies from the drawing-room; far from it. I would that drawing-rooms now silent might be restored again, and that the present ones might be even more frequented. The Parisian drawing-room perpetuates not only the traditions of wit and grace, but the more precious traditions of just ideas, noble manners, honorable and elevated sentiments. I know that in those drawing-rooms which have ever been the special honor of our nation, it is the Frenchwoman, the accomplished woman of the world, who has wielded this beneficent sceptre; it is she who, leaving to others the care of making laws and writing books, has chosen rather to inspire ideas, mould manners, and govern through them.

I make no attack, then, on the reign of woman in the drawing-room. But what I do attack is the sacrifice of the home to the drawing-room, and above all, to that life of excitement and dissipation which is called, now-a-days, "being in society." Begin by living at home, and be—I am not afraid of the word, even for women of the loftiest position—be *housewives;* a common-sounding word, but in reality sublime! That is your empire, the empire of the earnest woman; be housewives, watch over the realm of home; be the educators of your servants and your maids—of your *domestics.* The very word might tell you this—dwellers in the house—I had almost said, members of the family. Domestics were the strength and glory of the society of former days; they are the peril and the scourge of society in our day: it is in great part the mistress of the house that makes them what they are.

* * * * * * *

The *occupation* of the home coming in to confirm the two holy laws of its *possession* and its *transmission*, this is the delightful, lasting, and religious form in which domestic society appears to us as instituted by Providence.

I call to mind the patriarch Jacob, as he went to Mesopotamia to look for a wife worthy of him in the house of his kinsman Laban. The grandson of Abraham, destined to found and give name to the house of Israel, slept, one evening, after sunset, upon a stone which he had placed under his head for a pillow; and there, in the simplicity which marked the communication of God to man in ancient days, Jacob dreamed dreams which were more of heaven than of earth: he saw a ladder that rested on the ground beside him, but whose top pierced beyond the stars; the angels of the Lord descended along its steps and returned again, and at its summit the Lord himself appeared and said: "I am the Lord God of Abraham, and the God of Isaac thy father; the land whereon thou liest, to thee will I give it and to thy seed; and thy seed shall be as the dust of the earth, and thou shalt spread abroad to the west, and to the east, and to the north, and to the south."* And when in the morning the son of Isaac arose from his slumbers and his dreams, he looked at the stone upon which he had slept; he reared it with reverent hands, and anointing it with sacred oil, he set it up for an altar, and said: "Thou shalt be called Bethel, that is, the House of God."†

I am thinking, Gentlemen, of you! This ladder, which begins and ends in heaven, and does but touch the earth, is chaste and Christian fatherhood. This Jacob, son of the patriarch, father of the people of God, it is yourselves, both now and in the years to come. O young men, and you of riper years, who hear me, you have part in the vocation of Israel; you have a great race to build up, which shall extend from the south to the north, which shall invade the east and the west, which shall carry far and wide, in its peaceful invasions, its civilizing colonizations, the glory of France, the glory of the Catholic Church, the glory of your race and of your name! Ah! take that stone on which you lean your head, on which you rest your heart, the hearthstone of your home: take it with trembling hand, and say, "O sacred hearthstone, for a moment, perhaps, I had despised thee, I had counted thee a common thing; but no, the water of holy baptism, the benediction of holy wedlock, have rested upon thee; and each day, a common faith, a common prayer, a household Christianity, renew thy consecration! O hearthstone of my home, rise from the earth, stand thou as an altar-stone before the Lord, and thou shalt be called Bethel, the House of God! On thee rest family and country; on thee the very Church of God shall rest, more firmly than on the foundations of her temples!

* Gen. xxviii. 13, 14. † Gen. xxviii. 19.

THE NOTRE-DAME LECTURES.

ADVENT, 1868.

CHRISTIANITY AND THE CHURCH.*

LECTURE FIRST.

NOVEMBER 29, 1868.

THE CHURCH IN ITS MOST UNIVERSAL ASPECT.

[FATHER HYACINTHE, in his exordium, shows how the order of ideas followed from the very outset of these Lectures, five years ago, has its logical terminus in the subject of which he is to treat this year. In contradiction of errors that leave to God an ideal glory and a nominal

---

* This series of Lectures had been given, for substance, during the Lent of 1867, at Rome in the church of St. Louis of the French. At the close of the course, which was attended by throngs of French, English, and Americans, the preacher was received by the Pope with the most cordial testimony of his approval and regard.

The reports of these Lectures, which, like all the discourses of Father Hyacinthe, though carefully studied as to substance, were absolutely extemporaneous as to language, are more meagre and unsatisfactory than those of the courses of 1866 and 1867. It had been the intention of the preacher to reproduce these Lectures in full under his own hand, and accordingly less care had been taken to secure verbatim reports. But such as they are, these reports, the best extant, are valuable both in themselves, and as containing the sequel to the discourses on the Family and the State, and the prelude to the protest of the preacher, which followed after the interval of a few months.

supremacy only, by denying him a real existence and a conscious life, he had begun by asserting the personal God—the *God that liveth and seeth*, as the Bible expresses it. But living as we do in an age which is an age of thought, no doubt, but far less an age of thought than it is an age of action, it is not for us to linger on these metaphysical heights. In the pending discussions the question on which men are divided is, in fact, far less the personal existence of God in himself than his personal sovereignty over man individually and in society.]

The great question of our times is the kingdom of God. Is God to reign, or man?—man, emancipated from God by skeptical science, by "independent morality," by society organized independently of all influences, whether of religion or of church?—or God, finding in man not a slave but a subject, or rather a son sharing in his empire and sitting with him on his throne? This question, which was mooted in the times of the patriarchs and the prophets, in the time of Jesus Christ, in all times, in fact, presents itself more than ever at the present hour. Therefore it is that for three successive years we have been putting this question to the individual and to society; and the conscience of the individual, the fireside of the family, and the forum of free and prosperous nations have given back the same answer: "The Lord reigneth."

But, above family and country, there is a form of society higher and broader, into which man is received, not to be absorbed by it but to expand in it, and which is superadded to all other forms of society, that it may help them all in realizing the kingdom of God. It is the direct and sovereign instrument of this kingdom. This society is the Church.

Not without profound emotion do I approach a subject like this, amid the excitement of the mind of Europe, which is intent, at this moment, rather on religious than on political questions. I approach it, however, not by that side which irritates and divides the minds of men—by considering the external constitution of the Church and its relations to the State; I come at once to the innermost seat of life, a region at the same time most divine and most human, in which, awaiting God's appointed time, lie the fruitful and peaceful solutions of the future.

My Lord Archbishop, having to speak of the Church that you represent in the midst of us, permit me to salute, in the episcopate with which you are invested, its most elevated order; in the throne of Saint Denis, upon which you sit, one of the most constantly illustrious and most justly influential sees of Christendom; in your person, finally, that best of all dignities—the dignity of conduct and of character.

Let us proceed, now, to consider the Church successively as a visible society, and as an invisible society; or to use the language of theologians, let me speak, first, of the *body*, second, of the *soul* of the Church. Thence we derive the complete notion of the Church in its most universal aspect.

That which strikes us, at first glance, in the Church is its hierarchy, "beautiful and terrible as an army with banners."* The Church should not, however, be confounded, as it too often is, with the clergy in general, or even with the episcopacy and the papacy. It is always a grave error to confound society with its government. The family is not the father, and, Louis XIV. to the contrary notwithstanding, the state is not the prince.

* Song of Solomon, vi. 4.

But nowhere else would this confusion be so false and so fatal as in reference to the Church, in which the government is a ministry, not a domination. The Church is a fraternity divinely constituted in the hierarchy. "Be not ye called Rabbi; one is your master, and all ye are brethren—one is your Father, which is in heaven."* The Church, say the Scriptures again, is a body, "the body of Christ."† The life is not in the head alone, it is in all the members. Let not the laity, then, lose interest in the Church, as an institution foreign to them, one from which they can, at most, experience the remote results. Together with the hierarchy, they themselves are the Church.

The Church, then, must be understood as the whole body of religious society, believers and pastors together; or, to return to Saint Paul's comparison, the members with the head. In the present age of the world this society has a determinate form, and its proper name—the Roman Catholic Church. But although of divine origin and definitively instituted, this form is not the only one that the Church has borne. Before being *Catholic*, in the modern sense of the word, it was patriarchal and Mosaic. It is important, then, since we are contemplating the Church in its most universal aspect, not to confound it with any of its forms, not even with its present form, the most perfect of all, and henceforth unchangeable. The Church does not date from the apostles but from the patriarchs; its cradle is not in the "upper chamber,' but in Eden; and as Saint Epiphanius hath said (and therein he does but echo the voice of all tradition), "the Catholic Church is the beginning of all things."

The Catholic Church, considered as a visible organi-

---

* Matthew, xxiii. 8, 9. † 1 Corinthians, xii. 27.

zation may be defined, then, as "that universal fellowship in which the true God has always been known and worshipped, and the only mediator, Jesus Christ, promised or given, looked for or possessed; having "one God, and one mediator between God and man, the man Christ Jesus."*

[Father Hyacinthe takes up, in reverse order, these three elements—universal fellowship, the living God, the only Mediator.

He shows us the living God—that is, the one only and personal God, always known and adored on earth;—the one God, in opposition to the gross plurality of polytheism; the personal God, in opposition to the cold and unconscious abstraction of philosophy. "I live, saith the Lord."† He adverts, in the course of his argument, to the positivist theory, which represents mankind as beginning, in its religious life, with fetichism, and making its way gradually through polytheism to monotheism and at last to the positive philosophy, and he refutes it by the incontrovertible fact of the monotheism of the Bible.]

Next comes the One Mediator, the expectation and "desire" (under divers names and in divers forms) "of all nations,"‡ as all systems of worship bear witness; but especially, and in a form so precise that it is, as it were, his prophetic portrait and anticipated history, the expectation and desire of that chosen family, and at a later period of that favored people, who preserved intact the notion of the true God.

Having but one God and one Mediator, the Church also knows but one people of God. Whilst everywhere else the unity of our race is forgotten or denied, the old Hebrew scripture alone refers to *one primitive pair* the

* 1 Timothy, ii. 5. † Ezekiel, xxxiii. 11. ‡ Haggai, ii. 7.

diversity of races; and despite the narrowness too habitual to the mind and feelings of the Jews, they have never repudiated this tradition of Genesis, and the character of universality which belongs to the religion that flows from it. They had in their temple the Court of the Gentiles, whither, from all the corners of the earth, the worshippers of the true God might come and worship. Through all the phases through which it has passed, the spirit of this religion has ever been love—the love of God and the love of man. For this twofold love is no exclusive characteristic of the Gospel. In that commandment which he calls new, and which indeed, in every age, is new to Pharisaism, Christ himself sums up the law and the prophets—that is, the entire Old Testament—" On these two hang all the law and the prophets."*

I pause at the end of this first reflection; but, in pausing, indulge me, Gentlemen, in a personal reminiscence. It has been said: The audience and the preacher are brothers. It is true; I have felt it for four years. There is no reserve among brothers, because there is no giving and taking offence among them. The reminiscence that comes to my mind at this moment depicts admirably this essence of the Church, the city of God.

I was a boy of seventeen years, and, after the manner of that age, when nothing is yet in blossom, but everything still shut up in buds and leaves, I was wondering, in my vague way, what it was to love; when God, who watches over the steps of the least and humblest of his children, led me into a church at one end of my little town, one evening in Whitsuntide. They were singing, at Vespers, that brief but beautiful psalm, *Ecce, quam bonum*—" Behold, how good and how pleasant it is for

---

* Matthew, xxii. 40.

brethren to dwell together in unity!"* I remember how I entered, boy as I was, with all my vagueness of thought and feeling. I was greeted by that soft and majestic harmony, by all that multitude that sat singing before the tabernacles. It seemed to me like a voice coming down from heaven, and the psalm said to me, "Behold! behold, how good and pleasant a thing it is for brethren to dwell together in unity!"

The psalm went on to say: "It is like the precious ointment upon the head, that ran down upon the beard, even Aaron's beard, that went down to the skirts of his garments. Behold, it is like the dew of Hermon, that descendeth upon the mountains of Zion."

At last the psalm ended with that cry of the heart, so piercing and so delightful, "For there"—in love, in unity, in the fragrance of the ointment, in the freshness of the dew—"there hath the Lord commanded his blessing, even life forevermore!"

I know not whether there were tears in my eyes, but I am certain that they were streaming and overflowing in my heart! I had understood not only human love in its purity, but love in its sublimest realization—the fellowship of souls in God and in Jesus Christ.

II. There is no use in attempting to disguise from ourselves the weighty objection that may be urged, and with which constant attempts are made to disparage the Church: Your edifice is very long, indeed, since it reaches back to the beginning of the world; but is it not somewhat out of proportion, for it is exceeding narrow?

From the very beginning, as the Bible bears witness, the division which separates our race into two hostile camps, the children of God and the children of men,

* Psalm cxxxiii.

as it calls them,* ran on into the universal corruption punished by the deluge.

This formidable chastisement is soon succeeded by idolatry, and the city of God is confined within an obscure and despised corner of the globe; for Judea was not more than twenty leagues in breadth. To-day, even, religious statistics show lamentable results: out of one thousand millions of human beings, we find 139 millions of Catholics, and, in all, 260 millions of Christians. A discouraging spectacle, it must be admitted; especially after two thousand years of Christianity.

To begin with, we might reply by pointing to the hope of the future. But even if the future were holding in reserve the most ample compensation, it would not affect either the past or the present. Therefore, although fully believing in the compensations of the future, I do not rest satisfied with them, either for myself or for my hearers. I feel that the objection calls for a direct and decisive answer; and this answer I seek and find in what theologians call the *soul* of the Church. Hitherto we have spoken only of the visible forms of the Church; we are now about to explore the invisible riches of its prolific life.

Just as a large number of those who share in the profession of its faith, in the exercises of its worship, in the action of its government, belong, nevertheless, only to the *body* of the Church, that is to say, are attached to it only by external ties, so it may be that a great number of those who have not this form of life are still, in reality, of the Church, because they are really God's by the state of their souls. The soul of the Church is the invisible fellowship of all the righteous who have faith, at least an " implicit faith," in the

* Genesis, vi. 2.

one God and in the Redeemer, and who, cleansed from sin through the efficacy of the blood of Christ, abide in the grace of God.

Thus, beyond the boundaries of orthodoxy, vast and mighty regions are held by heresy and schism. But, in the bosom of heresy and schism how many truly believing and well-meaning souls there be, who are, in reality, neither heretical nor schismatic!

One day, when Jesus had just expounded the great commandment of love for one's neighbor, a Pharisee asked him: "Master, who is my neighbor?" And the Master—resorting to that teaching by parables of which he was so fond, whether for the purpose of presenting invisible truths in a more evident and palpable form, or to escape the perfidious machinations of the scribes and the Pharisees—the Master said to him: "A certain man went down from Jerusalem to Jericho, and fell among thieves, which stripped him of his raiment, and wounded him, and departed, leaving him half dead. And by chance there came down a certain priest that way."*

This priest was of the body of the Mosaic Church, the then visible Church; he had orthodoxy, an inflexible, perhaps implacable orthodoxy; but, assuredly, according to the Gospel narrative, he had not that prime condition of the true priest, that "tender mercy of our God whereby the Dayspring from on high hath visited us."† He looked upon that man with an unmoved, tearless eye; he hunted in his casuistry for an excellent motive for not stopping, and so he passed by.

After him came a Levite; he paused longer, hesitated more; but he also passed by.

And the next man was a Samaritan. The Samaritans were the heretics and the schismatics of those days.

---

* Luke, x. 25-37. † Ibid., i. 78.

When the Jews had exhausted upon our Lord the old vocabulary of injurious epithets; when they had told him that he was possessed with a devil, they added, as the climax of all that triumphant argument: You are worse than that—you are a Samaritan. And the Lord Jesus answered them not; he meekly suffered himself to be classed with the Samaritans, those poor, despised heretics.* Pope Saint Gregory the Great has remarked upon the fact that Jesus Christ did not deny that he was a Samaritan.

So, then, the Samaritan comes along. He sees the wounded man. Without hesitating, he sets him on his own beast; he brings him to the neighboring inn; he examines his wounds through the tears of a tender sympathy; he binds up his wounds "with the sweetness of oil and the strength of wine," and leaves him with the host, saying: Keep this man, and take care of him; in two days I shall pass this way again, and whatsoever thou spendest I will repay thee.

"Which, now," said the Master to the doctor of the law, "which of these three thinkest thou was neighbor to him that fell among thieves?" And the Pharisee, confused and ashamed, answered, "He that showed mercy on him." "Thou hast well said," added the Lord; "go thou and do likewise."

That is the *soul* of the Church. Whoever has the grace of Jesus Christ, which is not without faith, at least, "implied faith," whoever has the great spirit of the Gospel, its great, all-prevailing charity—the love of God and one's neighbor—whatever may be his involuntary errors, he belongs to the soul of the Church.

I hold, with all theologians, that whoever knows the Roman Catholic Church for what it is—for a fact,

---

* John, vii. 20; viii. 48.

divine, authoritative, is bound to enter it. Yes, whoever, looking upon it, not, in spite of one's self, by the fault of birth and education, through prejudices that render it fatally odious, beholds it as a fact, divine, authoritative, is bound to enter it. But if it does not depend upon the mind thus to see it, so long as there is Jesus Christ and his love in the heart, every such a one is my brother and my sister.

Now these are not theories, they are facts. Have we not at our very doors, across the Channel, a striking instance of this? People demand facts, positive science: let us then have positive science in religion; let us leave abstractions and come to realities.

There is in England a choice company of Protestant pastors, admirable both for learning and for virtue, who, after long years of study, prayer, and hesitation, have entered the Roman Catholic Church. Not one of them has acknowledged any want of good faith before his conversion; on the contrary, they have all declared their perfect sincerity. I shall only cite one of them by his illustrious name. Obliged to defend himself against the charge of hypocrisy, or at least, of culpable reservations, he has produced a book entitled *Apologia pro Vita Sua*, a book whose entire honesty is only equalled by its soundness and its eloquence—John Henry Newman, the first theologian and the first writer of Catholic England! And in this book he was able to write this noble declaration: "*I have never sinned against light.*"

If that profound genius, that generous heart, that man who has awaited, if not the hoary hairs of age, at least the maturity of manhood, before re-entering into visible unity—if that man has not sinned against the light, by what right, ye unjust and violent men, would you brand all who live in Protestantism with the stigma of falsehood and sin? Never, never will I tolerate such utterances as this! I myself have but just now returned from the most Protestant of all countries—from England; and I owe it to the truth to bear this testimony—that I have found there, not only great citizens, but great Christians. When I clasped them by the hand, when I mingled my thoughts with theirs, when I came in contact with them, soul to soul—for that, after all, is the only way to know men. . . . . . There are barriers, you say. I know it: there are great gulfs, if you will; but cannot faith remove mountains? And cannot charity fill up great gulfs? Not violent discussions, not bitter controversies will re-establish unity; but charity, love, the noble virtues of truly Christian hearts. . . . Permit me then to take by the hand, to press to my bosom, these Christians, sincere in their error, but sincere in their love of God, of Jesus Christ, of men; and, in that embrace, let me take up again my psalm, "How good, how pleasant a thing it is for brethren to dwell together," if not in the same body, at least in the same soul, in the invisible unity of the Church and of Jesus Christ!

Even beyond the pale of Christianity, a like phenomenon is not impossible, and, without wishing to define precisely in what proportion it exists, it is not presumptuous to affirm that it does exist, if it is true, as taught by the theologians of Salamanca, that great school of the Bare-footed Carmelites, that "implicit faith" in the Redeemer is sufficient for the salvation of unbelievers. In that case, the place of baptism with water is supplied by the baptism of the Spirit.

[After briefly indicating this consideration—upon which time does not permit him to dwell—Father Hyacinthe closes this lecture by asking himself whether he has indeed told all the height, all the breadth, all the depth of the temple and the city of God.] The earth is but a point in the immensity of heaven, and the race of Adam is but a petty tribe in the universal Church of God and his Christ. Are not the stars inhabited by beings analogous to ourselves; and, if so, do not these beings form so many Churches scattered abroad throughout the heavens, but blended, in the sight of God, into a unity which we cannot see? Science does not give us the right to say this; but faith does not forbid our thinking so. On the contrary, the psalmist calls upon the stars to praise the Lord,* and the prophet affirms that "the host of heaven worshippeth him."†

But what need have we of these suppositions? Faith teaches us that our Church upon earth is joined to a Church that was before it, and is above it—the Church of the angels. Doubtless the angels have, in the bosom of God, a life peculiar to themselves. But they have also, among us, a mission in which we are concerned,—"sent forth to minister to them that shall be heirs of salvation."‡ This world of spirits is infinitely more populous than the world of men. It far more exceeds our power of measurement than does the universe of matter.

And even this last, has it then no place nor part in the Church? Has not St. Paul declared that "the whole creation groaneth and travaileth with pangs of birth?" But with what is it in labor? With "the manifestation of the sons of God!"§ This material world is God's offspring. He created it as well as us; and it shall be joined with us in the final transformation that is to give to God's elect new heavens and a new earth. "And I saw," saith St. John, "a new heaven and a new earth. And I saw the holy city, the

* Ps. cxlviii. 3.   † Neh. ix. 6.   ‡ Heb. i. 14.   § Rom. viii. 19, 22.

new Jerusalem, descending out of heaven from God as a bride adorned for her husband!"*

And here I pause, my eyes fixed upon the coming glory of the Church. I remember that eulogy which the Bible pronounces upon the prophet Isaiah: "By an excellent spirit he beheld what should come to pass at the last, and he comforted them that mourned in Zion."†

We are all mourners in Zion; and I first of all. O Zion! O Jerusalem! O ancient city of God, of old so happy! How art thou left, exclaims Isaiah, as a cottage in a vineyard, where one finds shelter for a moment from the heat of the day!‡

Yes, we mourn in Zion. We weep among the ruins that our enemies have made; and (why shall we not confess it?) among the ruins we have made ourselves! But the "tender plant"§ of the Lord is there. It shall grow and lift itself above the kingdoms, above the sons of Judah. This is "that which shall come to pass at the last." Gaze upon it, O ye that mourn in Zion, gaze with firm heart and fearless eye, and be ye comforted!

* Revelation, xxi. 1, 2.   † Ecclesiasticus, xlviii. 24.
‡ Isaiah, i. 8.   § Isaiah, liii. 2.

LECTURE SECOND.

DECEMBER 6, 1868.

THE CHURCH OF THE PATRIARCHS.

[FATHER HYACINTHE first points out that the Church, in its progress, has taken the same course as humanity itself, which, before embracing in its unity the prodigious diversity of peoples, has begun with the *family*, and then passed into the *nation*. So, before receiving its appropriate and definitive form in the Roman Catholic Church, religious society has been successively outlined in the patriarchal Church and the Mosaic Church—under the form, first, of the family, and then of the nation.]

In Adam and in Noah, those two fathers of the human race, religion existed, of course, in the family form, but it was coextensive with the human race. In Abraham it is restricted to a particular family, which is separated from others—the "house of Israel." Idolatry had invaded the country where Abraham dwelt, and even the family of his own father. Then it is that he hears, in his reason and conscience, that sublime call, coming from a source higher than his conscience and his reason, even from God himself, which is termed "the vocation of Abraham:" "Get thee out of thy country, and from thy kindred, and from thy father's house, unto a land that I will shew thee."

Thus, at the foundation of the Church, this especial work of God, there is an inner voice addressed to a wandering shepherd, a mystical contemplator of nature; a man at once profound and simple. Nothing here of human reasoning; and on the other hand, nothing of miracle, nor of scripture, nor of doctrinal authority. All this grand edifice rests, on God's part, upon an inner voice, and, on the part of Abraham, upon a faith not blind but yet obscure. "He went forth, not knowing whither he went." The voice of God cannot deceive, and when invested with the conditions without which it never demands our assent, it is the firmest of all foundations for our faith, our hopes, our sacrifices.

Now this grand individual inspiration has for its object to restore the kingdom of God upon earth by founding a new *family* of true worshippers.

The object of the Church in the midst of the corruption of the world, is always one and the same—to save men by the law of God; that is to say, by truth and righteousness; and toward this object it has, from the very beginning, laid out two paths which always stand open—that of the patriarchs and that of the prophets.

To the prophets, to the apostles, God says: Ye shall have no wife, no child of your flesh; ye shall leave your family, ye shall renounce all worldly goods, and, what is harder yet, all delights of the heart: let the dead bury their dead. In exchange ye shall have offspring of your lips, a race of spiritual children, begotten of your prayers and of your words, and ye shall be founders of the kingdom of God.

To the patriarchs and their successors, to laymen, to fathers, to Christian husbands, God says: And ye, too, get you forth out of corruption, get you forth out of idolatry of mind and heart, and be the founders of a race; be the fathers of children—spiritual children indeed, above all, but likewise of children of your blood and of your flesh, a posterity on which you shall stamp your own seal, and with it the seal of the living God.

With these two vocations, the virgin apostles of the New Testament and the prolific patriarchs both of the New Testament and of the Old, the clergy and the laity, the man of the household and the man of the sanctuary, joined closely hand in hand—with these two vocations, I say, the world is to be reformed!

No doubt great kings, great popular assemblies have their uses in the reformations of the world; no doubt the councils of legislators and the aspirations of the masses are necessary; great pontiffs, great bishops, councils in which God is present—all this is useful, is necessary to the moral and religious reformation of the world; but all this will come to nothing, if there is not, by the side of this force, that other force, less apparent but not less fruitful of results—the force of husbands and fathers laying the foundations of the Church in the Home. Get thee out of thy country; get thee out of thy corrupted dwelling; get thee away from past idolatry, and come forth into that home which I will show thee!

This Abrahamic inspiration of paternity in the name and for the cause of God, handed down in the patriarch's family, becomes there a domestic tradition, the characters of which arrange themselves under three main heads, the three grand acts of human life: birth—love—death.

I. The fact of *birth* is hallowed by the rite of *circumcision*—a rite of immense interest by reason of its antiquity and of the vast regions throughout which it has been practised from the earliest generations—a rite both human and divine, since Jesus Christ was subject to it.

But it is not enough to bow down before a fact, even though it be both human and divine—we must endeavor to understand it; and in this fact of circumcision I recognize two ideas—*separation* from the rest of mankind, special *consecration* to the true God.

1. *Separation* from the rest of mankind. This was doubly necessary, since the point was to establish a family, and a religious family. Do you think that a family, however strong its sympathies, can do otherwise than separate itself—hold itself more or less aloof from other families? Were it to lose its proper character, its special individuality, it would cease to be a family; and if we should ever get so far as to disregard the right, the necessity of a separation, an isolation between families, we should have at our doors, not socialism, but communism.

Separation, then, is necessary. Within the great bonds of justice and charity, there must be personal character, jealous individuality, distinguishing the race from all besides. But when the question is how to establish a religious family in the midst of intellectual and moral depravity, when the very object of establishing this family is that it may be a new ark, and a surer ark than that of Noah, upon the waters of this new deluge then, most of all, there must be separation.

Never, ye chosen families, whoever ye may be, family of Abraham of old, Christian French family of our own day, no, never, when it becomes a duty to separate yourselves from error and sin, while holding fast to every tie of justice and sympathy, never can ye build your walls too high, never can ye dig your moats too deep.

"Be ye separate, my people; go ye out of the midst of Babylon!"*

And how effectually is he separated by this inexorable circumcision—separated by the material seal that he bears in the flesh, by the whole physiognomy of his being, both moral and physical!

Do you ever meet a Jew without recognizing him? Do you ever look with a moment's hesitation or doubt on that exotic beauty, at once so sad and so fascinating—those deep eyes, so full of intelligence and passion? Do you ever hesitate when you encounter that blood, so pure, so proud, so aristocratic above all others, which has flowed on through the ages and through the races, refusing to mingle with any other?

Above all, have you studied, you men of thought and of political science, organizers of families and society, have you studied the original constitution of the Jewish family? To-day, even under our very eyes, in Europe and in Asia alike, the organization of the Jewish family has survived the downfall of all its external supports. It had a monarchy, a political organization: the political organization, the monarchy, have crumbled to pieces centuries ago. It had a priesthood; it had a religious synagogue : something of these still remains, but their genealogies are lost; their worship has fallen into dust. They have no more sacrifices, nor Church, nor kingdom, and the Jewish family, *sua mole stat*, is standing by its own strength! It finds within itself the power of preserving unimpaired, against modern civilizations as well as against mediæval barbarisms, the tradition of its blood and the tradition of its God!

I know that people say: It is the mark of Cain that this race wears on its forehead; it is the curse of Cal-

* Jeremiah, li. 45; 2 Corinthians, vi. 17.

vary. Ah! I do not deny the heinous crime of Calvary. I do not deny these millenniums of expiation. But I know that if this people has said, "His blood be upon us and upon our children," a better and mightier voice has said, "Father, forgive them, for they know not what they do!" And the Apostle Paul, also, acknowledging them to be guilty, has declared that the sons shall be "beloved for the fathers' sakes."* It is not the mark of Cain, then, that I behold; not the immortality of wrath: it is the immortality of love; it is the mark of Abraham, the great seal of the patriarchal family, that God himself has placed upon the foreheads of this people, and which this people preserves in spite of itself, and in spite of us. "My covenant shall be in your flesh for an everlasting covenant." †

2. Circumcision is not only a sign of separation from the rest of mankind, it is also a solemn *consecration* to the worship of the true God. In the moment when the father, in the presence of the agony of childbirth, that agony of unequalled danger and distress, receives the new-born child in his arms, without knowing whether he receives it from the hands of death or of life, two profound feelings take possession of his soul—the sense of the sovereignty of God, and the sense of the unworthiness of the child. This child comes to him from God, to return to God: it is from God, and for God: it is a son of God rather than a son of man, and yet it is "a child of wrath!"‡ The words of Saint Paul attest it; so do these heartrending cries, these tears that have not learned to flow, this blood that is our first garment, these obstinate struggles between life and death, contesting the possession of this cradle, which is perhaps

---

* Romans, xi. 29.   † Genesis, xvii. 13.   ‡ Ephesians, ii. 3.

to be a coffin! The sequel confirms this sad testimony. Nothing so pure as the child's brow, except its heart. And yet nothing so perverse as this heart! It contains, without doubt, the germs of every human virtue, but choked by the more powerful germs of every vice. If this nature, fallen through original sin, is not restored by an education as firm as it is mild, as energetic in repression as it is intelligent in counsel and affectionate in feeling, this child will be the victim and the cause of terrible disorders.

The religion of Moloch, spread over Western Asia in the age of Abraham, had preserved, under its horrible forms, these two great truths which are now-a-days denied—the sovereignty of God over the child, and the unworthiness of the child in the sight of God. Hence the atrocious custom of sacrificing children, especially the first-born. Heartless parents placed them on the red-hot arms of the brazen idol, and in a few moments those frail and delicate bodies vanished in a funereal smoke. Abraham struggled all his life against this worship of death. In his supreme trial he himself believed that God had called for this sacrifice from him. He led his son Isaac to the summit of Mount Moriah which is said to be the same as Calvary, to immolate him with his own hand to that God who had given him as the tardy consolation of his old age, and the sole hope of his race. But the angel of the Lord caught his arm ready to strike, and a voice from on high said: "Lay not thine hand upon the lad; for now I know that thou fearest God, seeing that thou hast not withheld thy son, thine only son, from me. . . . Blessing, I will bless thee, and multiplying, I will multiply thy seed as the stars of the heaven, and as the sand which is upon the sea-shore; and in thy seed shall all the nations of the earth be blessed."* This trial had for its object to strengthen Abraham in a better faith, by revealing to him that the true sacrifice is not a sacrifice of death, but a sacrifice of life—that of the Messiah, who should die only that he might give life to the dead, and whose blood should reconcile with divine justice not only the seed of the patriarch but all the nations of the earth. The scanty drops of blood shed under the circumcising knife of stone symbolized this sacrifice both in its benignity and in its sternness.

II. From birth, I am brought at once to death—so close is the connection between the cradle and the tomb! One act, however, separates these two extremes of our life—the supreme act in the order of nature! Between the tomb and the cradle I behold the nuptial couch, and I greet it with those grand words of the apostle Paul: "Let marriage be honorable in all things, and the marriage-bed be undefiled."† For love, holy love, forms between this ascent of birth and youth and this declivity of old age and death, the summit of human existence on earth.

Of all divorces, the most senseless, the most disastrous, is the divorce between the ideas of religion and the ideas of love. Love—I am only saying the same thing over, I know; but let that pass; I am not aiming at rhetorical art, but at facts, at results—love, in its nature, is the most religious of all human feelings; it tends toward the ideal, the infinite, and if, since the fall, it slides all too easily down the steep course of human degradation, is not that one reason the more why the religious man, and above all the priest—the apostle and

---

* Genesis, xxii. 12, 17, 18.
† Hebrews, xiii. 4. The rendering "in all things" which the original will bear indifferently with the rendering "in all *persons*," is naturally preferred in Roman Catholic versions.—TR.

prophet of the New Testament—should revive and restore it by surrounding it with the most stimulating and invigorating atmosphere of the divine life?

Yes, love and religion are the indivisible basis of the family. I make bold to put the question, when man and wife have not put God in their love, when perhaps they have not put love in their hearts, what do they come for at the foot of our altars? What use is there to them in a benediction, sacred, most assuredly, in the intention of the Church that gives it, but formal, pharisaical, or rather utterly worldly, in the mind with which they receive it? Does that consecrate marriage? Does that bring down God into their hearts? No; not unless their choice itself is holy, not unless love itself is there already. For marriage is not the union of two names, two fortunes, two material beings: it is the union of two souls in the immaterial and divine cement of love. Yes, divine, for this cement would have no solidity, but that it had been prepared by the hand of God. And that is what I admire in the patriarchs; that is what the Bible, in its smallest details, in that book which is too little pondered, the book of Genesis, the book for all Christian families after the Gospel—that is what the Bible teaches me; it teaches me the religious care, the moral and divine inspiration that presided over the love of the patriarchs and the marriage of their children.

These unions have a twofold character—*purity* and *fecundity*.

1. First, *purity*. This was necessary in the wives of the patriarchs, in the women who were to be the wives of the saints, the mothers of the chosen people, the ancestresses of the Son of God himself. Health, beauty—above all, that moral beauty which shines through

physical beauty, purifying and ennobling it,—virtue in the habitual exercises of the will, religion in the habitual exercises of the soul, that is what was needed in Sarah, in Rebecca, in Rachel, in all those strong and tender women " which did build the house of Israel."*
So, neither distance, nor the difficulties of the journey deterred the patriarchs when they wished to form an alliance for themselves or for their sons. They held in horror the fair but lewd daughters of Canaan, among whom they lived, and they sent their servants, or went themselves, to those high table-lands of Asia, where the family of their fathers had continued to dwell in their primeval purity. The marriage of Isaac and Rebecca affords a memorable instance, the spirit of which is summed up in this final passage of that touching history: " And Isaac brought her into his mother Sarah's tent, and took Rebekah and she became his wife; and he loved her: and so Isaac was comforted after his mother's death."†

Such were these families. Monogamy was already their prevailing spirit, and thus it is that amongst them love had a purity, the wife a dignity, not to be found elsewhere in all antiquity, at least in the same degree.

Polygamy makes its appearance among them, it is true; but it is very much restricted, and surrounded by all the correctives of morality and religion. It is only accidental. It is not mentioned in connection with Isaac, and if Abraham and Jacob resort to it, that is only to compensate for the absolute or relative sterility of the principal wife; in the quaint and striking language of Rachel, " that she may bear upon my knees, and that I may also have children by her."‡

2. The mission of these families and their power lie,

* Ruth, iv. 11.   † Genesis, xxiv. 67.   ‡ Genesis, xxx. 3.

in fact, in their *fecundity*. Each of these men wishes to be the father, each of these women the mother, not of a son but of a people. The splendid vision of Abraham, contemplating in the innumerable company of the stars the prophecy of his posterity, remains their ideal.

God had said to Abraham: "Sarah shall be the mother of nations!"* Mark this, Gentlemen. Not of a man, not of a narrow family, but the mother of a people, " a great people." And does not history show us, in fact, that two great nations have issued from the loins of the old man,—by Sarah, Isaac and the Jews—by Hagar, Ishmael and the Arabs; two nations, brothers and yet enemies? The one has covered the world with the prolific fragments of its exiles and captivities; the other with the proud, invading waves of its conquests. And each has seemed to emulate the other in contributing largely to the civilization of the globe.

Yes, the sons of Isaac and the sons of Ishmael! I know that allowances, vast allowances, must be made; but permit me to be just.

France is mourning—she will be mourning to-morrow—by the side of a grave forever illustrious, for that incomparable orator who ever defended the traditions of the past without repudiating either the grandeurs of the present or those of the future. One day, when the men and the deeds of the revolution were attacked in his presence, he uttered that exclamation which admirably depicts the sublime impartiality of his soul: "I shall never forget that the Convention saved my country!" For myself, Gentlemen, I shall not be sublime, but I shall be impartial, and say: I cannot forget that Mohammedanism, despite its errors and its deeds

* Genesis, xvii. 16.

of violence, enthrones, this day, the idea, more than the idea, the genuine sentiment of the unity of God, over one hundred millions of my kind. From the shores of Morocco to the foot of the Himalayas, from the recesses of Yemen to the centre of Europe, one hundred millions of men bear witness, in the teeth of paganism, to the unity of God! And it is the sons of Ishmael who have done this.

I make no recriminations against the unjust detractors of the Mohammedan nations. You blame these peoples, and you are right, but do not blame them beyond measure; blame first the decay of Christian civilization. Physician, heal thyself! For we sons of the Crusaders, heirs of Christianity, what have we done with the traditions of Sarah and Rachel? and has the blessing of a numerous family been changed for us into a curse?

I shall not dwell upon this point. I merely point out and denounce that covenant of which the prophet spoke, that covenant made with death by surrendering to him the sources of life! "Your covenant with death shall be disannulled, and your agreement with hell shall not stand."* I point out and denounce, with hand and heart and soul, that constitution of the family which tends to introduce itself even into the internal arrangements of the house, a superb palace, a palace of pride and voluptuousness, that can never allow room enough for oriental luxury, and has no place for a cradle!

III. After the woe of that people which cuts itself off from the future by sacrificing its cradles, I know none greater than that of the people which cuts itself off from the past by removing its graves. Blind people!—

* Isaiah, xxviii. 18.

that has lost the twofold faith in which the greatness of our race resides, that it may shut itself up in that circle of narrow selfishness and barren voluptuousness, which it calls the present! . . . .

[In this manner the speaker approaches the subject of the consecration given to death by the care of funeral rites. He shows that the family spirit strives after fellowship in death, by means of a common place of burial.

He shows how this spirit animated the patriarchs, and wrought in them the more vigorously from the fact that death, presenting itself to the mind of the ancients under the image of a sleep, invested the sepulchre with a higher importance.

He refutes, in passing, the refined spiritualism which, no less than the coarsest materialism, leads to the neglect of the grave. The body is the casket, the instrument, the companion, of the soul; it is a part of immortal man; it claims our respect for the sake of the recollections of the past, and of the hopes for the future. Let it rest, then, in an honored and cherished grave, guarded by the memory of life, and the expectation of the resurrection!

But not only is Abraham's sepulchre desired by all the prophets as the place where they shall lay their bones. Abraham's bosom is to the Jewish mind the glorious and living sepulture of the just. Thither, as Christ himself declared, Lazarus was borne by angels to receive the recompense of his reward, and was beheld "afar off, in Abraham's bosom."

This, in brief, is the thought with which the discourse concluded.]

LECTURE THIRD.

DECEMBER 13, 1868.

THE CHURCH IN THE FAMILY.

"But I would have you know that the head of every man is Christ; and the head of the woman is the man; and the head of Christ is God."*

What I have to say to you is nothing more than a comment on these brief but profound words; and therefore I invoke them at the very outset of my talk with you.

The Church of the patriarchs was not wholly buried with them in the cave of Mamre. It was its own survivor in the vigorous organization of the Jewish family within the *national* Mosaic church.

It survives in the still higher constitution of the Christian family in the bosom of the *universal* Church of Jesus Christ. For not in vain has the Lord said, "I am the God of Abraham, of Isaac, and of Jacob; this is my name forever." The supreme Artist, in fact, does not destroy the studies with which he preludes his works, but perfects them, and incorporates them in his masterpiece as integral parts. This masterpiece is the *Catholic* Church, the Church of all mankind united in God by Christ. In this final form are to be found, sub-

---

* 1 Corinthians, xi. 3.

ordinated, but not impaired or crushed, the preparatory forms of the *patriarchal* Church and the Mosaic Church; the domestic and the national Churches are still living in the bosom of the grand and perfect catholic unity.

The Church of the patriarchs is still the subject, then, that is proposed for to-day's discussion. Only, instead of studying it in its remote past, we will take it up at the very fireside of the Christian family. We have already, for one year, spoken of the Family; but we have not yet considered it in its special relations to the priesthood of the Catholic Church. Moreover, there need be no fear of repetition in such a subject. The great concern, both of the speaker and of his hearers, is not to bring out a discourse or a volume of artistic symmetry, it is to bring out facts. We proceed, then, to consider the family in its *domestic priesthood*, and this domestic priesthood *in its relations with the hierarchical priesthood of the Catholic Church.*

I. It is obvious in how many invidious and ridiculous ways this word *priesthood*, in our times, has been abused. To apply this word to the family is not to add another to the list of these profanations. Rather, we are true to tradition and to the most exact theology, when we assert that in the proper sense of the word there is a priesthood in the Christian family.

In baptism, every Christian is invested with a priesthood, by virtue of the character which this sacrament confers; to wit, a participation in the priesthood of Jesus Christ. This sacerdotal character grows in Confirmation. It achieves its full development in the sacrament of Orders.

St. Irenæus, Tertullian, Origen, and many other Fathers speak of this first degree of priesthood common to all Christians. The Greek Church has maintained, and still professes this doctrine, distinguishing two kinds of priesthood: one *spiritual or mystical*, which is the common lot of all orthodox Christians; the other *sacramental*, peculiar to those who have received the sacrament of ordination. The Council of Trent makes the same distinction in different terms. It admits an inward priesthood, which all should exercise, alongside of the outward priesthood, the privilege of a few. So that the heretics of the sixth century did not err in teaching that every Christian is a priest, but only in confounding this priesthood with the hierarchical priesthood, or in reducing the latter to the proportions of the former. Is this not the meaning of those words of the Apocalypse: Christ "hath made us kings and priests unto God and his Father?"*

And what are those "spiritual sacrifices" of which St. Peter speaks,† if not the sacrifice answering to this priesthood? The Christian has even an active part in the public sacrifice of the Altar. "Pray," says the priest to the faithful, "pray, my brethren, that my sacrifice, which is also yours, may be acceptable to God, the Father Almighty." *Orate, fratres, ut meum ac vestrum sacrificium acceptabile fiat apud Deum Patrem omnipotentem.*

Now this lay priesthood reaches its perfect fulness only in the Christian who has become a husband and father. From being inward and private, it then becomes social, exerting upon domestic society, so far as this society is Christian, an action of its own, although subordinate to the action of the hierarchical priesthood.

This domestic priesthood has, in fact, three chief functions, which correspond to those of the hierarchical

---

* Revelation, i. 6.   † Peter, ii. 5.

priesthood—*religious and moral instruction, the government of consciences, the exercise of worship.*

1. *Religious instruction.*—In the lectures on The Family, it has already been shown how the authority to teach is, in the father, a natural authority, derived immediately from the fact of fatherhood.

But when, in the Christian who has been consecrated in his whole being by baptism, paternity is at once raised into the supernatural order by the sacrament of marriage, this authority of instruction becomes *supernatural* in him, and constitutes in the Church a sacred function.

Obligatory upon the father toward his children in the patriarchal family, by virtue of a positive decree of God,* the exercise of this authority is still more obligatory in the Christian family, in which Jesus Christ has not only not abolished it, but has confirmed it.

It is principally the right and the duty of the father. For, although the mother is the first to reveal the good God to the fruit of her womb and of her heart, still it is the office of the father to perfect and confirm this revelation in the soul of his son, who comes down from the mother's lap and stands by his side to be initiated by him into life.

So little does the principal part in religious instruction devolve upon the mother, that she herself is obliged to resort to the lessons of her husband. This is the teaching of St. Paul. He would have the woman, if she has not understood the public instruction of the priest in the temple, to question her husband in the privacy of home, and to be a silent learner in his school.† The husband, then, according to the apostle, is the private, home-interpreter of the public instruc-

---

* Genesis, xviii. 19.   † 1 Corinthians, xiv. 35.

tion given by the hierarchical priest. That does not mean that he is free to alter the instruction of the Church; he is no more free to do that than the Church is free to change revelation. But because all outward instruction needs to be interpreted—the Scriptures and tradition being interpreted by the Church, the word being interpreted by the priest in its name—the words of the priest, also, will be interpreted by the father of the family, and his words, finally, by the Christian conscience; for the comprehension of religious truth depends, in the last analysis, upon the good or evil disposition of the conscience and what theology so aptly terms the light of grace, the light of the Holy Spirit. Hence nothing is more futile, be it said in passing, than the hope with which narrow minds flatter themselves, of creating within the Church, by an exaggeration of doctrinal authority, a sort of vulgar precision, a sort of tyrannical uniformity, which are no part of God's designs toward the soul of man.

Such, then, is the legitimate share, both large and wise, that the Church gives, within its own fold, to lay-instruction.

2. *The government of consciences.*—It is not only the instruction of the children that is given into the hands of the parents, and especially into the hands of the father; it is their *education*, the practical formation of their will, their heart, their conscience, their entire soul; their preparation from early life for the choice of a profession; the settlement of that vital affair, their marriage; in a word, their moral and religious guidance, immediate and supreme, during the early stages of their life, and, in all its subsequent course, indirect but always efficient. None of these things would be possible, if the conscience of the children did not unfold itself to

the parents, especially to the father. Yes, the father must be the first guide, and to a certain extent, the first confessor of his children.

Still more. A certain knowledge and guidance of the conscience of the wife herself falls to the husband. The order of nature demands it, and the order of grace. The order of nature, because of the difference of age and of sex. In the early stages, at least, of wedded life, the wife is as much of a child as of a companion, with respect to her husband. He has received her, young, ignorant of what awaits her in life, lacking in the teachings of an experience which she has not yet undergone personally, and which she has not even witnessed in others. This child, in order that she may become indeed a wife, must have a higher education that shall make her equal to her new position. The type of this education is to be met in the primeval fact related to us in Genesis—Eve born of Adam. The wife should always be born of the heart of her husband, should know all its secrets, and share all its emotions and feelings. They should be one, not only in the outward intercourse of life, but in the close community of all human and divine possessions. They should vibrate in unison in the presence of those three great and increasing objects of affection—the cradle of infancy, the love of married life, the tomb of age. And as they should view the things of earth with an undivided glance and an undivided heart, so they should soar toward God with one common aspiration and in one common flight. The law of sex perpetuates what was first rendered necessary by difference of age; and this order, established by nature, is consecrated by grace.

The institution of Christian marriage, in fact, places the wife in the same dependence toward her husband that the Church is in toward Jesus Christ. "Therefore," says St. Paul, "as the Church is subject unto Christ, so let the wives be to their own husbands in everything."* This subordination extends to the affairs of the soul, since, on the one hand, it is universal, "*in everything,*" and, on the other, it finds its model in the very union between Christ and the Church, "*as the Church is subject unto Christ.*" And this is so true, that, in accordance with the general teachings of theologians, the husband has the power to invalidate, in the forum of conscience, vows made by the wife, after marriage, without his consent, when these vows affect, in any way whatsoever, the conjugal relation. Some theologians of great weight and authority even go so far as to free the marital power from this limitation, and to subordinate to it all vows made by the wife without the husband's consent after marriage, whatever may be their object. They only limit this sovereign power by the general condition requisite to the validity of dispensations—to wit, that they should have a reasonable motive; but of this motive the husband alone is judge.

Doubtless, in behalf of the children, and still more so in behalf of the wife, we must make important reservations touching the rightful independence of the human conscience, and especially of the Christian conscience. For if it is true that there is a government of the conscience by outward authority, it is no less true that there is a self-government of the conscience under the eye and the hand of God, who alone sees into the depths of the heart, according to that fine expression of Saint Thomas: *Deus solus illabitur animæ.* But these reservations apart, we should not hesitate to conclude, not only from the temporal point of view, but also and

---
* Ephesians, v. 24.

especially from the spiritual point of view, that the father of the family is the head of his house, the king and the priest in one. "I would have you know, that the head of every man is Christ; and the head of the woman is the man, and the head of Christ is God."

3. *The exercises of worship.*—Private worship is necessary. "When thou prayest, enter into thy closet; and when thou hast shut the door, pray to thy Father which is in secret."* Public worship, also, is necessary: "not forsaking the assembling of ourselves together."† But the two, even when scrupulously observed, do not suffice: there must be another—family worship, indicated by these words, so often employed by Saint Paul: "the church that is in the house."‡ This worship is rendered in the peasant's hut of schismatic Russia, by the worship of holy images; and in the heart of Protestantism, in the aristocratic families of England, by family prayers. Family prayers, which have almost disappeared from among our French customs, especially evening prayers, are, in fact, the solemn act of domestic worship. It is not the mother but the father who presides, who is the high priest. What religious ascendency this example gives over the wife, over the children, over the servants themselves, who are not strangers nor slaves, but adopted members of the family, admitted to a share in its worship as well as in its labors and its prosperity!

But there is another prayer that goes from man to God without crossing the lips, and that is mental prayer. This too should be common to father and child, and especially to husband and wife.

Do you remember that page of the *Confessions of Saint Augustine,* beautiful above all the rest? The

---

* Matthew, vi. 6. † Hebrews, x. 25.
‡ Romans, xvi. 5; 1 Corinthians, xvi. 19.

personages are not man and wife, but mother and son: but no matter—they are two souls wedded in tenderness and purity. A few days before Monica's death, Augustine was with her in her house in Ostium. They were both there, one evening, watching the sky, the sea, the land, that Roman scenery, so sad and so beautiful, that speaks so deeply of the infinite. Their hearts were going up in mental prayer, for they spoke not, or at least they spoke but little; they were going up to invisible things, to ideas, to moral sentiments, to the soul, to the eternal types of the true and the beautiful—to God himself, the source of all these great things. There came a moment when they attained unto God, *ictu oculi, ictu cordis,* with one outstroke of the intellect and heart, like those who, sailing into port, touch the shore before they are able to land. Even so, at last, they had touched the shore of the Infinite. A moment fleeting as time, but full as eternity. What happened to Monica and Augustine is the history of mental prayer in Christian families: the history of religious life between man and wife, the truest, sweetest, most enduring of all loves! Yes, when a man and a wife have made common property of their conscience and their reason—as I said before, I do not understand marriage without a community of reason and conscience—when this wife, understanding her husband, and this husband, understanding his wife, read together the great masterpieces of human genius, Homer, Dante, Shakespeare, or better still, the divine masterpieces, Genesis and the Gospel; when they contemplate the scenes of Nature, now grand, now beautiful; when they experience in common the vicissitudes of the family, grouped around these three centres—birth, love, death, like the statue of the ancient desert, which responded with harmonious murmurs to the first rays of the sun, their soul also responds to this sun of Nature, of the human mind, of the family, of revealed faith, this divine sun—for all this comes from God!—their souls blend in the same prayer, and the husband, as "the head of the wife," presides at this unuttered prayer, this love which is prayer, this prayer which is love!

Ah! that man has never known what it is to love—he has talked about love, he has not understood it—who has not known these secrets of God in love, and of love in God. In these hours we feel God, we gaze upon him, we discern him—at least when our heart is pure—and wiping away a tear, we exclaim: "We thank thee, Lord! for in these hours the old curse has been suspended, the saddest of our pangs has ceased, and those flowers, united of old in Eden, but separated ever since, have mingled their splendor and their perfume on the stem of human life—the flower of love and the flower of virginity!" This married pair, are they indeed husband and wife? These virgin ones, are they still virginal? They are virgin spouses, and espoused virgins! God is in their love, their love is in God. The husband is priest, because he has been the *teacher* of his children and his wife; because he has *governed* their conscience and their will; he is priest because he has *prayed* with his lips in the midst of them, with his heart in their heart, and with his soul in their soul. Such is the priesthood of the household. "I am the God of Abraham, of Isaac, and of Jacob, the God of Sarah, of Rebecca, and of Rachel; that is my name for evermore!"

II. Having established, as the teaching of revelation, the existence of a domestic priesthood, of which the father of the family is the priest, it is my next duty to take up the reproach cast upon the Church, of having brought about the downfall of this priesthood. I listen to this objection, often violent and hypocritical indeed, and yet, again, too earnest not to be sincere. It is summed up as follows: The influence of a Catholic institution, compulsory confession, has destroyed in the family the moral and religious authority of the father, by yielding up the conscience of the mother and the children wholly into the power of a stranger, the priest, and this substitution has consummated the moral divorce of man and wife.

It is first to be considered whether the fact which serves as the starting-point for this objection is true or false; and it is capable of proof, as a general rule, that in the city populations of France—for we confine our attention to France, and particularly to the cities—the priesthood of the father of the family has disappeared entirely, or almost entirely; the moral and religious guidance of consciences, where it still survives, has passed entirely, or almost entirely, into the hands of the Catholic priest, who thus cumulates the two priesthoods, the hierarchical and the domestic. The fact, then, must be frankly admitted, not, however, without observing that there are exceptions so numerous and respectable that they must not be left out of the account.

Still, the fact exists, and we will not seek to justify it in itself. On the contrary, we do not hesitate to pronounce it abnormal, for this fact implies profound degeneracy in the character and authority of the head of the family, and, in the families infected with it, a moral and religious disorganization which passes into anarchy or despotism, and the incidental results of which, more profound than is imagined, make themselves felt throughout the whole structure of society.

But admitting the existence and the danger of the fact, it remains for us to seek its true *cause* and its true *remedy*.

1. First, the *cause*.—Those who would throw the responsibility for it upon the Church, will do well to ponder this question: Is it the Church that has *usurped* this authority, or you who have *abdicated* it?

If the question were one of particular acts, due, not to the Catholic institution, but to a want of enlightenment or of rectitude in this or that minister representing it, doubtless it must be admitted that in certain cases the priest has usurped. I willingly admit that all of us in the Church—laity, priests, popes—we are all liable, both to error and to sin. Jesus Christ alone is holy, with his Church taken in its universality—"Thou only art holy." . . . . "I believe in the holy Catholic Church"—and I do not deem it either expedient or right to retort in an inverse sense the tactics of the school of Voltaire—"Keep lying; some of it will stick!" Falsehood is even more hateful and more baneful when it pretends to serve the Church than when it pretends to ruin it.

But it is not a question as to particular acts, but as to a condition of affairs already general, or, at least, tending to become so, which condition is said to owe its existence to the Catholic institution itself. In this view the priest has not been guilty of usurpation.

No! it is no usurpation when we fulfil the universal mission assigned us by Jesus Christ for the salvation of souls. . . . . He has told us to go to all, without distinction of husband or wife, master or slave, considering them all as one in Christ Jesus. We have no right to turn away from any one. He has also told us: "Whosoever sins ye remit, they are remitted unto them." . . .

"Whatsoever ye shall loose on earth shall be loosed in heaven."* We have exercised this beneficent ministry. Far from being the enemies of the family, we are its benefactors, when we bring, in the name of Jesus Christ and the Church, what the father of the family is powerless to give—the outward means and the moral assurance of the forgiveness of sins; when we dispose the heart to receive this pardon, and when we pronounce that absolution which betokens grace and produces it in the heart prepared for it. We are the benefactors of the family—not its disorganizers, when, in the majesty and sanctity of the sacrament, we receive confidences necessary not only by virtue of the law of the Gospel, but also by reason of the most imperative needs of the human soul,—confidences, however, which cannot and should not be made at home. We are, finally, the benefactors of the family when we make known to each of its members, with the authority of our ministry, "as though God did beseech them by us,"† the counsels and practical exhortations that enlighten the ignorant, and restore and strengthen the feeble.

It is not we, then, who have usurped, but it is you who have *abdicated*.

You have abdicated your domestic priesthood in the bosom of a Christian family, in that you have abdicated the exercise of Christian duty. Is there any instruction, any government, any family worship in your homes? And if there be such, is it you who preside over them and conduct them? In the sanctuary of the Church and in the sanctuary of the household, do you lead the family in the performance of religious duties? And with regard to morality, do you put in practice the morality of the gospel, or the morality of skepticism and

---

* John, xx, 23; Matthew, xviii. 18.   † 2 Corinthians, v. 20.

lust? Perhaps you have renounced the Christian faith. How then could you have any religious conviction, and any conscience of right and wrong in common with your wife and children? Perhaps you have even lost all religious belief whatever, and passed over from the ranks of the deists to the ranks of the materialists, or at least of the skeptics? Once more, how would you be able to instruct the mind, give counsel to the conscience, and direct the soul?

Yes, you have abdicated, and by that fatal abdication you have become the authors of the vast and profound evil of which you complain, and from which you all suffer. *Children* must have religion, their education is impossible without it. Even skeptics generally admit this, and, on this ground, they admit religion into their families. Besides, the *wife* is not enough to guide the children. She, too, must be religious; and because her mind acts rather by intuition than by reasoning, because her heart, more than man's, is made for suffering and loving, there are invincible affinities and connections between her and God. But, in moral and religious matters, as in everything else, indeed especially in them, woman cannot do without the man's government. The great apostle comes back continually to this point, "man is the head of woman, as Christ is the head of man." To hear him, one might suppose that the husband is a necessary mediator between woman and Christ, as Christ is himself the mediator between the Church and God. Now all this you have lost sight of. You have held yourself aloof, or have even attempted to invade the domain of the Christian conscience. And then, alarmed at your encroachments or your abdication, the wife has taken her soul, and with it the cradle of her children, and has laid them both at the feet of the priest; she has put them in his keeping, waiting for better days. We then have usurped nothing; it is you who have abdicated everything.

2. But is there no *remedy* for this evil? O God of our salvation! wilt thou not revisit thy people and build up our ruins?

It depends upon you, fathers, to bring about a better future for the whole world; it depends upon you to realize it from this very day, beneath your own roof. Learn to have some higher aspiration; learn to be, in the full meaning of the word, the father of the family—the head of the house; learn, we beg of you, to send us back within our proper limits, to have us confine ourselves to the exercise of our priesthood; and, to that end, resume the exercise of your own.

I remember that several years ago, eight young men, under the guidance of the immortal Ozanam, founded the society of St. Vincent de Paul..... But no, an earlier and nobler example rushes to my mind. Eighteen centuries ago, twelve young men, gathered by Christ among the towns of Galilee and the boats of the sea of Tiberias—twelve young men became apostles and regenerated the world.

Take heed, brethren and friends, young men who hear me—take heed, not to the office of apostle, but the office of patriarch. This day let a blessing attend upon my words; may they prove to be the calling of eight, of a dozen true men to this divine office of father, and they will have done more for France, for society, for the Church, than the political and religious parties by which they are rent and torn.

Yes; let a blessing rest upon these words of mine. Ah, young men, may each one of you say to himself, There is a priesthood that has perished from the world, the most ancient, and, in one sense, the most indispensable of all—the priesthood of the husband and father. I will raise it up in my person. Henceforth I will put away the speculative seductions, and, still more, the practical seductions of materialism; I will remain pure, I will keep myself worthy, some day, of loving; and, when that day has come, I will take my bride from the hands of God, "the wife of my youth;"* I will take her to my arms, I will press her upon my heart as upon an altar, and, commingling my soul with hers in one song, one flame, one incense-cloud, I will lift her up before Jehovah as a victim, a glorious sacrifice of tenderness and purity; I will love her "as Christ loved the Church." I will offer up myself for her, "as Christ also gave himself for the Church," that through the power of love "he might present it to himself a glorious Church, not having-spot nor wrinkle."† This will I do. In my love I will be a priest—priest of the fellowship of our consciences and our prayers. I will be a priest in my fatherhood: God shall be in the fruitfulness of my fatherhood as well as in the chastity of my love! Woe! woe to the bastard races born only of flesh and blood! Woe to the races that have no origin save the gross will of the animal man! But blessed, on the other hand, the men who are born of God, whom their father has begotten with his soul, whom he has begotten a second time in his affection, upon whom he has stamped the divine impress of his conscience, his justice, and his religion. That is what I would be—let the Christian youth say to himself. I would be a husband and a father; I would know, here on this earth, where people no longer seem to have any idea of it, what it is to love a woman in God and for God—what it is to beget children in God and

---

* Proverbs, v. 18.   ‡ Ephesians, v. 25, 27.

for God. I would be a priest! O God of Abraham, of Isaac, and of Jacob, grant me thy blessing!

Thus it is, Gentlemen, that the priesthood after the order of Abraham, Isaac, and Jacob will rise from its ruins, and stretch forth its hand to that other priesthood after the order of Melchisedek, that had no father nor pedigree, says St. Paul—the priesthood after the order of Jesus Christ and the Apostles. And when these two hands have been laid in mutual fraternity upon every family—the hand of the Catholic priest and the hand of the household priest,—the hand of the father respected in his independence and in his government of hearts, and the hand of the Catholic priest appealed to sincerely, faithfully, as he that is to help and complete the work of the domestic priest, then the world will be saved, and not before. Yes, whatever you may do, you will be powerless, utterly powerless, so long as the priesthood of the father of the family is not resuscitated, and its hand does not rest in that of the priesthood of the Church!

LECTURE FOURTH.

December 20, 1868.

THE JEWISH NATIONAL CHURCH.

In taking leave of the domestic Church of the patriarchs, we give it our parting salutations as one of those pregnant ideas which teem with inexhaustible fecundity—one of those central points around which we must build if we would leave behind us anything useful and lasting. We shall come upon it again—we shall return to it more than once as we proceed. But just at this moment we are to study its transformation into the Jewish national Church. For above the family comes the nation; and in the order of history, as well as in the order of logic, the work of Abraham is the preparation for the work of Moses. The domestic Church of the patriarchs leads to the national Church of the Jews. In a future discourse I will consider the internal constitution of this Church. To-day I propose only to consider in a general way the tie which, under the Mosaic law, united the religious life with the life of the nation.

On the summit of Mount Sinai I hear God uttering his voice; at its foot, I behold a people forming itself into a nation. But this people is at once a people and a Church; and this God is at once the God of this Church and the King of this people. So that the

Church, in this second phase of its development, unites and merges its own life in the life of a particular people, thus giving the pattern of what it is to do hereafter, after the coming of Jesus Christ, in other forms, and without weakening catholic unity, for each one of the nations that shall be gathered into its fold. Now the life of a people, viewed according to what is most general and most essential, can be summed up in its *agricultural* and its *political* life. What have the institutes of Moses had to do in respect to each of these two elements?

I. The prosperity of nations, as of families, results especially from the connection that they form with the soil. Patriotism is not a purely moral sentiment; like all the feelings of our hearts, it needs an object incarnate in matter. *Our country* takes to itself a body in the *land* of our forefathers, and the love that it inspires is merged in love for the soil. In its soil does the fatherland wish to be loved and served. The surest source of a nation's wealth, and the source nearest to its moral life, is the soil made fruitful by human labor.

But what shall consecrate this wedlock of man and the earth? What shall give to the earth that sacred character of which it has need, not to charm but to fix the roving heart of man? What shall bring down upon man's labor that strong, sweet anointing, beneath which patriotism shall flourish, while the fields are clothed with harvests? There is no close and lasting union of a nation with its soil, except that which is consecrated by religion.

With the Jews, the land is the object of an unparalleled consecration. This is the land, above all others, that deserves to be called the Holy Land, and to exert upon strangers an irresistible charm. Our fathers, the early pilgrims, bedewed it with their tears; our fathers, the Crusaders, bathed it with torrents of their heroic blood; we, ourselves, have learned at our mothers' knees to name it and to love it, until we scarcely know which is dearer to us, the land of France or the Holy Land! And do not its exiled sons, to-day, on the hospitable banks of the Seine, as they did of yore on the hostile banks of the Euphrates, still mingle the recollection of it with all their dreams, with all their prayers? "No;" they say to-day as they said of old: "We will not sing while sitting by the waters of Babylon. At the remembrance of Zion we have but weeping and tears." "By the rivers of Babylon there we sat down; we wept, when we remembered Zion. If I forget thee, O Jerusalem, let my right hand forget her cunning, let my tongue cleave to the roof of my mouth."

Situated at the junction of the three continents that formed the ancient world, on the shore of that sea that was the centre and the highway of the civilization of antiquity, so near to everything and yet so isolated from everything by that sea, by that other sea whose sandy waves served it as a rampart, by the impregnable fortress of Lebanon, Palestine was the abode destined by God for his people, promised with an oath to the patriarchs, and given at last to their posterity.

But this land, favored in so many respects, is not one of those enchanted and prodigal regions that charm their inhabitants to sleep in voluptuous idleness. It is not like Egypt, watered and fertilized by the Nile; it is a mountainous country, in which there is especial need of the constant toil of man, and the constant blessing of God. So God would continue to be, in the strict sense of the word, the owner of the land, insomuch that no portion of it might ever be alienated, and the

Israelites might hold only as tenants. "The land shall not be sold forever; for the land is mine, and ye are strangers and sojourners with me."* And the Jewish people, on its part—because it is the typical people, and because, as such, it is to bring out in relief the essential traits of national life, leaving in the shade everything secondary—is a people of husbandmen and shepherds. It is the most *agricultural* and the most *religious* of all nations.

By reason of this close union of rural life and religious life, the three great feasts of the Mosaic institute have reference to the work of the field. The Feast of the Passover celebrates the time when the ears of grain begin to show; the Feast of Pentecost, the time when the ripe crops fall beneath the sickle; the Feast of Tabernacles, the finished harvest. Then the head of the family, still invested with the patriarchal priesthood, notwithstanding the legal priesthood invested in the tribe of Levi, went up to Jerusalem with the first-fruits of his flocks and his fields, followed by his wife, his children, and his servants. He came into the temple to offer all that he had from the bounty of the Eternal and his own labor. Then the people made merry together before their invisible Master. These were joyous festivals, intermingled with chaste dances and religious songs.

What a lesson for rationalism and for overwrought mysticism! In their excesses they come all the nearer together, from the fact that they are extremes. They would fain separate religion from the things of the earth, and from the present life; they would shut it up in its sanctuaries, seclude it to the contemplation and expectation of future happiness. That is, without a

* Leviticus, xxv. 23.

doubt, the sublimest part of religion, and it is the special mission of Christianity to develop it. But, since the Christian does not, any more than the Jew, cease to dwell on the earth, Christianity cannot be indifferent to any earthly interests or labors. With its own divine breath it should fill the sails of commerce toward distant isles; it should speed its course over the vast continents; it should bless the hard struggles of industry, and consecrate its conquests, and animate, in a word, the production and the distribution of wealth, the evidence and the instrument of the universal brotherhood of nations! But upon agriculture especially should it bestow its sympathies and its benedictions. For agriculture is the essential labor of nations, while commerce and industry are only their luxury—a necessary luxury, no doubt, but after all a luxury.

And since I am speaking of agriculture among the Jews, permit me to revert to France, that France which has been called by great popes "the tribe of Judah of the Catholic Church," and to view it in its country provinces. Its cities are great, but so are its fields. Let us, then, Gentlemen, greet in its country homes—the most intelligent and prosperous of all homes, as they are the most Christian—that hardy race of French peasants with their practical treasures of wisdom and goodness, in our day too little appreciated. Here I behold, upon our soil, in the midst of our brethren, the daily realization of the beautiful figure, at once positive and poetical, under which the prophets depict Messiah's reign. Henceforth let there be no more swords, nor spears. Lift up your heads! Beat your swords and spears into ploughshares, and with these peaceful weapons pierce the earth with fruitful wounds! Be every man the owner of his field and vineyard. Sit down beneath the shade of your own vine and fig-tree, and talk together of the joys of heaven, indeed, but also of the good things of the earth, that are the prophecy and preparation of heaven.

And as we are speaking of our splendid peasantry, suffer me to pause a moment before that man whom I shall call, with the poet, " a ploughman clad in mourning." Beneath his black cassock, what simplicity! what goodness! I behold his abode, the poorest, perhaps, and yet the brightest—the quietest, and yet the most cheerful, looking out on one side upon the village and the fields, on the other upon the church and the graveyard. I know him well; it is the country parish priest, the obscure and sacred link between the catholic life and the national life of our Church of France. The country priest, one of the most deserving servants of our native land, one of the most essential ministers of our Church.

II. Man does not live by bread alone. So a people worthy of the name does not live solely by agricultural labor. There are national events, social institutions, a *political* life. From one point of view, it is of the utmost importance that religion should be separated from politics. It may not belittle itself to the proportions of the parties, whatever they be, with which it might be involved. People must not be able to say, instead of the catholic Church, the catholic *party*. But from another, and no less correct point of view, it is extremely desirable, it is necessary, that religion should not hold itself aloof from any element of national life. Whether they are to be legally united depends upon circumstances; but in every age and in every country, they should be morally united. History, in every age, and particularly in our own, shows that the most powerful peoples are precisely those in whom this union is most strongly impressed upon thought and character.

Nowhere has it existed as it did among the Jews. With them, the religious and the national spirit were but one, and the name that people bear is literally true —*the people of God*. From God indeed, from God directly and by miracle, they received those three grand things that constitute political life—*liberty, law, government*. The three agricultural feasts of which we have spoken above were also three political feasts. The Passover celebrated *liberty*—the deliverance from Egyptian bondage; Pentecost, the promulgation of the *law* from Mount Sinai; the Feast of Tabernacles, the fellowship of the people dwelling happily in its tents under the safeguard of *government*.

1. *Liberty*.—It is with liberty in the public life of nations as with love in the private life of families. No more disastrous divorce than that between the idea of religion and the idea of liberty. Through this divorce, liberty degenerates into license; it becomes a scourge. Allied with religion, it remains itself, fruitful and glorious. "If the truth shall make you free," says Christ, "then are ye free indeed."*

Jewish liberty was the daughter of Jehovah. The Hebrews were slaves in Egypt; worse than that—they loved their bondage. They groaned beneath the blows of Pharaoh's taskmasters; but when their daily task was accomplished, they would sit down with sensual delight to their flesh-pots, the remembrance of which called forth their regrets during the painful beginnings of their deliverance—"the land of Egypt, where we sat by the flesh-pots and ate bread to the full."† This satisfaction of their sensual appetites had such dominion

* John, viii. 32, 36.   † Exodus, xvi. 3.

over them, that Moses had a harder fight, perhaps, against these than against Pharaoh's resistance, although he came to them bringing the gift of liberty from the hand of Jehovah, saying, "I AM hath sent me unto you."* And it was only with great difficulty that this heroic ambassador of the Lord succeeded in delivering them both from their political bondage to the tyrant, and from their religious bondage to idols.

From this twofold deliverance, thus simultaneously effected, was derived the divine character of liberty, which always, among the Jews, continued true to its religious origin. Bondage never ceased to be, in the hands of God, the most terrible of punishments, as liberty was the most precious of rewards. Hence that hatred of slavery which animated the Jews, and which, though free from fanatical excess, at least in the brighter days of their history, carried with it, into the wars so aptly named "the wars of the Lord,"† all the fiery zeal of religious passion.

After a few years of liberty, those Hebrews had grown out of all recognition, for liberty is an educating power, just as (in an inverse sense) slavery is. Behold their struggles in the land of Canaan; see how this love of independence is confounded in their soul with the love of God, and how there was developed in them a passion—a wild passion, as I must call it, when I listen to the accents of Deborah's song—a wild but most noble passion, at once the most human and the most divine— the passionate love of country and of God. They rose up against their adversaries; and when the men came not up to crush the tyrants, the women were ready for the work!

I have mentioned Deborah, the wife of Lapidoth—

* Exodus, iii. 14. † Numbers, xxi. 18.

Deborah the prophetess, who, sitting under a palm-tree, judged all the children of Israel assembled unto her to settle their disputes at her feet.* Deborah, seeing her people under the yoke of the king of Canaan, beneath the sword of his general Sisera, unfurls the banner of liberty, calls upon the warriors to follow her; and when the warriors, who had no man to lead them to combat, saw this woman braver than the men, they followed her, and victory went with them! And when the enemy was defeated and put to flight—when the prophetess of Israel had secured the triumph of liberty and religion, she sang this song:

> " The mighty ones were no more in Israel,
> The warriors had ceased,
> Until that I Deborah arose,
> Till I arose, a mother in Israel!"
> " Awake, Deborah, awake!"—

thus she speaks aloud to herself, calling forth the enthusiasm that was thrilling in her veins;

> " Awake! awake! utter a song!
> And thou Barak, son of Abinoam,
> Arise and lead captivity captive!
> The stars fought in the height of heaven,
> They fought in battle array against Sisera.
> The river of Kishon has swept them away,
> That ancient river, the river Kishon.
> O my soul, thou hast trodden down the mighty ones!"†

Thus it was that, among the Jews, the love of God, joined to the love of country, kindled even women's hearts to a blaze of patriotism.

And in their internal organization what entire lib-

---

* Judges, iv. 4, 5.   † Ibid., v.

erty! Civil equality, political equality, I was almost going to say social equality, were graven on their laws in the name of God. All Jews were equal in the eye of the law, and before the tribunal of the elders, who were chosen for this high office with reference to their age and their virtues, the experience they had acquired in life, and the position they occupied at the head of families. All employments were alike open to all, except the ceremonial priesthood, which had devolved upon the tribe of Levi, that the fathers of families in other tribes might be eased of the burden of it, and which was dearly bought by exclusion from all share in the distribution of property.

A mere shepherd, like David or Amos, might become a king or a prophet. There were no classes in this society; all were "sons of Abraham, and never in bondage to any man."* No Israelite was a slave. "Over your brethren, the children of Israel, ye shall not rule with rigor; for they are *my* servants which I brought forth out of the land of Egypt; they shall not be sold as bondmen."† Nor did the law wish that there should be beggars or paupers, at least paupers condemned to perpetual and absolute poverty.‡

A special statute of limitation secured the success of this legal provision against misfortune, and even against fault. The homestead could not be alienated forever. By the decree of God, every fifty years, when the jubilee trumpets sounded their glad and piercing peal, the homestead reverted to those who had lost it.§ They were, indeed, as Moses had said, a people of *kings* and *priests;* for the sovereignty of the fireside is the foun-

---

* John, viii. 33.   † Leviticus, xxv. 46, 42.
‡ Deuteronomy, xv. 4. Margin: "That there be no poor among you."
§ Leviticus, xxv.

dation of true national sovereignty, just as national religion draws its life from the religion of the fireside.

Doubtless it is out of the question to think of reviving these forms among ourselves. But it is indispensable that the same spirit should animate society amongst us; that, as it was among the Jews, the idea of the nation should be in full harmony with the idea of religion, and that both should find a firm foundation in the constitution of the family. The Jewish people is the typical people; above all other nations it is the people of the homestead, the people of religion and of liberty.

No! neither the nations of Greece and Rome, nor the Germanic races of the middle ages, nor the great nationalities of modern times, have equalled this type of society. And, besides the religious reason why God permits this singular race to exist in its dispersion among the nations of the earth, is there not a political reason for the strange phenomenon? May we not find some indication of this in the words of Scripture: "He set the bounds of the nations according to the number of the children of Israel."* Yes; if they have to learn from us Christianity and the Gospel, we have yet to learn from them the Pentateuch and liberty.

2. But what was the use, you will perhaps say, of delivering them from bondage, only to give them forthwith a *law*, and, soon after, a *king?* Because a nation is not conceivable without a body of laws and a government. What, then, is the *legal system* of the Jews? What is their *government?*

In the Mosaic economy, contrary to the custom of all other national constitutions, the first and principal place is assigned to the moral law as it is graven upon

---

* Deuteronomy, xxxii. 8.

the human conscience, though not always recognized by it; to the moral law as it remained after Jesus Christ came to fulfil, not to destroy it; to the Ten Commandments of God, which are not only the teaching of the Church, but the teaching of Nature herself, the soul of civilization and true progress. Such is the law brought by Moses to the people, written by the hand of God himself on the tables of Mount Sinai, and in that temple without images, where the Invisible shall dwell between the outstretched wings of the cherubim, the book containing this law shall be the only image among men of God's justice and goodness! And in every age, and in every land, obedience to this law shall be the condition upon which depends the dignity of man and the liberty of nations.

Such being the nature of the Jewish law, we cannot cherish any doubt as to the nature of their government or the person of their king. This government is theocracy in its most extreme, but also its purest and most efficient form; not the government of society by priests or by kings acting in the name of God, but government in the hands of God himself, speaking directly to the conscience of a people at once free and religious. The Godhead was not to be represented in the temple of the Jews by any image, lest it should be exposed to the idolatrous propensities of the people. So, also, there was to be no visible royalty among them, because political paganism almost always converted kings into tyrants.

To-day, Christianity preserves us from this social idolatry. In those days there was but one possible preventive. "Your king," exclaimed Samuel, in the presence of the faithless people that asked for a king like the other nations, "your king is the Lord your God."[*]

---

[*] 1 Samuel, xii. 12.

And Gideon, rejecting the sceptre which they offered him in return for his services, and which they wished to make hereditary in his family, had before replied: "I will not rule over you, neither shall my son rule over you; the Lord shall rule over you."*

And when Samuel was wroth at this passion for servitude that he could no longer repress, the Lord comforted him, saying: "They have not rejected thee, but they have rejected me." And yielding to their foolish desires, God gave them a king; but by the side of this royalty, or rather above it—above even the Levitical priesthood itself, he raised up the ministry of the prophets, through whom he continued to reign, delivering his orders to kings and priests and people.

Such was the Jewish people in its liberty, in its laws, in its government—a people essentially religious. And if we seek for the lowermost foundation of this structure, so massive even in its ruins, we are surprised—the skeptic, who believes only in material organizations, would be stupefied—to find at the base of this nation-Church and Church-nation, nothing but an idea!

One day in the desert the Hebrews said, in sight of the manna that rained down to them from heaven: "Our soul loatheth this light food."† So there are some modern consciences and reasons that would revolt at this foundation of a Church and a nation—only an idea! And yet that is all we can find there. But what idea? It is the idea of the living God!

Look at the beginning of the book of Exodus; you will find there the same things that you have found in Genesis, at the commencement of the history of Abraham, Isaac, and Jacob; a vision, and in that vision, God. To Abraham, God the only Sovereign, Creator, and Pre-

* Judges, viii. 23. † Numbers, xxi. 5.

server had revealed himself under the name Elohim and Adonai. To Moses, the shepherd wandering in the desert, feeding his flock forty years in solitude, at the foot of that Horeb that was afterward to behold him as a nation's lawgiver, God reveals himself once more. He is ever the same God, of Abraham, Isaac, and Jacob.

But in this revelation there is an advance, the last advance in monotheism. Elohim now calls himself *Jehovah*. Beneath this new name there is a new conception, a new idea; it is no longer merely the Creator and Governor—it is the *Being*. With painful effort human philosophy lifts itself thus high; it can rise no higher. In the burning bush Jehovah said: *I am that I am. Thou shalt go to the children of Israel; thou shalt bring them hither, that I may make my covenant with them. If they ask thee, Who is the God that hath sent thee to us? thou shall say: I AM hath sent me.** And there, no longer at the foot of the mountain, but on its summit—there Jehovah sees them gathering themselves together unto him; there he enters into covenant with them.

Ah! it is well that he does not call himself Lord and Master, as in the days of old. It is well that now he calls himself Jehovah, for this covenant is a covenant of supreme liberty. He could have forced himself upon them, for he was strong: he did not; he suffered himself to plead with them, for he was wise and just! He imposed nothing—he merely proposed. Moses was the ambassador that went up from the people to God, that came down from God to the people, and God and the people held converse with one another. He proposes the covenant with its conditions; the people accept it freely. A living idea, the idea of the living God,

* Exodus, iii. 13, 14.

has been revealed in one word: "Ye saw nothing," said the lawgiver to the people, "ye saw no similitude; ye heard only a voice; but it was Jehovah!"*

Between this living idea and this people an alliance is formed, formed beneath this rock riven by repeated thunderbolts; fit shelter for the stormy wooing between the faithless people and the jealous God! It is more than an alliance freely contracted; it is a wedlock! It is to pass down through centuries of discord and centuries of peace, through ages of glory and ages of ignominy; through the prosperities of David and Solomon, the captivities of Nineveh and Babylon, the scattering abroad to the four winds of heaven: it will subsist despite all changes, and throughout all ages. Always, and despite his anger, Jehovah will be faithful to his people. Always, and despite their rebellions, the people shall be faithful to their God; and together they shall afford for all time the glorious, the unique spectacle of a nation indestructible because it is a Church, a Church immortal because it is a nation.

Yes. This people has lost everything; everything has tended to cast it down into the bottomless pit of destruction; the land of Canaan has been taken away from under its feet; it has been torn up by the roots, and, as if it had been the prey of ravening beasts, its bleeding fragments have been carried off by the nations on every side. The throne of David, the altar of Aaron —all is in ruins. But when its conquerors are nothing more than a handful of dust, nothing but a name in history, what has this people still left, that it should live on and not cease filling the world with its woes and with its glory? It has its God! This people remains a people because it still believes in the God of Sinai!

* Deuteronomy, iv. 12.

And this God—I do not mean Jehovah himself, for he is our God, indestructible by virtue of his own might—but this God, considered as the God of the faith and the obsolete worship of this deathless people, what is there left to him that he should survive all his misfortunes? For everything has gone against him, everything has been battering into ruin the religion which he instituted. Logic is against it; and, what is worse, facts, all history are against it. This waiting for the Messiah is the grandest, wildest perseverance that ever the world saw! And yet the religion of the Jews stands firm; the God of the Jews abides still, despite the confutations of logic and of history. Why? Because on the side of God there is something mightier, in one sense, than logic and facts—there is the faith of this people!

Be this a lesson to us, to all Christian nations—a people immortal because of its God, a God that cannot be forgotten, because of his people.

LECTURE FIFTH.

DECEMBER 27, 1868.

THE JEWISH CHURCH IN ITS RELATIONS TO THE CHRISTIAN CHURCH.

THE Church of the Jews presents two very different aspects, according as we look at it in the light of the *national* life of this people, or in the light of the *religious* life of mankind. From the first point of view, it is only a national Church, the finished model for the several Churches which, within the pale of the great Catholic Church, derive their life from this common source, and infuse it more directly into the life of the nations whose names they bear; such as the Church of France, the Church of Spain, and, in the happy days of unity, the Church of England. From the second point of view, it expands to the dimensions of the human race itself, it carries in its womb the germ and inception of the Catholic Church.

"But what is the use," I hear some inattentive and fretful spirit say—"what is the use of talking to us so much about the synagogue? We are no longer in the synagogue, but in the Church." True, but the synagogue is only the Church begun; and the Church is only the synagogue developed and completed. The Church of the Jews is the court of which our Church is the temple. Before entering the temple we must cross the court, and even pause there a moment in pious meditation. "Our feet," says the psalmist, "shall stand within thy gates, O Jerusalem! Jerusalem is builded as a city that is compact together." In so doing we shall do the Church a service. A philosopher who, in many respects, is worthy only of contempt, but whose bold spirit seized and formulated many a truth, Machiavelli, has said, that "in order to the preservation of society, it should constantly be brought back to its beginnings." And Tertullian, who is in all points a higher authority, especially in the Christian pulpit, has stated the same law in these terms: "Christianity maintains itself by means of its holy antiquity, and in no way can we better repair the ravages with which it may be attacked, or threatened, than by bringing it back to its beginnings."* To speak of Judaism, then, is to speak of the Church, and to speak of it in a way eminently adapted to be useful.

But before considering Judaism *in its relation to the Church*, it is important to clear the ground of one objection that starts up of itself. How can Judaism stand related to the Church in its character of universality—Judaism, whose distinguishing character is just the opposite, narrow and exclusive? Because its mission was one of *conservation*. It was to preserve for better times the true religion, the constituent elements of the universal Church; and that could only be by sequestrating those elements from the influence of the rest of mankind, then almost wholly corrupt and idolatrous. When we wish to keep some precious perfume that is apt to diffuse itself and evaporate, we shut it up

---

* Omnino res christiana sanctâ antiquitate stat, nec ruinosa certius reparabitur quam si ad originem conseatur.

in a strong, well-sealed vase. So did Moses. This vase he himself carved from the rock of Sinai; or rather, he fashioned it in the body and the soul of this energetic, obstinate race, so inaccessible to outside influences. "A stiff-necked people," as he often calls them, whose stiff-neckedness, however, faulty as it was, was none the less a qualification for its special mission.

Isolated in this little country, twenty leagues in breadth, shut up between the sea, the sand, and Lebanon; isolated in its purity and pride of blood, that has kept itself irreconcilably aloof from all admixture; isolated by its unsocial character, and that contempt for the stranger which the stranger has repaid with usury —the Jew was especially isolated by his *law*. And here I am not speaking of the Decalogue, strictly so called, but of the whole body of the Mosaic law, so far as it was peculiar to the Jewish nation. So understood, this law enveloped the Jew, and held him bound up, as it were, in a network of religious and civil prescriptions, as numerous as they were minute and complicated. It gave to his entire existence a foreign character, that found no analogy in the rest of the world, and was so exclusively peculiar to his land that this law does not seem possible outside of Palestine. This is so true that the gigantic labor of the Talmudists, after the dispersion, had for its object to render it less impracticable by dint of interpretations and dispensations. "The people," exclaimed Balaam, "shall dwell alone, and shall not be reckoned among the nations!"*

Still, under the forms of this religion that is so narrowly and exclusively national, we find the constituent elements of the grand and eternal religion of mankind —Christianity. These elements are *doctrine, morality,*

* Numbers, xxiii. 9.

and *worship*, which are identical, for substance, in the Jewish and the Christian Churches.

1. *Doctrine and Morality.*—The doctrine is summed up in the idea of God, and in the idea of the Messiah. Of the latter I shall speak by and by. In the present discourse we shall consider only the former. It is in the Jewish race that the successive developments of the idea of God have been accomplished, by the threefold revelation of the patriarchs, the prophets, and the apostles. To the patriarchs, God is Elohim—that is, the Almighty Ruler. He reveals himself to them in his connection with the external world, as Creator and Preserver. To Moses and the prophets, he is Jehovah—that is, the Being of beings, the Absolute. He reveals himself in his self-existence—"*I am that I am.*" Sublime definition, which man hath not made, on which he scarcely dares to comment, and which all the schools of philosophy must borrow from the sacred echo of the desert.

Monotheism is complete. There is nothing more to be added upon the nature of God; and when the Gospel unveils the Trinity it does nothing more—if we may so speak—than deduce the consequences of the principle laid down, and name by their mysterious names the three personal terms of that life which subsists in the Absolute Being—the Father, the Son, and the Holy Spirit. "And the life was manifested."* And yet these names had already been uttered by the prophets, and if they resound with new solemnity in the synagogue as it is about to be transformed into the Church, it is because they are uttered by the lips of Jewish apostles, called to teach them to the nations that without their preaching would never have known them.

* 1 John, 1. 2.

"Go ye into all the world, baptizing the nations into the name of the Father, and of the Son, and of the Holy Ghost." Thus shall be fulfilled the word of the prophet Isaiah: "The toilers of Egypt, and the merchants of Ethiopia and of the Sabeans shall come over unto thee, and shall fall down unto thee, saying: 'Surely God is in thee, and there is none else; there is no God beside.' "*

You remember that noble, erring spirit, who, having just drunk from the broad rivers and the grand epics of India, found the lake of Tiberias but a pool in comparison with the Ganges, and the Bible insignificant by the side of the Ramayana. And yet the God of humanity is no more Hindoo than he is Greek. The God of mankind is the God of the Jews! In vain would modern thought, abusing the powers that it derives in part from revelation, seek to change in the future this law of the past, and to create to itself a sublimer and purer God than the historic God of the Old Testament. Smitten with giddiness, it would reel between pantheism and atheism, these two forms of recent paganism. "Thus saith the Lord, the King of Israel, and his Redeemer, the Lord of Hosts: I am the first and I am the last; and beside me there is no God!"†

It is from the Jews, then, that mankind has received, in Christianity, the complete idea of the living God; and had it received from them no more than this, it would owe to them a debt of eternal gratitude. But the idea of God is not all. Along with it and the entire dogmatic system of which it is the germ and the sum, man has need, besides, of morality. Assuredly, Gentlemen, we do not desire morality independent of doctrine; but no more do we desire doctrine independent

---

* Isaiah, xlv. 14. † Ibid, xliv. 6.

of morality. Away with the God who should not say, like the God of the Jews, "Be ye holy, for I am holy!"* Away with the God who should demand of his adorers only a pharisaical preciseness in dogmatic formulas and the ceremonies of worship, and should suffer himself to be venerated by men prostrate in the meanest of all mire, the mire of mysticism! We would have a God with "*a law in his hand.*" *Et lex in manibus ejus!*

Now, such is the God of the Jews; and as they have given us God, so they have given us the *law*. Not now that narrow law of which I spoke at the outset, that has been rent, together with the veil of the temple;—and in vain do the Talmudists seek to put together the fragments. The law that the Jews have given us, the law that we are keeping, that we may some day return it to them, is the law of the Decalogue, a law grand, holy, majestic like Jehovah, a universal law to which the philosophical or religious legislators of antiquity have never been able to attain. I know that there are admirable things in the religious codes of the East, in the grand philosophical systems of the West. I am foremost to admire the nascent splendors, the dawning glories that shine in these ethical systems. But how inferior, when confronted with the morality brought down from Sinai—with the Decalogue of Moses! There is not, to-day, in Europe, a thoughtful scholar that would dare to make the comparison; there is not in the whole world a civilized people that would dare to risk the exchange. The morality of mankind is that which was elaborated in the Jewish code, that which was written by Moses, magnificently commented by the prophets. That is our system of morals. It is an everlasting system!

---

* Leviticus, xix. 2.

Let it not be said that morality varies with the individual, and still more so with the race and the century. No. Morality never varies; it is immutable as God—inflexible as conscience. The applications only of moral principle vary with a most harmonious flexibility, a most productive liberty. But as to morality itself, I repeat, it varies no more than God varies in the circle of the heavens—no more than conscience in the depths of the human soul. It is immutable; the old commandments of Sinai are, for all time, the rule for nations, families, and individuals. The Gospel of Christ and the apostles has but thrown additional light upon it, and cleared away all shadows, especially those of Pharisaism; and by vindicating morality against the Pharisees, the Gospel has vindicated Judaism itself, which they had corrupted.

Were the Christian law, in fact, superior in substance to the Mosaic law, that could only be because the Mosaic law had failed to recognize *inward righteousness,* or because it had failed to recognize charity, which rises superior to the law of which it is the crown. But neither of these hypotheses is admissible. The law of Moses did not merely condemn the *act*—it did not merely cleanse the outside of the cup, like the Pharisees, leaving corruption within; but it sought to make inside and outside, the visible deed and the inspiring intention, both pure in the eyes of God. Therefore it is that Moses, prohibiting the act, has also forbidden the desire; he has uttered that word which is at once the glory and the sting of the human conscience, "Thou shalt not covet."

You deem yourself no murderer, because you have refrained from the act—because your hands have not been imbrued with the blood of your fellow-man. You consider yourself pure, because you have not attacked the life, nor the property, nor the honor of your brother; you think yourself exempt from God's judgment and the pangs of conscience, because you have not robbed your neighbor of his chief honor, his chief treasure—dear as life itself—the love, the fidelity of his wife. . . . If you have coveted the blood of your brother, if you have coveted his gold or his honor, if you have looked upon his wife to lust after her, you have committed murder, robbery, and adultery in the dark recesses of your conscience! "Thou shalt not covet." They are the words of Moses.

And he adds, Even though you should not have done this in the depths of your heart, even though you should have respected inward and outward righteousness, take heed! righteousness is a very narrow, and contracted, and impotent thing, when it comes short of *love!* "And now, O Israel, what doth the Lord thy God require of thee," exclaims the lawgiver, at the end of his commandments—"what doth the Lord thy God require of thee, but to love him with all thy heart and with all thy soul?"*

And Saint Paul, commenting upon Moses, has said in his turn: "He that loveth another" (for, as Saint John says, let no man think to love God whom he hath not seen, when he loveth not his neighbor whom he hath seen,†) "he that loveth another hath fulfilled the law. For when the law says, Thou shalt not kill; thou shalt not steal; thou shalt not bear false witness; thou shalt not commit adultery, it is briefly comprehended in this—Thou shalt love."‡ How can we commit murder, falsehood, adultery, when we love? Love, stronger than righteousness, restrains us in the

---

* Deuteronomy, x. 12.   † 1 John, iv. 20.   ‡ Romans. xiii. 8–10.

presence of all those boundary lines that passion would transgress. Saint Paul was right. "Love is the fulfilling of the law," even the law as Moses understood it. Saint Augustine is right when he concludes: "Love, only love, and thou shalt do what thou wilt." *Ama et fac quod vis.*

Love, then, is the last word of Deuteronomy, and it is the first word of the Gospel. Jesus Christ only called this commandment "new" because it was new to the Pharisees of his age, as it ever has been and must be for all Pharisees in every age; but he said: "It is the great commandment of the law: Thou shalt love the Lord thy God with all thy heart, and with all thy strength, and with all thy mind,"[*] also; for God must be loved with the mind as well as the heart. And the second commandment is like unto the first: Thou shalt love thy neighbor. The patriarchs and the prophets have summed up everything in these two commandments.

I conclude, Gentlemen, that our morality is the morality of the Jews, as their doctrine is our doctrine; and consequently, when I speak of the synagogue I speak of our own religion, our own Church. When I sit down with the patriarchs and the prophets, I sit with my masters, my teachers, my forerunners in Christ! "Search the Scriptures," said Jesus Christ, at a time when as yet there was no New Testament; "search Moses and the prophets; they are they which testify of me!"[†] I am right, then, in saying, with St. Augustine, that Christianity is Judaism completed, as Judaism was Christianity begun. "*Vetus testamentum est occultatio novi, et novum revelatio veteris.*"

2. *Worship, ceremonies, sacrifices, prayer.*—Worship

[*] Matthew, xxii. 28.   [†] John, v. 39.

is the living bond between morality and doctrine, the complete and supreme unfolding of the religious idea in the human soul and of the religious soul before God. And yet it is the most varying part of religion. We know what diversified forms it assumes and presents even in the Catholic Church itself. The primitive Church beheld the prevalence, at one and the same time, of the greatest unity of love and faith, and of the greatest freedom of usage and rite. Later, much later, a movement toward uniformity manifested itself, providentially designed, no doubt, by that Spirit that does not cease to govern the Church. But, even to-day, is not the Latin ritual, in certain Churches and religious bodies, diversified with authorized or rather consecrated differences? And is there not, alongside of the Latin rite, the Greek rite, or rather the Oriental rites?

It is understood, then, that the *ceremonies* of the Church of Moses have not all been transferred to the Christian Church. But a great number of them are perpetuated here, and the child of Israel, assuredly, would not feel himself altogether in a strange place were he to consent to sit down in our temples, and look around him. Astonished and delighted, he would see once more what he had believed to be buried and lost beneath the ruins of Zion; the golden candlesticks with their mystic lights, the ever-burning lamp attesting the presence of Jehovah; the smoking censers, the instruments of music, the songs, and the rhythmic march of our processions, recalling the sacred dances before the ark. He would find, along with the numberless choristers, the Levites, clad in robes of white linen, and the priests in their glittering vestments, standing around the altar like a grove of cedars of Lebanon.*

---

* Psalm xcii. 12, 13.

He would gaze upon the water flowing as in the ancient purifications, but with greater efficacy, and the shew-bread upon the altar, and those religious and fraternal feasts of the new Passover; and that Lamb, eaten without the breaking of a bone of it, Lamb ever immolated, and yet ever immortal! He would recognize his Passover festival in ours, his Sabbath in our Lord's day, and how many other features taken from his Church and preserved in ours! And are not our basilicas and our cathedrals the worthy inheritors of Solomon's temple, and the more glorious temple of Zerubbabel?

Some, it is true, of these ceremonies of the Hebrew ritual, so rich and so varied, have disappeared; the others have been preserved in the Catholic ritual: but still we can say of them all, that they have survived in this ritual, survived in newness of life, for they were all symbolical, all prefigurative of the future worship of Christian humanity.

But however great the *ceremonies* may be, they are only the outward vestment of the worship; the body is not there, still less the soul. The body of worship is the *sacrifice;* the soul is *prayer.* Here, then, the similarity, I go farther and say, the spiritual identity becomes more striking.

The sacrifices of the Jews! Be not alarmed, Gentlemen, lest I enter here into details; we will come back to them subsequently; for I shall not grow weary of the Church of the Jews any more than of the Church of the patriarchs, and I shall always revert to the sources of our Catholic Church, to reinvigorate myself and you with the spirit of our origin. For the present, I shall only ask myself, What is the origin of the Christian worship, from the sacrificial point of view? and I reply: It is the blood-offering of Judaism.

Oh! what an odor of blood in the temple at Jerusalem! It is worship—the expiation of sin by blood; it is the reconciliation of God and man by blood. Saint Paul, explaining Moses, says in his epistle to the Hebrews, "And by the law are almost all things purged with blood; and without shedding of blood is no remission."*

O ye plains of Bashan, ye broad pastures of Gilead, ye fertile hills of Judea, how many flocks ye were wont to feed! But your lambs, your many bulls, did not exist merely for the wealth of families; every year they were led by thousands to the temple at Jerusalem; they were brought lowing and bleating to the brazen altar, whose unquenchable thirst was always crying out for blood. The priests, exclusively engaged, so to speak, in this sacred immolation, raised the knife, thrust it in, and drew it reeking from the bowels of these victims. Blood flowed in torrents through the gutters around the altar. But never did the sacred stream spring up that could cleanse the world! The prophet—the priest of the spirit, elevated, according to the real institute of Moses, above these priests of matter—the prophet said to them in the name of the Lord: "Enough, I am full of your burnt-offerings. Will I eat the flesh of bulls, or drink the blood of goats? I am full."† "Cease, ye priests of matter, cease ye Pharisaic priests," exclaims Malachi, "or I will spread dung upon your faces, even the dung of your solemn feasts."‡ There was something more, then, than this blood; the prophet knew it, he told it in bold language, and the priests listened to him.

What shall wash away sin? Ah, in these times we have got beyond the feeling of sin, and the need of expiation. You remember, Gentlemen, the hero of Shak-

---

* Hebrews, ix. 22.   † Isaiah, l. 11; Psalm, l, 13.   ‡ Malachi, ii. 3.

speare's tragedy, who, alone, in the dead of night, looks at his hand, stained with innocent blood, and cries:

"What hands are here? Ha! they pluck out mine eyes!
Will all great Neptune's ocean wash this blood
Clean from my hand?"

Nothing but blood can cleanse blood; it is only the blood of a God that can wash away sin; the sweet savor of the blood of Christ alone that can remove all spots, ransom all crimes. The prophets knew this; they lifted up their hands to the future, they lifted up their eyes to the hills, and pointed to a cross!

Behold the true blood! Behold the sacred stream that has purified the soul! Behold the worship of the synagogue restored to its true idea. Jesus, by his blood, has taken away all our shame. Worship through blood, expiation by blood, is what makes the Christian. The man who should believe in the divinity of Jesus Christ, without believing in the efficacy of his blood—in the necessity of Calvary, in the only and sovereign expiation of the cross, that man would no longer be a Christian; he would no longer have the worship of the Catholic Church; he would no longer have the worship through blood, the atonement for sin and the reconciliation with God through blood. The Christian is the one who has the worship of the cross—the worship of Calvary; and, if he pursues to the end the needful understanding of this blood, this Christian is the Catholic who goes from Calvary to the altar, and says, with Saint Paul, the shedding of this blood is no longer needed for our ransom; "for by one offering he hath perfected forever them that are sanctified."* But this blood, that it

---

* Hebrews, x. 14.

may be applied to us, must flow over us individually, as it has flowed over the race of man universally. "This bread that we break," adds St. Paul, "is it not the communion of the body of Christ? The cup of blessing which we bless, is it not the communion of the blood of Christ?"* That is the worship of the Catholic Church —the worship of the blood on Calvary and the blood on the altar.

But, however high the sacrifice may be above the ceremonies, it has need of a soul, a voice that shall interpret it: this voice is the voice of *prayer*. Now the prayer of the Jewish Church is the *Psalms*.

Strange people! One day there arose among them a man who united in himself all their faults and all excellencies, a man more astonishing than the people itself—David! A nature essentially religious, like the Jewish nature, and, like it again, ardently, profoundly passionate; thrown upon life as upon a stage, amid the adventures of the warrior and the visions of the prophet, under the touches, so diversified and yet so harmonious, of human life on one side and supernatural revelation on the other, David resounded like a harp, and from his heart-strings, now wrung with anguish, now thrilled with joy and happiness—from his heart, open now toward earth, and anon toward heaven; from the breast of the adulterous and bloody lover of Bathsheba, the wife of Uriah; from the humiliated, repentant, and sanctified breast of the forefather of Jesus Christ, there came forth cries—O my friends, cries that have not their like in the records of the human soul, and yet to which everything in the human soul must tend.

Mankind has not heard their like before nor since, and thus it is that it never wearies of repeating them. . . .

* 1 Corinthians, x. 16.

Tears and sobs—tears of the heart and groanings of the soul! Nights spent upon that guilty couch, wet with his tears, clutched in his arms, gnashed upon by his teeth, upon which he tosses in the thorns of remorse or the thorns of temptation! Nights spent in prayer upon that guilty and solitary couch, on that penitent couch from which he now rises, in the sweet and happy calm of pardon won, with quivering lips, with trembling bones: "All my bones shall say, Lord, who is like unto thee!"*—to thee who leadest me down to the pit, who leadest me back from death unto life, from hell unto heaven!

Behold the prayer of the Jew who thought but of himself, his adulteries, his murders, his son dead at eight days old, to whose icy feet his lips were pressed, of his throne contested by an enemy, of the grand hopes of his future, that "of the fruit of his loins should be raised up Christ to sit upon the throne."† And while thus pouring out his soul, while making the confession of his life, this man becomes, as he has so well been named, "the prince of prayer!"

Yes; the prince of individual, the prince of universal prayer. Gaze toward the setting of the sun, listen toward the rising thereof, wherever the Catholic Church is to be found—what do I say?—wherever the synagogue, wherever the place of Christian worship is to be found, whether in the fold of the schismatic but Christian East, or in the fold of Protestantism—everywhere I hear lifted up the grand prayer of the Psalms of David! All mankind is praying with his words, weeping with his tears, hoping with his hopes. David had said, "My praise shall be of thee, in the great congregation."‡ And at the same time, outside of the temples, in the

---

* Psalm xxxv. 10.   † Acts, ii. 30.   ‡ Psalm xxii. 25.

sanctuary of each household, behold that young man struggling against his youthful passions, that old man shuddering before the open grave, that wife, that mother, that poor weeping woman, whose tears have been her meat in the night-season—what do their lips murmur? *Miserere mei, Deus!* "Have mercy upon me, O God, according to thy loving kindness." "Out of the depths have I called unto thee, O Lord! Lord, hear my voice! If thou, Lord, shouldst mark iniquities, O Lord, who shall stand? But thou art good; more than in any human heart, with thee there is mercy, and with thee is plenteous redemption."*

Let us, then, my friends, remember Israel and Zion, and, summing up Israel and Zion in one great and eminently practical fact, let us remember the *Bible*. Israel is not the tents of Shem, not the tabernacles of the desert, not the temples of Solomon and Zerubbabel. All these have vanished away. What gives Israel its unfailing life is its God and its Bible. Israel has embodied itself in its Bible; the whole of it is the work of Israel; and that, says Saint Paul, is its crowning glory.†

The Church of Jesus Christ, the Catholic Church, has not the gift of *inspiration*. We have not among us a single sage, a single inspired pontiff that has the power, even had he the wish, to write a line that should be the word of God. We have pontiffs, doctors, councils *assisted* by God, but not *inspired* by him; assisted to study, to understand, to explain the inspired word of the Church of the Jews, the word written, from the first book of Genesis to the last word of the New Testament, by a Jewish pen! The Jewish Church, from the prophets to the apostles, has been the only mouth

* Psalms, ll. 1; cxxx. 1, 2, 3, 7.   † Romans, iii. 2.

inspired of God, of whose utterances it could be said, "The mouth of the Lord hath spoken them."*

And yet what do we do with the Bible? Is this book the object of our study, our preaching, our teaching? Is it the light that shines upon the family, the State, the soul? Let it not be said to me: The Church prohibits the reading of the Bible. That is a terrible calumny! The early Christians read the Bible and meditated upon it day and night, and the more zealous ones learnt it from beginning to end by heart. The early Christian priests had two equally sacred compartments in their tabernacle, the one for the eucharist, the food of the heart, the other for the Bible, the food of the mind. Since when has the Church changed? Since when has the spirit of the Church been divided against the spirit of the Church? It is a terrible calumny, I repeat. What the Church does forbid, is reading it without legitimate precautions, reading it without the spirit of docility, in a spirit of rebellion, heresy, and schism. But reading, meditating upon the Scriptures, is evermore the true spirit of the Church of Jesus Christ!

What then? Do we read the Bible? Do we not too often seek our knowledge in merely profane authors, in the discoveries of man? And when we refer to the traditions of the Church, do we not practically give the first place to mere church-doctors! No one venerates more than I do the Fathers of the Church—Athanasius, Basil, Augustine; the great school-men of the middle ages—Thomas Aquinas, Bonaventura, Scotus; the great modern theologians—I need name only the king of them all, Bossuet! Yes. But Bossuet, Scotus, Bonaventura, Thomas Aquinas, Basil, Athanasius, and all the rest, are not *the book*. Give me *the book*, the in-

---

* Isaiah, xl. 5.

spired word! Let me rest upon the foundation of the apostles and the prophets; let my thirsty roots penetrate even to the fatness of the fruitful olive-tree. The Bible, the Holy Scriptures, the light of the family, of the nation, of the soul, this is the book of the Church! And our branches will be thin, and our foliage withered, and our blossoms will fall before they can bear fruit, as long as we do not steep them afresh in the knowledge, in the light, in the practice of this divine book!

While rationalism, this modern force from the cloisters of German universities, is trying to find its way into the book independently of the Church and of the Spirit that inspired it, thereby transforming it into one of the most active and formidable poisons, *corruptio optimi pessima;* while rationalism is doing this scholar-like but mischievous work, we shut the book, or rather we do not open it, nor seek in it for a remedy.

"I looked," said Ezekiel, "and behold a hand was stretched out to me from heaven; and lo! a mysterious book. It was written within and without—without, in an earthly language, and in human characters; and within, in the language of heaven, and in letters from the hand of God. It was a closed book, and the hand reached it forth to me; and a voice said: Eat this book!" Woe to him who, able to read it, reads it not! But woe also to him who reads it only with the eye of a haughty intellect! It must be eaten with the heart. "O son of man, rise and eat this book! And I took the book, and it was in my mouth as honey for sweetness; and I was filled with its substance; and the voice said to me, again, Son of man, go, get thee to the house of Israel, and speak with my words unto them."†

* Ezekiel, ii. 8.

Rise, then, O Church of Christ! Rise as one man! Take the book from the divine hand that offers it, meditate upon it with your understanding, devour it with your love and your heart, and then shall you be the masters of the world; you shall speak to the children of idolatry; the world shall hear you, for your lips shall be no longer your own, but God's! The lips of the Christian soul are for the word of the Lord, and it is that word which they never cease to declare!

LECTURE SIXTH.

January 3, 1869.

CONFLICT BETWEEN THE LETTER AND THE SPIRIT, IN THE JEWISH CHURCH.

The Letter killeth, but the Spirit giveth life.* I take this text of Saint Paul as the starting-point and summary of this whole discourse. I have already remarked in the Jewish Church two elements mutually opposed, but alike necessary to the object of this Church: an element of *separation,* in order to the conservation of the sacred deposit of revelation, and an element of *universality,* in order to the diffusion of this revelation among all mankind. These two elements I call, in the words of the apostle, the *letter* and the *spirit*. By the letter, the Bible, that is, the Old Testament, tends to separation; by the spirit, it tends to universality. The intestine struggle between these two elements makes up the whole interior history of Judaism; and the open rupture between them, in the time of Christ, is the commencement of the Christian era, and the inauguration of the Catholic Church. As sons of this holy and infallible Church, we no longer need to fear the triumph of the letter; but as members of a Church composed and governed, after all, by fallible and sinful men, we ought not to pass over its internal conflicts. Let us,

* 2 Corinthians, iii. 6.

then, observe the instructive spectacle of the combats between the letter and the spirit within the pale of Judaism, considering in order, in the Jewish Church, the representatives of the letter and the representatives of the spirit.

I. *The representatives of the letter.*—These were the *kings* and the *priests.* The kings represented it in politics—the priests, in religion.

1. David exclaimed, "He shall have dominion also from sea to sea, and from the river unto the ends of the earth. .... Yea, all kings shall fall down before him, all nations shall serve him."* And beholding, in this radiant future, that one of his descendants, whom he called the Anointed, *the* Christ, as above all others, he said, or rather God said through him, "Sit thou at my right hand until I make thine enemies thy footstool. Rule thou, and thy people shall be willing in the day of thy power, in the beauties of holiness from the womb of the morning: thou hast the dew of thy youth."†

In this throne of the son of David and of the Son of God, there were, then, two royalties united: the temporal kingdom, that should reign over the house of Jacob, restricted to the narrow limits of its own blood, —" He shall reign over the house of Jacob,"—and the kingdom that should extend over all mankind within the broad bounds of the faith of Abraham—" Of his kingdom there shall be no end."‡

The danger was of confounding these two kingdoms, and, as always happens in such cases, of absorbing the heavenly kingdom in the earthly. It was to this danger that the synagogue succumbed.

In a national Church, or in a religious nation, nothing is easier, nothing more fatal, than this confusion be-

* Psalm lxxii. 8, 11.   † Psalm cx. 1-3.   ‡ Luke, i. 33.

tween religious forms and political forms. Great even in its merely human character—for it is human both in its function and in its origin—the business of government becomes greater yet when it gravitates toward the heavenly spheres of morality and religion; but religion belittles itself, abdicates its own dignity, shocks all the instincts of human nature, and at the same time wounds all the attributes of divine majesty, when it puts on the forms of politics, catches up its ideas and characteristics, and pursues its paltry interests.

Yet such was the kingdom that the kings and their followers perpetually dreamed of bestowing upon humanity. For a single moment, under David, the prophetic ideal briefly seen and described by this prophet-king, shines with a pure lustre. But it soon veils itself behind the worldly, let us say the heathen, ideal of Solomon.

Solomon was a great king, especially at the outset; he was always great, even in his errors and his crimes. But, intoxicated with the knowledge of nature that he possessed, according to the inspired word, "from the cedar of Lebanon to the hyssop that groweth on the wall," Solomon, not content with the knowledge that lifteth up to God, wished also to possess all the riches and all the amorous delights of earth; he built palaces little like the palm-tree beneath which Deborah judged Israel, or the tents under which David and his soldiers camped; palaces so sumptuous that the queen of Sheba came from far Arabia to admire them. He had harems filled with women, mostly strangers and idolaters: seven hundred sultanas and three hundred concubines! And then, this intoxication, rising—I will not say from his heart, but from his senses, to his reason—he fell down with his wives at the feet of all their idols, venerating, under these poetical symbols, that great nature which is the handiwork of God, yet which so easily usurps the place of its Creator!

Such was the spectacle presented by Jerusalem under David's successor. A revolting spectacle, but extenuated, at least during the reign of Solomon himself, by a glory which he was not mighty enough to bequeath to his heirs in Judah, and his rivals in Israel. He bequeathed to them only his pride, his sensuality, and his idolatries, and when the two hostile but kindred monarchies finally succumbed beneath the blows of those powerful neighbors, those northern conquerors, whose favors they had so often courted, whose arms they had so often defied, they left behind them, in the history of the holy people, only a long trail of blood and filth.

That is the kingdom of Judah, the kingdom of Israel; that is what was proposed to the world under the name of the kingdom of God!

The Jews had been so perverted by their kings, or rather—let us not be unjust to the kings—the Jews had been so perverted by their national pride, that they could not rid themselves of this gross ideal, and they forever dreamed of ruling over the nations, under the desecrated name of the kingdom of God, with the sword and the rod of iron. When Jesus, their true Messiah, came to them, they knew him not; and this was, in a great measure, because he had rejected this kingdom, too narrow and too low for him, and because he had proclaimed the true principle of the kingdom of God, the spiritual kingdom which is in the world, but "not of the world," a spiritual kingdom that "comes to bear witness to the truth."* They preferred the seditious

* John, xviii. 36, 37.

Barabbas, who had fought and shed blood in the streets of Jerusalem to deliver them from the Romans; they preferred all the false messiahs, all the lying, impotent christs, who ended their senseless intrigues by bringing on the ruin of the nation, the city, and the temple that they pretended to save.

Break, then, thou vase of national Judaism, that God, by the hand of Moses, had fashioned with such loving care ;* royal, priestly vase, be broken, since thou wouldst have it so! Thou shouldst have preserved for all men the treasures of religious life; thou hast chosen rather to shut thyself up in jealous selfishness; be broken, and from thy scattered fragments let that fragrant balm go forth, which is for the healing of the nations!

"The vase was broken," says the Gospel, "and the house was filled with the odor of the ointment."*

2. What the kings did in politics the priests did in religion. In truth, if it is a fatal error to confound religious and political forms, it is a still more terrible blunder to confound, in religion itself, the accidental, accessory forms with the essential ones. Every religion, especially the true, the Christian religion, which extends back to Moses, Abraham, Adam, is not merely a religious idea, a religious sentiment, as contemporary rationalism is pleased to say. It is a fact, and therefore it has positive forms; it is a living fact, and therefore it has a settled organization. But the religious fact, existing in time and space, should take into account the conditions of space, so diversified, and the conditions of time, so changeful. Its organization is to exercise its functions amid the most dissimilar, even the most contradictory surroundings. Hence, besides the substantial

* John, xii. 3.

and permanent forms, the accessory and shifting forms, with which the former are, so to speak, invested, according to the exigencies of race or epoch. By endeavoring to confound religion with its accessory forms, peculiar to such and such a country and race, we should cut it off from the great current of humanity in the present. By endeavoring to bind it down to worn-out forms, we should cut it off from the great current of humanity in the future. We should be forgetting what Saint Paul said to the old synagogue: "That which waxeth old is ready to vanish away."* We could not render religious unity a worse service. Now, it was on this very rock that the Jewish priesthood made shipwreck.

I would not speak of this priesthood otherwise than with great respect. Last Sunday we breathed the perfume of its censers, and listened to the harmony of its chants. The rod of Aaron had not budded for nothing in its hands, and in its tabernacle we have almost adored the body of Jesus Christ prefigured in its manna, the word of Jesus Christ anticipated in its Decalogue. But, after all, however respectable the Levitical priesthood might have been in its origin and in its essence, it no longer deserves our respect in the corruption that came over it toward the end—at least over the greater part of its members. This corruption has retained its special name, *Pharisaism*.

Is Pharisaism hypocrisy? No; whatever our dictionary may say, Pharisaism is not, in the biblical sense, hypocrisy, unless we mean that most subtle form of hypocrisy, the most innocent and at the same time the most fatal—the hypocrisy that knows not itself, and considers itself sincerity. Jesus often said, "Pharisees, hypocrites!" but he explained this word by another—

* Hebrews, viii. 13.

"thou blind Pharisee!" And the great Apostle Paul, himself a Pharisee, brought up, as he says, at the feet of the Pharisee Gamaliel, pays them this remarkable tribute, that they really had "a zeal for God, but not according to knowledge."*

Pharisaism, then, in its deepest aspect, is religious blindness—the blindness of priests who are put in trust with the letter, who think that the less they explain it, the safer they keep it; a blindness that extends to every point of the sacred deposit; blindness in doctrine —the predominance of formula over truth; blindness in morals—the predominance of outward works over inward righteousness; blindness in worship—the predominance of outward rites over religious feeling.

Blindness in *doctrine*.—The Pharisees taught the truth. "The Scribes and Pharisees sit in Moses' seat," said Jesus Christ; "believe what they say, but do not what they do."† There is no revealed idea, enlightening and quickening the world, without a word to contain it—*lucerna verbum tuum, Domine.*‡ The Lord's light is in a lamp. But if the word closes itself together, and shuts up the idea as in a narrow and jealous prison—if it darkens it, stifles it—that is Pharisaism. This is what the Apostle Paul called keeping the truth, but keeping it captive in unrighteousness.§ This is the thing which extorted from the mild lips of the Saviour Jesus that terrible anathema, "Woe unto you! Ye have taken away the key of knowledge; for ye enter not in yourselves, and them that are entering in ye hinder.‖ Woe unto you!"

In *morals*, it is outward works, the multiplicity of human observances, piled up—a miserable and tyranni-

---

* Romans, x. 2. † Matthew, xxiii. 2. ‡ Psalm cxix. 105.
§ Romans, i. 18. ‖ Luke, xi. 52.

cal burden upon the conscience, making it forget, in unwholesome dreams, that it is an honest man's, a Christian's conscience. The Pharisees said to Jesus Christ, " Why do not thy disciples wash their hands before eating, according to the tradition of the elders?" And the Saviour answered them, "Why do ye trample under foot the commandments of God to keep the commandments of man?"*

As to the *rites*, they are necessary in worship, as formulas are necessary in doctrine—woe to him who rends asunder the formulas of biblical revelation or the formulas of the Church's definition!—as works are necessary to morality—woe to him who slumbers in a barren, dead faith, without works!

Worship! why, it is the very blossoming of the religious soul; the emotion of the heart ascending fragrant and harmonious into the presence of God. It is the action from within outward; it is also the reaction, no less legitimate, no less salutary, from without inward. The ritual arouses religious sentiment, gives birth to inspiration in the conscience and the heart.

But when there is no longer any religious feeling, when the heart and the conscience are bending under the burden of outward observances, "Full well," says Christ, again—for the Gospel is full of these things, the Gospel is the perpetual condemnation of Pharisaism— "full well did Isaiah prophesy of you, This people honoreth me with lips and hands, but their heart is far from me."†

This is the yoke of which Saint Peter spoke—" a yoke put upon the neck of the disciples which neither our fathers nor we were able to bear."‡ This is the smothered and oppressed inspiration that they thought to send

* Matthew, xv. 1-6.   † Ibid., xv. 7.   ‡ Acts, xv. 10.

forth over the face of the earth to renew it. This is Judaism—not the Judaism of Moses, but the worn-out Judaism of the Scribes and Pharisees! When the whole world, by the eloquent voices of Greece and Rome, was calling on the East for deliverers; when by the agitation of barbarian tribes, moving, all at once, in the depths of Germany and Scythia, the world was craving light and civilization—that is what they offered it! Judaism made itself more and more of an impossibility the more the world had need of it; blind and fanatical Pharisaism threw itself across the threshold of the kingdom of heaven, to prevent the generations of man from entering!

Get ye behind me, ye men of the letter! get ye behind me, ye foes of the human race! "They are contrary to all men," as Saint Paul has said. And thou, Lord Jesus, arise, my Saviour and my Lord—thou who in all thy gentle life wast but twice in anger! . . . Jesus had no wrath against poor sinners; he sat at their table, and when the adulterous woman fell at his feet, blushing with shame and weeping with remorse, he lifted her up, only to absolve her: Go in peace and sin no more! He had no anger against heretics and schismatics; he sat upon Jacob's well beside the Samaritan woman, and announced to her, with the salvation which is of the Jews, the worship which is in spirit and in truth. But twice was Jesus angry: once, scourge in hand, against those who sold the things of God in the temple; once, anathema in mouth, against those who perverted the things of God in the law.

Rise then, meek Lamb, in thy pacific wrath against the enemies of all men and against the real enemies of the kingdom of God; rise, and drive them from the temple!

Thus it was that the synagogue perished, and the Christian Church arose.

II. *The representatives of the spirit.*—I have told you, and you know already, that we have nothing to fear from the triumphs of the *letter*. Still, we cannot ignore the combats, the temptations, not merely of every priest, but of all piety; the temptation of believers as well as priests is to the predominance of the letter over the *spirit*. Let us glorify God for having suffered us to be born in an infallible and holy Church, which Jesus Christ protects and shall protect until the final accomplishment of his work, through succeeding ages, against all the errors of our mind and all the weaknesses of our will!

But what voice is this that strikes upon my ear? It is no longer the harsh voice of earthly dominion or carnal legislation; still, it is not a Christian voice, not the voice of Jesus Christ that I was repeating just now; and yet, although long before Jesus Christ, how it resembles him!

"Hear," says the voice, "hear the word of the Lord, ye rulers of Sodom; give ear unto the law of our God, ye people of Gomorrah," and yet it is speaking of the Church of Sion! "To what purpose is the multitude of your sacrifices unto me? I am full of the burnt-offerings of rams, and the fat of fed beasts; and I delight not in the blood of bullocks, or of rams, or of he-goats; your new moons and your appointed feasts my soul hateth; they are a trouble unto me; I am weary to bear them; your incense is an abomination unto me. When ye spread forth your hands, I will hide my eyes from you; yea, when ye make many prayers, I will not hear! Wash you; make you clean; put away the evil of your doings; cease to do evil; learn to do well; seek judgment, relieve the oppressed; judge the fatherless, plead for the widow. Come now, and let us reason together, saith the Lord. Though your sins be as scarlet, they shall be white as snow!"*

This is the voice of the religion of Moses, in all its energy and all its clearness. What a difference between it and Pharisaism, of which I have just spoken, that letter which stifled, with its fatal constrictions, the reason, the conscience, and the heart! And how like the Gospel, that law of Jesus Christ which has but two commandments; an insatiable hunger, an unquenchable thirst after righteousness, and a heart ever open in compassion! Ah! I feel that we have here no longer a local law, a national organization, a restricted and temporary code, we have the law of all nations and all ages, and it needs but the breath of Saint Paul to waft it from one end of the world to the other.

But the voice of the spirit continues, and this time it no longer speaks of the *carnal law,* but of the *earthly kingdom:* " And it shall come to pass in the last days, that the mountain of the Lord's house shall be established in the top of the mountains, and shall be exalted above the hills, and all nations shall flow unto it. And many nations shall go and say: Come ye, and let us go up unto the mountain of the Lord, to the house of the God of Jacob; and he shall teach us of his ways, and we will walk in his paths; for out of Zion shall go forth the law, and the word of the Lord from Jerusalem. Come, let us beat our swords into ploughshares, and our spears into pruning-hooks, for the Anointed of the Lord shall reign in justice and peace, all the idols shall be utterly abolished, and the Lord alone shall be exalted in that day!"†

That is the future which the kings and their succes-

---

* Isaiah, 1. 10-18.   * Ibid., 11.

sors had marred. Mark it well, it is not oppression, it is deliverance! It is the property of the letter to prevail by force, that is its necessity. It has no other way, if that is indeed a way. It is the property of the spirit to appeal therefrom to the liberty of man, to the liberty of God. "Where the spirit of the Lord is, there is liberty." That is why I do not behold in the hands of the Messiah a blood-stained sword; but I see the nations rising spontaneously like the sea murmuring in its depths; all nations shall flow unto him; they arise, they ascend toward the God of Jacob; no subjugation, but emancipation; the reign, not of Messiah the conqueror, but of Messiah the deliverer.

But, you will ask me, what is this voice that preaches to priests the spiritual kingdom, and to kings and nations the divine royalty? The voice shall tell its own story; it shall give its origin and mission.

It was "in the year that king Uzziah died," that Isaiah beheld in the temple the vision of Jehovah, high and lifted up, and heard the continual cry of the seraphim, Holy, holy, holy! And at the voice the settled columns of the temple heaved and rocked, and the house was filled with smoke. Then said Isaiah, "Woe is me! for I am a man of unclean lips, and I dwell in the midst of a people of unclean lips; for mine eyes have seen the King the Lord of hosts." Then flew one of the seraphim unto me, having a live coal in his hand, which he had taken with the tongs from off the altar; and he laid it on my mouth, and said, "Lo, this hath touched thy lips; and thine iniquity is taken away, thy sin is purged." And I heard *the voice of the Lord*, saying, "Whom shall I send, and who will go for us?" Then said I, "Here am I; send me." And he said, "Go, speak to the people."* Such is the commission of the prophet.

And why should there not have been need of prophets and saints in the Jewish Church, seeing there is need of them in the Catholic Church? Those two mendicants who, in the dream of Pope Innocent III., support the crumbling basilica of the Lateran, that seems to symbolize the decline of the hierarchical Church of the Middle Ages—those two mendicants, Dominic de Guzman and Francis of Assisi, what are they, then, but prophets of the New Testament, sprung, not from the hereditary succession and tradition of the centuries, but from the burning kiss of the Lord's altar-coal? Yes, there is need of saints, of prophets, that is, men of love, of martyrdom; men of vision, who read not only by the letter but by the spirit, "whose eyes have seen the Lord of hosts" in the vision of their reason enlightened by faith, in the ecstasy of their conscience quickened by grace. There is need of men who speak with God face to face, like Moses; and above all—above all, Gentlemen, there is need of men who love God heart to heart, and who march on amid the strifes of days and centuries—strifes whose full meaning can be apprehended only by such as "see afar off the things that shall come to pass at the last, and comfort them that mourn in Zion."† Such were the prophets.

1. They were *seers*. They beheld the future. They did not look merely at the present—this present that so satisfies the capacity of narrow minds and hearts. They did not even turn back, with craven tears, to the irrecoverable past. It was the part of the Gentiles, of all heathen antiquity, to dream of a golden age forever lost. The prophets looked forward, and they saw this

---

* Isaiah, vi. 1-9. † Ecclesiasticus, xlviii. 24.

lost golden age of Eden appearing in a more complete, more lasting form, at the vestibule of heaven, but yet upon the earth.

The prophets believed in the future because they believed in God. They believed in progress; they were, in all antiquity, the only men of progress. Antiquity had no faith in progress—did not even know it by name. The prophets believed in the most incredible and most essential of all progress—progress in morals and religion. They believed in it despite the fall, or rather because of the fall and the redemption. To them evil did not lie in the essential corruption of our nature, nor in the inflexible decree of fate; it lay in man's freedom, and the remedy was found in God's freedom. If God had suffered that by reason of sin the starting-point of human nature should be set back to hell, it was that the goal of humanity should be carried forward and upward to heaven. From these heights to which their faith had soared, they looked down and beheld salvation spreading from the individual to the nation, from the nation to the human race, from the human race over all nature.

Such was progress to the mind of the prophets. Such was the universal Zion which they hailed in the future. Isaiah prophesied it during the existence and comparative prosperity of Jerusalem. Jeremiah mingled it with his tears over the smouldering ruins of his beloved city. Ezekiel, in captivity, described Zion, not now the city of the Jews, but the metropolis of humanity, a city in which every nation should find a home; and he inscribed over its portals these immortal words: "The name of the city shall be, THE LORD IS THERE."* *Jehovah-shammah.*

---

* Ezekiel, xlviii. 35.

2. This is what the prophets, believing seers and seeing believers, believed and looked for. This, also, is what they loved, for they were not merely men of intellect, but men of *heart*.

I have no love for Utopians; I do not admire the mind that dwells exclusively in the future, that lives upon barren and chimerical dreams; I love the men of the future who are men of the present, who meditate, but also work. The prophets were workers; they did not love the future in the future, but in the present, which contains it in the germ; they did not love mankind in mankind—too abstract, as a mere conception, too vast, as an aggregate of individuals. They loved humanity in their nation; they loved the typical Jerusalem of their visions in the earthly Jerusalem of their daily lives.

O how I love to see them, as I read their pages, standing up to confront every national, every religious act of that grovelling people! confronting every evil act to denounce it, every act of duty and religion, of beneficence and progress, to bless it in the name of the Lord! How I love to see them as they wend their way down the dark valley to the brink of that brook Kedron—that "brook in the way" of which Messiah was to drink ere he should "lift up his head,"* and then climbing again the steep path that led to the citadel and the temple where Jesus was to teach, frequenting the public places where at times the desert wind, as if in mockery of their hopes, would stir the hot and parched dust, and fling it in their faces! But then, in the dark valley of Kedron, in the citadel and temple of Zion; in the streets swept by the whirlwind—everywhere, throughout the city which they cherished with their affectionate devotion,

---

* Psalm cv. 7.

they beheld that Zion which was to grow and expand from within until it should embrace the whole world. Thus loving the house of Abraham and the Church of Jesus Christ, they loved the future and humanity in God.

In the presence of these great examples, suffer me to say to you about love of country what I said to you about love of family; we have forgotten, or at least we do not sufficiently remember, what it is to love a country, a people, a city, in God and in man—to see and love therein the commonwealth of man and of Jesus Christ, the commonwealth of time and of eternity.

3. The prophets were men of vision, men of love: they were also men of *war;* and, when necessary, men of *martyrdom*—soldiers and victims. Not without a struggle, in truth, do we cross that Red Sea that separates the present from the future. We stand upon its brink, pent in between the inquietudes of the past and the forebodings of the future. The prophets have crossed it, bearing on their stalwart shoulders the ark of God and the ark of the human race. But what fightings! what struggles!—struggles magnificent as their visions, as their love! They shrank—in the weakness of their human nature, they shrank from these struggles. They knew that the word of God is, sooner or later, the death of them that bear it. "I have slain them," saith the Lord, "by the words of my mouth."* "Ah! Lord God," exclaimed Jeremiah, "why dost thou call me? Behold, I cannot speak, for I am a child." And the Lord said unto him: "Say not I am a child; for I shall put my word in thy mouth, and thou shalt confound all my enemies; I shall set thee to root out and to plant, and to pull down and to build up. I shall

---

* Hosea, vi. 5.

set thee over the kings and priests of Judah, over all the nations of the earth: they shall fight against thee, but they shall not prevail, for I am with thee."*

And to Ezekiel, the colleague and successor of Jeremiah, God always spoke this language of battle: "Fear not. I send thee to a rebellious nation, but I shall make thy face strong against their faces, and thy forehead strong against their foreheads. As an adamant, harder than flint shall I make thy forehead: I shall set thee as a wall of iron and as a city of brass, for I shall be with thee."†

After this fashion did the prophets struggle for Zion, that resisted, that rejected them. Never did they abandon her; they ever loved and served her.

We are about to separate, Gentlemen, for one more year. Suffer me, at this moment, to entreat you to unite with me in an act of self-consecration to this kingdom of God, this Church whose outer courts we have been treading together. Christianity is not a thing of to-day, nor of yesterday: it is not only of the historic epoch of Jesus Christ and the apostles; it is of David, of Moses, of Abraham—it is of Adam, the father, king, pontiff of us all. In this one religion, then—in this Church whose form may change, but whose substance abideth unchangeable, ah! Gentlemen, and—suffer me this word, for it is in my heart—friends, brothers, let us consecrate ourselves, as did the prophets, to the love and service of the kingdom of God! The kingdom of God is formally constituted in Christianity, in the Church, catholic, apostolic, and Roman; but this Church, as I have but just now been saying, must ever go on changing from form to form, "from glory to glory," until it shall have spread its mild

---

* Jeremiah, 1. † Ezekiel, ii., iii., iv.

dominion over the whole world, until it shall have reached, with all the human race, "the stature of the perfect man in Christ Jesus."

Do we not wish to labor for this reign? And what do we, if we do not this? What are the works of our private and our public life, if these works do not bear ultimately upon the kingdom of truth, justice, charity, all that is included in Christianity—all that makes up the Church, catholic, apostolic, and Roman. I do not ask you to love this Church as it does not wish to be loved—to love it as one loves a sect—as the grovelling Jews loved the synagogue, with a mind and a heart shrunken up within the letter; I do not ask you to love our great Catholic Church by glorifying the infirmities of its life (which are your infirmities and mine), and condemning all the truths professed and all the virtues practised outside of it by men who are often unwittingly its sons. No; away with all sectarian love! I ask you to love the Church with the heart of the Church itself, with a heart that measures itself only by the heart of Christ. "Be ye also enlarged!" I say to you as Saint Paul said to the Corinthians—"*Our* heart is enlarged. Be not straitened in your own bosoms. Be ye also enlarged."*

Suffer me, Gentlemen, before we part, to tell you the secret of my soul, the secret of my youth; how, on the day of my ordination to the priesthood, here in the nave of this cathedral, not thronged as it is to-day, as I lay prostrate on its cold pavement, with burning, throbbing heart, the thought that sustained, that entranced me, was the thought that I should have henceforth but one love, one service—the kingdom of God in man.

Yes, Gentlemen, let us love the Church in every man,

* 2 Corinthians, vi. 11—13.

and every man in the Church! What matters his condition? Rich or poor, ignorant or learned, *omnibus debitor sum*, "I am debtor to every man," says Saint Paul. What matters his nationality? Frenchman or foreigner, Greek or Barbarian, *omnibus debitor sum*, I answer with Saint Paul: I am debtor alike to barbarism and to civilization. So far as concerns our loving the man, what matter is it, even, in one sense, what is his religion?

If he be not a son of the Catholic Church according to the body, the outward unity, he is, perhaps, he is, I hope, according to the soul, the invisible unity. If he be not a son of the Catholic Church according to the soul or according to the body—either according to the spirit or according to the letter—at least he is such in the preparation of God's counsels. If he have not the baptismal water on his brow, I am grieved, but nevertheless I behold there the blood of Jesus Christ; for Christ has died for every man, opening to the whole world his great arms upon the cross! The world belongs to Jesus Christ, and therefore the world belongs to the Church, if not actually, at least potentially. Let me, then, love every man; and you also, with me, love every man, not only in himself, not only in his narrow and earthly individuality, but in the great Christian fellowship, the great divine fellowship which invites us all.

THE EDUCATION OF THE WORKING-CLASSES.

SPEECH BEFORE THE CHURCH CONGRESS AT MALINES, BELGIUM.

SEPTEMBER 6, 1867.

YOUR HIGHNESS, MY LORDS, AND GENTLEMEN:— I will not attempt to hide the deep emotion which I feel. I look about me and am abashed—abashed by this very assembly from which I am to gather inspiration for the words that I shall speak. I see before me one of the princes of the Church—a prince indeed, by wisdom and virtue. I see this illustrious group of bishops, my fathers in the faith. I see eminent statesmen, masters of learning and eloquence, and I find this desk still warm and throbbing with the hands that have pressed it, and the tones that have thrilled it. I see this great assembly, gathered from the four winds of heaven to discuss, here in this free corner of the earth, called Belgium, the religious interests of the Catholics of the two worlds. Gentlemen, I was abashed, but I am so no longer. I feel that I am not here as a stranger. I am among my brethren; and these cheers with which you greet me I accept, because they are not meant for the individual, which is nothing, but for the cause, which is much—I had almost said, which is everything. This cause I define in two words—the Catholic Church; and the Catholic Church in the nineteenth century.

On that day which no priest ever forgets—the day when, prostrate on the pavement of the church, I took for my chaste and only spouse the holy Church of Jesus Christ, with lips in the dust, eyes in tears, bosom rapt in ecstasy and heaved with sobs—I vowed in silence to love her well, and, so far as in me lay, to serve her well, not only in her great past, which never can return, in her great future, which is yet to come, but in her present, at once so grievous and so grand—her present, such as History, and therefore God, has made it.

Now, in this service of the Church of the nineteenth century there arises a question which, of all questions, is the most perplexing and threatening—the Working-Class question.

It is an immense question, but I shall confine myself to a single aspect of it, *the Education of the Working-Classes*. The hope of the harvest is in the seed, and Leibnitz might well say, "Give me the instruction of the youth for a century, and I will change the face of the earth." But this transformation can be accomplished only in so far as the education of the working-man is effected under the conditions prescribed by the nature of man, and the general harmony of the divine plan.

There are three grades in this education—primary education in the family, business education in the shop, religious education on the Lord's-day.

I. *Family Education.*—I put the family in the front rank. It holds this rank in the order of time; it should hold it in the order of influence.

Among the multitude of superior minds that concern themselves about the condition of the working-classes,

I am amazed that there should be so few to comprehend their real wants. For the cure of their ills, the means of their advancement, men go on a vain quest among new inventions and combinations, specious theories, and even special and accidental institutions. They are to be sought rather in the family—that institution, as old and as universal as mankind, which is rooted in the tenderest, strongest, inmost recesses of human nature;—that institution coming from the hands of God himself, rescued from the wreck of Eden, washed by Jesus Christ in his own blood, and raised by him to the dignity of a sacrament, that he might make of it one of the seven columns which are to bear up, to the world's end, the edifice of regenerate humanity. [*Applause.*]

It is the family, then, which must be sustained or restored in all classes of society, but especially in the working-class of our cities. It is to the family, more than to any other agency, that the primary education of the child must be remitted.

In primary education, there are two things that demand special consideration—the place, and the agent. The place is home; the agent is the mother.

Home! There the cradle is to rest; there the first years of childhood to be passed. Has not Providence implanted this instinct in the hearts of all his creatures, even of the inferior orders? Does not the bird build its nest in the fragrant moss, under the shelter of the hedge, or amid the branches of the tree? In every rank of nature is there not some special, some sacred place, where the earliest hopes, joys, sorrows of life are to be harbored? Surely, then, the human race is entitled to a spot where it may lay its young, more sacred than these cradles of the lower races; it is entitled to a home neither mean nor murderous—fatal neither to the body nor to the soul of the little child. This home is to be of itself the primary education of the young soul, the nascent imagination and feelings. These walls are more than walls; this roof is no mere putting together of timbers and tiles; these bits of furniture are no vulgar objects. All these things speak a deep language, and exercise a mighty moral action. We Catholics, have we not, in our divine religion, sensible signs called sacraments—water, wine, bread, oil; material things, in short, but material things which reveal, and, in different degrees, communicate, things invisible? So, in the plane of nature, in what I would call household religion, there is also a mysterious influence of places and things—a secret communication of family habits, family virtues, family feeling, by material objects themselves. The little child sees what his fathers saw, mingles his life with objects full of their memories, and, as one might say, impregnated with their spirit. He receives therefrom some indefinable impressions, some indelible marks which he will carry with him through all the wanderings of youth, down to the gray hairs of old age.

If this is poetry, Gentlemen, it is "positive" poetry. It has its germ in facts, and its roots in the nature of things. And it shows us, withal, how important it is for the child to be brought up in the home of its parents, and not under a strange roof.

As I have said, the principal agent in household education is the mother. Not that I would disparage the father's share in it; on the contrary, I should be disposed, if I were to speak my mind freely on this subject, to reproach some Catholic authors for not taking sufficient account of it. We are in danger of forgetting the father, in presence of the mother—that ideal so pure, so graceful, so Christian. But I am not now attempting a complete treatise on family education; I am insisting especially on the importance of that primary education, the care of which is devolved almost exclusively on the mother. At this period of life, the object is to form the body and the heart of the child: by and by, the reason will have its turn; but it will never be fairly developed, except on this twofold basis, physical and moral—a body and a heart worthily prepared. Now, no hands but a woman's are capable of this *agricultura Dei*—this husbandry of God. No hands but hers are pure enough and gentle enough to handle this new-born, tender body, that might be chilled and blighted by one imprudent touch. No hands but hers are potent enough to waken within it that organ of the heart which, as science tells us, is the first to be born, the last to die—*primum saliens et ultimum moriens* —and in which, nevertheless, the very faculty of love lies so often extinguished or corrupted in the germ. Yes! as the hands of the priest are consecrated to touch the body of Christ on the altar—that glorious body, hidden beneath the limitations of the sacrament—in like manner the hands of the Christian woman, by the marriage benediction and the grace of motherhood, are hallowed that they may worthily touch the body of the little child,—that feeble and yet glorious body, since it is the shrine of a soul—I might almost say, the shrine of a God. For by baptism it has become a living member of Jesus Christ. [*Applause.*]

Home! Mother!—Where are they, to-day, for the people of our great cities? Ah! I have laid my finger on two gaping, hideous wounds of modern society—the bad condition of the dwellings of the working-classes, and the withdrawal of the mother from her home. These are two of the principles most active, and yet most commonly overlooked, at the root of the evils of society. Here, in the disorganization of the family, in the demoralization of the people, we see the gathering of those black specks which go climbing up the sky, and cover it with clouds, to burst, by and by, in a tremendous storm.

Do you call this, then, a home? Is it not rather a den—this dank, dark, fetid cellar, from which its tenants are absent all day, and into which, at nightfall, they come huddling back in a loathsome herd? Is it the abode of the living, or the sepulchre of the dead?—this close, stifling garret, in which, in order to stretch himself upon his Procrustes' bed (I am citing a fact that has lately come to my knowledge, in Paris), the weary laborer is obliged to open the dormer-window at night, and put his feet out on the roof? I put the question—Are such as these fit dwellings for free citizens of France and Belgium—for men redeemed by the blood of Christ? [*Applause.*]

If the mother were but there, her look and smile might irradiate that darkness, and transform that ugliness to beauty, and make a feast of joy in the midst of all this wretchedness. But Manufacture—tyrannous Manufacture—has dried up the fountain of her breast, and dragged her, feeble and staggering, into the great workshop, noisy with the din of labor and the din of blasphemy, where she can no longer hear the cries of the child that has been carried away from her and left in the careless hands of some mercenary stranger, from which it shall come back to her dead or blighted.

These are not exaggerations, Gentlemen, they are facts that are already far too common, and which tend to become the law in all the great manufacturing centres of population. Now it is the duty, the imperative duty of Catholics to enter into association among themselves, and with Christians of all Churches, with benevolent men of every class of opinion, to make one last effort in favor of the working-classes. Let us strive to give them back the family of which they have been robbed. Let us strive to give them a home, humble and poor of course, but honest and cheerful, where the mother may dwell with her children, and give them those cares of heart and body which nobody else in all the world is fit to give. [*Applause.*]

I am no Utopian, and am not so simple as to suppose that all these things can be accomplished in a day. Whatever might be that coalition of all powerful influences, all wise intellects, all generous hearts, to which my longings aspire, years must needs elapse, and years again, before the family, now so fatally impaired among the people of our cities, could regain its vigor and its beauty. Meanwhile, Gentlemen, what shall we do? Charity has been the mother of wonderful inventions. For the homeless she has opened *crèches* and asylums; for the motherless, she has trained up devoted hearts to the work of education, whatever their sex, or name, or garb. Especially has she been training up, now for three centuries, by the heart of Vincent de Paul, that extraordinary woman whose mission has been chiefly reserved for this nineteenth century, and for this great crisis of the laboring-classes, this helper of the workingman as of the soldier, on the battle-field of toil or of suffering—the Sister of Charity. If anything could fill the mother's place beside the cradles of the people, it would be this nun uncloistered and unveiled, living in the world but not of the world, and who, by an unexampled combination, carries a virgin's heart within a mother's bosom. [*Prolonged applause.*]

Leave the little one with the Sister of Charity. Leave it to the school-teacher, standing in the place of the parent, to the asylum or the school that must answer in the place of home. Do not suffer any hand, under any pretence whatever, to tear it out of the very cradle, and present to us that spectacle so loathsome, if it were not so pitiful—the eight-year-old factory-hand.

I am constrained to tell the whole truth to this great manufacturing interest, which has been, in turn, flattered to the point of sycophancy, and insulted to the point of outrage. I deal neither in flattery nor in insult. I deem it the noblest homage that can be rendered to any earthly power to believe it great enough to hear the truth. I say, then, to the manufacturing interest, that it has no right to lay its hand upon the child before the age marked by nature and religion. So to act is to commit a crime more heinous than that which so long defiled America, and which she has had to wash away in seas of blood. Among those men that were owners of men, there were good and upright ones, who were rather the benefactors of their slaves than their masters; and there were others that had neither conscience nor heart. They saw in the negro nothing but a machine, and enforced from him labor without measure or rest. This was the oppression of the body. But all oppressions, like all liberties, are mutually connected, and from the oppression of the body they passed to the oppression of the soul. If slaves get hold of the truth, the truth will make them free. No intercourse, then, with the sources of knowledge—with the audible teaching of men, or the silent teaching of books! And, finally, to intellectual oppression these studious and cruel tyrants added moral oppression. They were in the right, a thousand times over, for of all the confederates of liberty, the most dangerous is not knowledge, but virtue. No virtue for slaves! We have taken away the Gospel—now take away nature! And because, in the absence of the Gospel, and in the very wreck of human nature, so long as that nature has not perished altogether, there remain still two noble sentiments, two mighty roots from which, even yet, all may bloom again —conjugal love and parental love—they destroyed the family itself, so that in those woe-stricken cabins men might not even embrace in honor as in affection the partners of their misery and the offspring of their loins.

You shudder, O my friends, and you do well. And yet nothing is wholly ruined; however great the evil, it is not hopeless. This negro is a grown-up man, and if in a childhood more happy than his maturer years, he was nursed upon the bosom of a negro yet Christian mother—"black, but comely"—with the healthful and honest milk of chaste wedlock; if he has known the Gospel and loved the Saviour, he carries deep within his breast hidden resources; he will feel within him sudden and mighty quickenings of an honest conscience and of Christian dignity, and against the threefold tyranny of body, mind, and heart he will rise in victorious revolt!

Gentlemen, the being effectively oppressed, the victim incurably blighted, is not the man, but the child. It is the little white slave of Europe, that has never known its cradle or its mother, and that comes to its consciousness in the gloomy factory, a sort of earthly hell, over whose portals you might write,

"Who enter here, leave hope behind."

Its gasping lungs fill themselves with draughts of air that are nothing less than draughts of poison. Its puny limbs, bent under the burden of toil before the bones had hardened, are doomed from infancy to decrepitude. Its understanding, also, stunted in its early growth, is twisted, in the darkness, into miserable malformations. In vain, at a later day, with useless pity, you may make the effort to teach it some few truths. After years of brutal degradation, the negro may begin to remember; after some months only of this odious regimen, the child loses the faculty of acquisition. Never shall it hold in its hands those three common but sublime keys that unlock so many things in life and in the soul—reading, writing, and arithmetic! Never shall he possess those rudiments of knowledge which ought to be the common lot of all: something about the shape and the life of this world in which he lives; much of the glory and destiny of the country he is to love and serve. Never, no! never, shall he have the clear, strong revelation to himself of his own soul and of God. His soul and God! it is not only ignorance that has robbed him of them, it is vice. What transactions are those that take place in that gloomy factory, that hell of precocious and yet hopeless depravity? I will not attempt to say; I will only listen to what is told us by the mouth of one of our own poets, the eloquent interpreter of the frenzies and the miseries of wickedness in the human soul:

> "Man's virgin heart is like a deep, deep vase:
> Let the first water poured therein be foul,
> And ocean may flow over it in vain,
> And never wash it clean ; so deep th' abyss,
> And the stain fastens to its inmost part."*

> * " Le cœur de l'homme vierge est un vase profond :
> Lorsque la première eau qu'on y verse est impure,
> La mer y passerait sans laver la souillure :
> Car l'abîme est immense, et la tache est au fond."
> —*Alfred de Musset.*

EDUCATION OF THE WORKING-CLASSES. 273

Woe unto you, ye hands that have put a blight on childhood! Woe unto you, for all your grandeur, for all your skill, for all your wealth! Ye hands of merciless enterprise, ye shall be dried up and withered like the hand of the tyrant of Israel under the curse of the prophet of Judah: "the hand of Jeroboam dried up so that he could not pull it in again to him," because the Lord had cursed it.* Ye have been guilty of the most cowardly, the most revolting, the most irreparable of crimes! [*Prolonged applause.*]

II. *Factory Education.*—I have dwelt too long, perhaps, on this primary education of man. You must put the blame of it, Gentlemen, on your own attention and sympathy, and then on that empty cradle, that absent mother, that sorrowful home, over which we felt that we must pour out our tears and our hopes together.

The education of home concludes by a great religious act, the first communion, which is like a first coming of age of the child. More precocious, in this respect, than the rich man's child, the laborer's son enters, from that time forth, into a sort of public life. From the family, he passes to the factory. Am I mistaken, Gentlemen; and ought I to speak of the school as coming between the family and the factory—first, the primary school, and then the professional school? No! the school is not *between* the family and the factory; it is alongside of both. It does not form, with the family and the factory, a third grade of popular education; to put it all in one word, its function is not principal and independent, but secondary and subordinate. I have great sympathy and respect for these modest and self-denying instructors of the people. Whether they are connected with public

* 1 Kings, xiii. 4.

schools or private, whether they wear the garb of laymen or of some religious order, no matter, so long as they are faithful to the dignity of their calling. I, for one, will never have anything to do with the coarse and undeserved insults that have been flung at them, with different spirit, by extremists of all parties. But honorable as their calling is, I repeat, it is only secondary. Practical good sense refuses to see in the school what too many of our contemporaries think they see in it— the most effective instrument for the elevation of the working-classes. Permit me, Gentlemen, to cite the words of a master of economic science, a patient, impartial, sagacious observer, whose name and works I would be glad to find becoming popular among Catholics: "In free and prosperous nations," says M. Le Play, " the teacher has only a subordinate part. The real education is given by the family, aided by the priest; it is completed by apprenticeship to business, and by the practice of social duties."*

The factory, then, after the family, is the second centre—the second home of the education of the people. But what is a factory, correctly understood and rightly organized? It is a place where there is practical recognition of the personal rights and dignity of the working-man, and especially of the working-child. A personal being is always an end, never a means; he is not to be used like an irrational animal or an unconscious tool. If we expect service of him, if we derive profits from him, we are bound to deal toward him, as God does toward us, " with great respect"—*cum magna reverentia disponis nos.*† What is a well-constituted factory? It is

---

* " *La Réforme Sociale en France*, by M. Le Play, author of *Ouvriers Européens*, Commissioner-General at the Universal Expositions of 1855, 1862, and 1867. Third Edition, Vol, II., p. 369.

† Wisdom, xii. 18.

one which has at the head of it an honorable man as patron,*—a man really worthy of that title. There are those who object to this title as somehow ridiculous or invidious; to me it seems a very grand title, a very noble and Christian title. To my mind, it suggests the idea of a *paternal* relation, and in this very idea the practical solution of our social questions, by means of relations of mutual affection—by means of free, and yet close and lasting association between masters and workmen. In such a factory, under such a father of the people and of the laborer, it is possible to sacrifice immediate profits, however considerable, to the training up of intelligent and virtuous apprentices. In such a factory, it is not the only question how to turn off the most work in the shortest time, but how to make the business as honorable for its workmen as for its work—for its moral side as for its material side. In such a factory, they "seek first the kingdom of God and his righteousness," and all the rest is added unto them. For the righteous and the profitable are more closely connected than men think; and science has recently proved that in the productions of manufacturing industry are to be discovered indications of the grade, not only of the workman's intelligence, but of his morals.

With the aid of capable and faithful foremen, such a patron will make the factory under his direction the best of professional schools. The good workman is trained, like the good soldier, less by precept than by example—less by general and theoretical notions than by practical struggle with the realities of his business. Come on, then, my young conscript of labor! I would there were a great many more of your sort of conscripts,

---

* The title commonly applied, in French, to the master of a ship or of a manufacturing concern.

and a great many less of the other sort—[*Applause*]—
yes, conscripts of husbandry for those vast open workshops the fields, and conscripts of mechanic industry
for those narrower, but not less fruitful, workshops of
our cities—these make up the grand, pacific army that
constitutes the true power and the true preponderance
of a nation! [*Renewed applause.*] Come on, conscript
of labor! enter the battlefield of the shop! Go in to
those fights that are not always without danger—that
are never without courage and glory! And you, old
veteran of a foreman, captain of the noble host, follow
him, guide him, urge him on with look, and word, and
action. See how he will avenge his early reverses by
valiant feats of arms! How he will lay his victorious
hand on this wild beast—this brute matter in revolt
against mankind! He shall seize it by the forelock, he
shall twist his hand into its mane, and bring it down
at last, subdued, docile, broken to his will, to fetch and
carry the inventions of science, and the creations of
genius. [*Applause.*]

One word more, Gentlemen, as to the factory. It belongs to it to complete the formation of the moral and
religious man, as well as of the intelligent and skilful
artisan. It is not only the chief school of the profession,
it is the chief school of life. The family, with its auxiliaries, the school and the catechetical teaching of the
Church, has rather formed the theory of life than put it
into practice. Its teachings of good have fallen into the
child's soul under the form of a mysterious revelation,
the power and beauty of which he has felt, but the
whole bearing of which he has not been able to grasp.
Every theory, so long as it remains an abstraction, differs more or less from the reality. It has to descend
into the region of facts, and come into a contact with

them which does not destroy it; far from that, it confirms it, but at the same time modifies and makes it fruitful. This is the truth that there is in the tendencies of positivism. So soon, then, as the mother and the priest have settled that sublime, real, eternal theory of religion and virtue, it is for the factory to subject it to its inevitable and decisive test—to confer upon it, or withhold from it, "the freedom of the city" in practical life. If everything in this new school says to the young apprentice—"They have been deceiving you, or rather they have been deceiving themselves; the great movement of men and things is not, cannot be, such as they have told you"—if this contradiction of the belief of his childhood penetrates into his mind and heart by all the teachings of word and example, by all the influences of that moral atmosphere that acts upon us with so much greater energy than the physical atmosphere, there is an end of the principles inculcated by his parents and his early teachers; he will quit them as a broken reed, and will suffer himself to be drawn easily down the seductive slopes of doubt and pleasure. On the other hand, let the child happen upon one of those factories, such as we too seldom meet with now-a-days, that are a sort of continuation of home and school; let him hear and see there the practical commentary on all that he has been wont to believe and love; let him breathe there that wholesome spiritual atmosphere, the free, refreshing, bracing inspiration of the conscience and heart; and soon you will see coming out in him, in manly shape, those youthful virtues over which the two sacred wings of family and of religion have been brooding, and which have been warmed into life by the pressure of those two hearts of which I dare not say that one surpasses the other—in such equal tenderness and piety hath God formed them both to tend the cradle of human childhood—the heart of the mother, and the heart of the priest. [*Applause.*]

III. *Education by the Lord's Day.*—I have just been speaking of the priest and the mother in the same breath. In fact, Gentlemen, if I have ever spoken of the family and the factory separately, I have never meant, in so doing, to isolate them from religion. In these two primordial laws, of love and labor, whose respective centres, the family and the factory, I have indicated, there is involved, and, so to speak, interlaced, a third law, greater still, which, with them, makes up the web of human existence. I mean prayer.

We cannot be the disciples of the school of "Independent Morality," because we cannot be the partisans of the doctrine of an impersonal God. We have a morality which comes from the living God and returns to him; and in that golden chain which binds earth to heaven, all the links are not mere duties of man to man. If one would be an honest man, in the full and sacred meaning of that desecrated name, he must not leave out of view, in respecting the claims of personal duty, the first, the most living, the most sacred of all personalities. Now, this communion of the living and personal soul with the personal and living God is what we call prayer, in the largest and fullest sense of the word. It is not enough to think of God; we must pray to him. When men become accustomed to approach God only by the way of thought, they end by not believing in God at all. He vanishes away, or at least becomes transformed in those confused and chilly clouds—*evanuerunt in cogitationibus suis*—and of the Being of beings there remains nothing but a sublime but unsubstantial idea. There must be the heart, the acts, the movements of a soul whose respect and love reach out to the God in whom it has its being on the earth, to the Father who awaits it in heaven. Individual prayer, too, is not enough. There must be common prayer—the meeting and intermingling of souls in, presence of the same light and heat. Such prayer as this must have its sacred time and its sacred place—the Sabbath and the temple. It remains for me, Gentlemen, to say of this day and place that they are, not only before, but after the first communion, the highest school of the child, the youth, the man.

Therefore the first, the most necessary, of all the elements of popular liberty, is the liberty of the Lord's day. There are those who do not understand this need of rest to soul and body. Commonly they are among those who employ labor, not among those that do it—those who receive its profits without knowing its weariness. They are not among those who have torn their hands on the thorns and briers of the workshop—on the hard asperities of matter, or who have been bending for six days over the earth cursed for man's sake, the brow bathed in sweat, the soul exhausted with toil. Ah! I can conceive the nature of their objections to the law of rest—I see through their repugnance to the liberty of the Lord's-day! But the workingman, whenever he is not under the pressure of physical or moral violence—whenever he is left to his own instincts—the workingman claims as his dearest and most sacred right the enjoyment of that day which makes him indeed a free man, indeed a husband and a father, indeed a child of God. It is demanded in his behalf by the sense of the dignity of human nature—by the exigences of family life—by the religious wants of the soul—by the voice of whatever is noblest and most commanding in our nature.

I still remember the impressions of my childhood.

Suffer me this little reminiscence, which any one of you could recall from his own memory, and which might come from among our working-men as well. In the morning when I waked, how well I used to know that it was Sunday! In the clump of trees near the window the bird was singing more sweetly, and the church-bells were chiming more gladly, the air was fuller of music and perfume; the sky was so fair, the sun so splendid. It was always a mystery to me, and I used to ask myself sometimes how nature could so change its face and be transfigured on a fixed day. But afterward I came to understand it. Dear child, from off whose brow the baptismal water has hardly dried, upon whose cheek the mother's kiss still lingers, it is but the reflection of thine own religious soul that is cast upon the face of nature, making her more beautiful—more like thyself! [*Applause.*]

The child rises with delight, and betakes himself to the house of worship, which is the house of God, but also the house of the people. The rich have their palaces; they may be content, then, with a modest chapel. But the people must have their cathedrals. . . . [*Applause.*] They must have festivals such as are not given to the princes of the earth, such as religion alone can realize. The true popular fête—if I may use that much-perverted word—the true democratic festival, is the Lord's-day. In the vast basilica all the arts gather themselves together about the altar, to mingle their enchantments in one supreme enchantment—architecture, sculpture, painting, music, and, above all, eloquence. Yes, eloquence! how rude soever the words of the priest may be, by the very nature of the truths which he proclaims, by the very chords which he is sure to thrill in human hearts, the priest cannot but be eloquent. [*Applause.*]

Into that presence come the people, feeling their own greatness. The little children, as they cross the threshold, are welcomed like kings, with the majestic voice of the organs; they breathe the odor of incense and of flowers; they listen to those sublime and touching chants, those Latin words which they do not understand, and from which, nevertheless, they learn so much—words of eternity let fall into time—mysterious secrets of the far-off land, seen dimly from our exile. Transported with faith and hope and love, they go from hearth to altar, and from altar back to hearth, and bring back God's kiss with them to their mother, even as they carried their mother's kiss with them to the house of God.

And yet this is the day which certain "friends of the people," forsooth, would wish to extort from them. False friends, that think only of their bodies, that see in them nothing but their material wants, the toil and the enjoyments of the beast of burden! O ye courtiers of democracy, who flatter the people while you despise them, have some faith in the people's souls, *crede animæ;* and that you may have, do begin by having a little faith in your own! [*Applause.*]

Yes, this law of Sabbath rest, so religiously democratic, is now-a-days misapprehended on every hand. Patriotism imposes on me something more than an ordinary consideration for my own country, when I am speaking on another soil than hers. No, no! I mistake; my country asks of me nothing but justice, and I know that if men may say much in censure of contemporary France, they are bound in justice to say much in praise of her. I will speak, then, without constraint, and make my complaint of the violation of the Lord's day in the great manufacturing towns of France. It happens, now and then, that I have occasion to pass through their streets on my way to the church to preach the word of God. I am revolving in my heart the lessons of the Gospel, and all along the street there are the visions of hell, the ponderous carts, the shrieking axles, the smoking pavements, the clouds of dust that shut me out from the sight of the sun and of God! I hide my eyes with my hands, and groan, "O France, this is thy doing!"

But some one will answer me—"To be sure; but it is liberty. You must respect the liberty of France! You must respect the conscience of your fellow-citizens!" Ah, I have nothing to say against liberty. I speak of it with lips all the more sincere and earnest as they are more truly Christian and Catholic. The hour cometh, but is not yet, Gentlemen, when misunderstandings shall be done away. This century shall not have passed away before it shall be acknowledged that that pontiff so great, and at the same time so grievously misunderstood, Pius IX., who has battled so bravely against revolution, is the same who has made the boldest and most successful advances—yes, the most successful; I say it notwithstanding apparent failures—toward liberty in Europe. Let us not be guilty of that for which Saint Paul reproached the Christians of Corinth—let us not "divide Christ"—let us not separate Pius IX. in twain. For my part, I take him in the whole of his glorious career, from his most blameless prosperity down to his most touching misfortunes—from the time when the flag of progress and reform was unfurled by his priestly and royal hands, before 1848, down to the convocation of the Œcumenical Council, which is greeted at this very hour, not only with the applauses of Catholics, but with the sympathies of Protestants and of Rationalists.

No, we have no disposition to trench upon liberty. We would not interfere with the advantage of the workman, nor the exigencies of the manufacturing interest. What contemptible sophistries are these! Have you never heard of two great embodiments of liberty—two great organizations of industry, which are as good as your own, if not better—England and the United States? I have had the pleasure of visiting London. I never shall forget the emotion which filled me at the sight of that city like the ancient metropolis of the seas of which the prophet speaks—"the woman that sitteth upon many waters." And in those mighty floods, I saw no vision as of the abyss, but only a vast and solemn equilibrium, as it had been the majesty of a throne rocking and yet stable. There she sat, the great empress of the seas, giving law to isles and continents, stretching afar over kings and peoples, not, like them of old, the rod of oppression, but the beneficent sceptre of her riches and her liberty. And I heard the din of her vast industry, and through the streets there poured the living sea of men and vehicles. Then, by and by, there dawned a day which was like the days of my childhood, a day such as public life in my own land has not now to show, a day which was not like other days. No noisy wagons now in the streets; no throngs hurrying to business. The giant machine that had been roaring and thundering the day before, had suddenly stood still as if before the vision of God. The great movement of British industry was hushed, and in the streets I saw naught but families going their way, calm and cheerful, to the place of prayer; I heard naught but the sweet chiming of Protestant bells, that remember that they once were Catholic, and wait the day when they shall be Catholic again. [*Applause.*]

Let no one say, "England is an aristocratic and feudal power; her Sabbath rest is one of those relics of the middle ages which the breath of modern progress will soon have swept away." I look across the ocean, and there again I find this same Anglo-Saxon race clad in like grandeur under forms the most unlike. This time there is neither mediævalism nor aristocracy. It is the foremost prow of modern civilization under full headway on her glorious and daring course toward an unknown future. It is, I love to think, the people chosen of God to renew the face of the earth, and to prepare for those old truths and institutions which cannot pass away, newer and more enduring garments. Now, the United States keeps holy the Lord's-day, just like England, and sends back to us, across the ocean, that same answer of God's silence to man's profanations. [*Applause.*]

When I speak thus, Gentlemen, in eulogy of these great countries, I do not mean to recommend to you a servile imitation of them. Neither do I ask to have engrossed among our laws anything that is not settled in our character. The law exists in France, indeed, but it exists as a dead letter. I do not ask to see it enforced. I am satisfied that in countries like France and Belgium there would be immense difficulties in adopting that course. What I ask is not the enforcement, but the liberty of the Sabbath. Liberty through the Sabbath; and the Sabbath through liberty! [*Good, good; that's it!*] Yes; I say again the liberty of the people through the Sabbath, and the observance of the Sabbath through liberty!

If I had the right to speak to governments, I would do it with the respect which is due to them, with all their faults. We have been applauding here the no' words of M. de Maistre, when speaking of Russia: "I respect everything respectable, in sovereigns or in people." I would tell them, then, "Give your own example, and I ask no other support from you for the cause for which I plead. Let the public works scrupulously respect the Lord's-day, and the State will compel the individual to blush before it." [*Applause.*] And you, lords of the forge and the loom—organizers, legislators, monarchs of labor and wealth—you can do more for this cause than crowned heads can do. You have been mighty in crushing the liberty of the Sabbath; you shall be mightier yet in restoring it! [*Applause.*]

And now, Gentlemen, before I close, suffer me to make one last and pressing appeal to your zeal in favor of these three great restorations among the working-classes—the family, the factory, the Sabbath. Yesterday, in language such as only he can use, but such as spoke the feelings of us all, the Count de Falloux said to the illustrious Bishop of Orleans, "My lord, you have recommended to us early rising, and you have enforced precept with example; for we never fail to find you awake bright and early in every good cause." Now, I wish every one of us might be bright and early, too—that we Catholics might have the honor of leading all the rest in the practical understanding of what is getting ready for us in no distant future.

What is getting ready—men call it by an ill-defined name, a name that provokes excitement and contention—democracy. I tried to explain this word, nearly two years ago, at Notre-Dame, in Paris,* and was taken to task for it by some people. Since then, I have come upon a very similar definition in the recent work of that courageous bishop whom I have just named. I reassert

* Advent Conferences, 1865. Conference Third.

it, then, with pride, and say to all those who make use of this name:—There are two sorts of democracy in the world; of which sort is yours? Is it radical revolution? Is it the prostration of all greatness, and intelligence, and virtue,—of the whole social hierarchy—before the mere force of numbers? Is it the brutal levelling process which passes over everything to debase and crush? If that is your democracy, it is the worst of all barbarisms, and we will fight it, if need be, to the death. But if by democracy is meant the gradual and peaceful elevation of the toiling and suffering masses whom in the country we call the peasants, and in the cities the working-class,—their elevation to fuller education, to more settled prosperity, to a purer and more effectual morality, and, as a legitimate consequence, to a wider social influence,—we are on the side of that democracy, not only because we are sons of this generation, but because we are sons of the Gospel.*

Already it begins to dawn. In behalf of you all, I greet this Christian democracy that settles itself deep and firm by the hearth-stones of our homes, in the shops of labor, in the sanctuary of our temples. It will change history, which in past time has never known how to write of anything but the intrigues of the cunning and the conquests of the violent, the impotence of state-craft, the corruption, too often, of riches and of the arts. It will give as a subject for the meditations of sages, the intelligent and faithful fulfilment of those laws of private life to which public life itself is subordinate, if we did but know it. It will rear up a grand

---

* "If democracy is the elevation of the common people, the peasants, the working-men, to a higher grade of education, prosperity, morality, and legitimacy, then the Church goes for democracy."—*L'Athéisme et le péril social*, by the Bishop of Orleans [Dupanloup]. 1866, p. 166.

people, which shall seek the practical happiness of its existence, as well as the inspiration of its literature and art, in the affections of the family, the struggles and the joys of labor, the chaste emotions of worship, and the splendid festivals of religion.

Doubtless the crisis through which we are passing is one of the most terrible, one of the most profound, that our race has ever known. Let our efforts, our courage, and our faith rise to the height of these solemn events, but let us not doubt concerning the final issue. I can understand the ruin of the organizations of heathen society; but as for society that has been touched by Jesus Christ,—as for humanity which for centuries has had the spirit of the Gospel,—as for Europe, in a word, it may suffer, it may agonize, it cannot die. [*Prolonged applause. For a few minutes the proceedings of the Congress were suspended.*]

MEMORIAL LETTER

ON THE LIFE OF

MONSEIGNEUR BAUDRY, BISHOP OF PÉRIGUEUX.

[The religious and theological teacher to whom Father Hyacinthe gratefully ascribes the strongest and best influences that affected his student-life, was the Abbé Baudry, professor in the theological seminary of St. Sulpice, at Paris, and afterward bishop of Périgueux. The following Letter was addressed to the editor of a posthumous volume of Bishop Baudry, entitled, "Christian Thoughts on the Heart of Jesus," (*Pensées Chrétiennes sur le Cœur de Jésus*).]

MY DEAR FRIEND:—I wish to thank you for the noble book which you have given to the public; and I make bold to do it, not in my own name alone, but in the name of many others who, like us, are disciples and spiritual children of Bishop Baudry. You have done a work of filial piety, in which every one of us must feel an interest. Perhaps, without suspecting it, you have really brought out the best possible life of our common father. His outward life would furnish but little of incident. It was passed almost exclusively in the cloisters of our seminaries. It was that of the most regular and modest of Sulpitians—which is a great thing to say for the heavenly life, but very little for the earthly. His true life was his inner life, the life of his intellect and heart; but above all, of his heart, for with this great Christian spirit, both the root and the fruit of the intellect were in the heart. Has not Bishop Baudry really unfolded to us his own heart, while attempting to speak only of that Heart of Jesus which was the object of his constant thought, his intimate and confidential fellowship, and his practical imitation? How truthfully and charmingly you show him to us, at evening, in that dear little chamber where we knew and loved him so well, pressing out into his soul's cup the sweet or bitter juices of the day's experience, mingling and assimilating them into that highest unity of man, the unity of his love, and then pouring them out over these pages, written for himself alone, like the outpouring of his soul into the bosom of Jesus Christ.

But in point of fact it was not your direct or principal aim to reveal to the world one of the loftiest and most secluded souls that God has granted to his Church in our age; it was your main purpose to help in throwing new and vivid light on that devotion to The Sacred Heart which, in our time, is one of the strongest attractions of Christian piety. At its very origin a subject of controversy, and ever since, for many, even among believers, a subject of distrust, this devotion has most commonly been defended, just as it has been attacked, by superficial arguments, in its relation to the imagination and the sensibilities. Without disregarding either of these two aspects, our author goes deeper, even to the mysteries of man's moral constitution. Heathenism had placed the seat of life sometimes in the abstractions of the intellect, sometimes in the emotions of the sensibilities. Christianity puts it back where it belongs, in the heart, the centre in which thought and sentiment come together, the one to receive real life, the other to gain ideal purity, both to come under the fructifying control of the will. This is the point of view from which Bishop Baudry contemplated his subject. The life of man radiating from the heart, the heart of man having its object and its law in the heart of God manifest in the flesh, such is the substance of this book, full of instruction as it is of piety, and which, by a beautiful care of Providence, is brought before the public amid the joy and enthusiasm of the festivals in honor of the lover and evangelist of The Sacred Heart, the blessed Marguerite-Marie.

These pages, it must be acknowledged, bear the impress of a metaphysics sometimes so profound, and a mysticism always so tender, that they might seem hardly appropriate to the wants of society, in which, even among Christians, contrary tendencies unhappily prevail. The objection is so plausible, that I could pardon a less acute and earnest mind than yours for being alarmed by it. But, thank God, you understand that the prejudices of the day need not to be humored, but to be withstood. You justly believe that it is not for us to level down the summits of doctrine and piety, because too many of our contemporaries fail to reach them. In our own time, as in all past time, the two wings with which to mount upward to these summits are the metaphysical and the mystical—intellect and love. This powerful and harmonious flight characterizes all the *masters in divinity,* as they used to be called, from St. John and St. Paul to Origen and St. Augustine; from St. Bonaventure and Gerson down to St. John of the Cross and M. Olier. To reproach you with this publication as an anachronism, would be equivalent to reproaching Bishop Baudry for having continued among us that succession which can never fail, and that race which can never become extinct.

Be of good cheer, then, my friend. This unfinished book (you have called our attention, in advance, to its incompleteness), this artless book, the expression of which is forgotten in the thought, and has none but an unconscious eloquence—this book, whose very substance, full of beams of light, of horizons half unveiled, and of sublime but fragmentary studies, reveals less the labor of the intellect than the inspiration of grace—this book will do its own work, as did the life of which it is the sweet and touching memorial. The life, like the book, was unfinished, and yet how fruitful! As he used to tell us at St. Sulpice, and as you remind us in your affecting preface, our friend was only an *initiator*. It was his mission to think rather than write, and the works he has left behind him are not books, but disciples. This book, which is hardly to be called a book, because it is so much more, will be for many an initiation; it will scatter germs of thought and virtue in men's souls, and will join to us brothers and sisters unknown, but not unloved, in that spiritual family in which, unworthy as we are, it is our honor to be counted among the first-born.

Accept, my dear friend, with the renewed expression of my thanks, that of my fraternal attachment in our Lord Jesus Christ.

BROTHER HYACINTHE,
Of the Immaculate Conception,
Barefooted Carmelite.

PARIS, *August* 21, 1865.

APPENDIX.

LETTER OF MONSEIGNEUR DUPANLOUP,

BISHOP OF ORLEANS,

TO THE CLERGY OF HIS DIOCESE,

On the proposed Definition of the Dogma of Infallibility in the Œcumenical Council.

GENTLEMEN: In sending me your farewell greetings and prayers before my departure for Rome, you have spoken of the trouble and anxiety produced among the faithful of your parishes by the violent controversy that has been excited in the newspapers concerning the approaching Council, and especially concerning the definition of the doctrine of papal infallibility.

This anxiety I fully appreciate.

The Holy Father and his privileges are here in question—matters of closest interest to the Catholic heart. It is natural in filial piety to wish to invest a father with every gift and prerogative; and, on the other hand, how painful it is for sons to hear discussed what they would rejoice to have proclaimed by acclamation as their father's honor and glory.

Controversies, then, upon the infallibility of the sovereign Pontiff cannot but have enkindled in men's minds these two feelings, both of which are worthy of respect.

But, however sweet and dear these suggestions of filial love may be, there is, Gentlemen—you feel it—something more to be considered and listened to in the proclamation of a dogma than the impulses of sentiment. There are reasons *pro* and *con*.—reasons on which, in a question not yet settled, great minds have taken different sides; there are, besides, the very interests of the venerated and cherished Father himself, which might be compromised in the attempt to exalt them; there are, above all, the interests of the Church, which take precedence of his interests; there is, finally, the sacred welfare of souls, the present condition of minds, which must be taken into account; in a word, by the side of supposed advantages there are also objections which must be weighed deliberately and gravely. All this should not be forgotten, Gentlemen, unless we wish to expose ourselves, despite our good intentions, to the risk of mingling contention with love, and turning a matter of theology into a matter of enthusiasm or of anger.

God forbid, Gentlemen, that I should wish to give pain to a single one of my venerable brethren in the episcopate! Had bishops been the only ones to utter their views on this subject according to the inspiration of their conscience, I should have kept silence, and listened with respect to respectful discussions, without contradicting their doctrines for or against the question, or their views for or against its opportuneness. Without wishing to judge the conduct of any one, such would have been my own. And if, subsequently, at the Council, I should have been called upon to decide one way or the other, I should have done so, for my own part, in the simplicity of my conscience, in the truthfulness and charity of my soul.

Such, however, has not been the case—far from it; and the question, launched upon the public in a very different manner, has evoked the anxieties which you have made known to me, and upon which, according to my promise to you, I make it my duty to give you my opinion.

But, before doing this, I must recall to your minds what has been said and done up to this time, and how the question stands at this moment.

I. I shall begin, Gentlemen, by observing, that such a question was a matter for the Council, and should have been treated by it alone. Unfortunately, intemperate journalists have not left this task to the future Assembly of the Church. Storming the doors of the Council, even before, a long while before it could assemble, they have made haste to open the debates upon one of the most delicate theological subjects, and to announce beforehand how the Council should and must decide. It was an effort made to create a current in public opinion favorable to their desires, and to bear down upon the assembled bishops with all the pressure of this anticipatory judgment.

Shall I go so far as to mention the pious artifices resorted to for the same object? Some have gone to the point of distributing in the streets—I have seen it myself, two years ago; they are keeping it up to this day—thousands of little handbills, with the vow to believe in the personal and separate infallibility of the Pope. They have got them signed by good Catholics, many of whom, assuredly, would scarcely claim to be theologians, and certainly do not understand the first word of the question.*

Two papers especially, the *Civiltà Cattolica* and the *Univers*, have taken the most astonishing steps. While the Holy Father was enjoining prudent and rigorous silence upon the counsellors of the Roman congregations charged with the work of preparation for the Council, they did not hesitate to throw open to the public questions which, in their opinion, should be agitated and settled by the future Assembly. They announced, in particular, that the matter of the personal infallibility of the Pope would be defined by it; even more, that it would be defined by acclamation.

This delicate question having been raised after this fashion, and dragged into the street and the press, a Belgian prelate, my reverend friend Mgr. Dechamps, recently nominated Archbishop of Malines, has published a special work, entitled: *Is it opportune to define in the approaching Council the Infallibility of the Pope?* and he answered in the affirmative. The new Archbishop of

---

* In certain towns the laity have taken the initiative with their pastors, going to them and requesting them to sign either the vow of belief in infallibility, or one of the petitions to the Council on this subject.

Westminster, the pious and eloquent Mgr. Manning, had already, in a prior work, treated the same question, from the same point of view, and he has subsequently taken it up again, still more positively, in a second letter to his clergy. The English papers, Catholic and Protestant, have taken an active part in the controversy.

On the other hand, the German bishops, convened at Fulda— as announced several days ago by the *Mémorial Diplomatique*—in addition to that letter which all Europe has admired for its moderation, elevation, and dignity, have addressed the Sovereign Pontiff a memorial (without, however, exposing it to the greedy publicity of the newspapers), asking him not to permit the question of his personal infallibility to be broached at the approaching Council.

Such was the state of affairs when the controversy was revived in France among several of our venerated colleagues. Unfortunately, the papers immediately took it up with extreme ardor. The quick and keen simultaneousness of the attacks aroused the public: a certain portion of the press, under whose eyes this debate was carried on, has made deplorable sport of it, and well-known publicists have thrown ridicule upon what they call "*the Holy War.*"

Finally, other writers, laymen and ecclesiastics, in France, in England, and in Germany, following the example thus set them, have broken silence and expressed, in their turn, their opinions and their fears.

With this spectacle before one's eyes, it was difficult not to ask one's self: If the question is already treated in this manner before the public, what will be the case if it comes to be presented to the Council? And it was impossible not to feel, once more, the grievous fault of the journalists, who, with the greatest indiscretion, have been the first to start a question of this nature.

The question is indeed a grave one. For it is the question of proclaiming a new dogma, the dogma of the personal and separate infallibility of the Pope.

We say "a new dogma," not in the sense you understand, Gentlemen, that a dogma is created by the Council: the Church does not create dogmas, it declares them. And there must be no ambiguity here. I say a new dogma in this sense, that for eighteen centuries the faithful have never been held to this belief under penalty of ceasing to be Catholics.

It is a question, then, of obliging all Catholics hereafter to believe, on pain of anathema, that the Pope is infallible, even—I make use of the very words of His Grace the Archbishop of Westminster—even when he pronounces alone, "WITHOUT THE EPISCOPAL BODY, UNITED OR DISPERSED," and that he can define dogmas by himself, "SEPARATELY, INDEPENDENTLY OF THE EPISCOPATE,"* without any co-operation of the bishops, express or implied, antecedent or subsequent.

Now this, as you see, is no speculative dogma; it is a prerogative which, in its practical realization, would be fraught with the most serious consequences.

Such is the question that we see discussed every morning, and decided off-hand by an overweening press, with the strongest freedom.

Besides, many treat the matter just as if, in their eyes, there was no difficulty in it whatever. "It is enough," says one of them, "to know our catechism." Bossuet, apparently, did not know his; nor Fenelon, who had a very different idea of infallibility from Bellarmin's; nor even Bellarmin himself, who, on this point, did not agree at all with other Roman theologians. To hear these editors, one would suppose that the proclamation of the dogma of Papal infallibility is so necessary, so easy, and so certain, that the Council will not even have to examine it; and to doubt its decision, even for a moment, would be to insult it: it would also subject one to the suspicion, at least, of very lukewarm devotion to the Church and the Pope.

This is what they say, accompanied with such abuse of those who do not agree with them, that, in truth, all restraint is forgotten, and the debate becomes strangely acrimonious.

* Pastoral Letter of Archbishop Manning, on *The Œcumenical Council and the Infallibility of the Roman Pontiff.*—Póstscript.

Yet nobody knows in the least what the Council will see fit to do or not to do on this point—the Council that does not yet exist.

But meanwhile, Gentlemen, these excesses of controversy trouble the faithful, and place them in the evidently dangerous situation that you have indicated to me. For, if the Council should see fit not to follow the line so imperatively laid down for it, would it not appear, in the eyes of many, to have fallen short of its duty? It is asserted, and justly, that the bishops will have full and entire liberty at the Council. But, truly, what liberty is left them henceforth, by such discussions, conducted in such a manner by the newspaper-press? To judge from the way in which the debate has been carried on, do they not seem to denounce beforehand, as schismatics and heretics, those who will permit themselves to be of a different opinion?

These, Gentlemen, are common-sense considerations, presented to me orally and in writing, not merely by yourselves, but again and again by a host of the best and most Christian spirits, who are interested and agitated by these disputes that are raging near and far.

I have waited long before deciding to speak on such a subject. You have decided me. My anxiety was not, indeed, to know whether certain men would suspect, more or less, and calumniate my zeal for the Pope and the Church, but to know what I had to do to serve those cherished causes as I ought. I have examined at length, in all its aspects, and especially from a practical point of view, the question discussed in the newspapers. I have found in it, for my part, difficulties of more than one kind—difficulties which, it seems to me, should strike even those who are most convinced, theologically, of the Papal infallibility.

Assuredly, I have no relish for precipitating myself into so violent an affray. I deplore the controversy that is being carried on before the public, and if I write, it is not to aggravate, but rather to calm, and even, were that possible, to suppress it. For, for my part, I hold it to be very inopportune, much to be regretted, for the sake of the Holy See itself; and the quarrels that have just taken place have only strengthened my conviction, already of long standing, as to this inopportuneness.

These difficulties it is—without going to the bottom of the theological question—that I would simply set forth in this paper.

I do not discuss the question of infallibility itself, but only its opportuneness. And, moreover, the views that I shall present here are no merely personal views of my own. I have often discussed them with a great number of my venerated colleagues, both in France and elsewhere, and these reasons have seemed to us so weighty, to them as well as myself, that at the very least they are of a kind to bring the religious press to reflection, and to persuade it, at last, to leave such delicate discussions for the bishops.

II. These debates, as I have said, have no less astonished than saddened me. For, indeed, prior to this meddling and these noisy demonstrations on the part of a certain portion of the press, the question had not been raised. God be praised, silence had come over quarrels which it would be better, I have ever thought, to forget than to revive. Never had the authority of the Holy Father been more respected in the Church, never had his voice been better listened to. Never had the bishops been more ready to gather around the papal throne, hurrying—not by the order even, but at the simple wish of the Pope—from the ends of the world to the centre of Catholic Christendom.

Wherein, then, was it possible for the Council to be an occasion of provoking controversy upon papal prerogatives? Was it for this object, was it to have himself declared infallible, that the Holy Father wished to convene the bishops of the whole world? Did the definition of the doctrine of personal infallibility enter at all into the motives and the causes of the convocation of the Council? Not the least in the world.

When Pope Pius IX., in his two celebrated allocutions, announced to the bishops assembled at Rome, in 1867, his project of convoking an Œcumenical Council, he did not say one word upon the necessity or the expediency of having the future assembly set up his personal infallibility as a dogma of faith.

Neither did the five hundred bishops, then met at Rome, in their address to the Holy Father, in reply to this communication, say one word about this question.

Finally, in the Bull of Convocation, in which the Holy Father laid down the programme of the future Council so broadly and in such grand terms, there is again no mention made of his personal infallibility.

No; nowhere, in none of the acts of the Holy Father, does there appear, for a single instant, this anxiety to aggrandize his authority by means of the Council and under favor of that respect which the world pays to his virtues and his misfortunes.

You know, Gentlemen, that the Vicar of Jesus Christ assigns other and grand objects for the assembly of the representatives of the Catholic Church.

"To cure the evils of the present century in the Church and in society," that is the purpose for which the Pope has convened the Council; and therein, of a truth, what questions are contained that have been raised by modern times and by the present crisis! It is everywhere anxiously asked whether, in such an uncertain era—when from one moment to another events may start up to dissolve the Council before it can finish its task—the bishops will even have time to consider them.

And it is in the midst of such pressing and necessary questions that people wish to start a new, unforeseen, unexpected question, of unmistakable difficulty, and charged with tempests! and to run the risk—in the path laid down by the newspapers—of showing the world, instead of that grand spectacle of unity which it is expecting of us, a totally different one!

Alas! we can foresee already, by the bitterness of these preliminary debates, what discussions this question—if carried there—might give rise to in the Council!

But why carry it thither? Is there any constraining necessity? Do the perils of the times demand it?

Not at all! But I hear it said, we have to do here with a principle.

A principle? Well! I reply in turn, this principle, if it is one, is it then necessary to the life of the Church that it should become a dogma of faith? How, then, do you explain it that the Church has lived for eighteen centuries without defining this doctrine essential to its life? How do you explain it, that the Church has formulated its body of doctrine, produced all its doctors, condemned every heresy, without this definition? Evidently, there is no necessity here, and the solution of this question is no more indispensable than it was called for.

The reason, moreover, is simple. The Church is infallible, and the infallibility of the Church has answered every purpose until now. Do you fear lest, in future, it should become insufficient? and do you flatter yourselves that those who are unwilling to believe in the infallibility of the Church united with the Pope will be more ready to believe in the personal and separate infallibility of the Pope?

Is there in the Catholic Church any misgiving as to the infallibility of the Church? Are not all agreed on this point? Does not the least of the faithful know that he is in communion with his pastor, who is in communion with his bishop, who is in communion with the Pope? Does not that suffice abundantly for the security of our faith? And have not the faithful, in this marvellous harmony of evidence, a sure guarantee against error?

Do you fear lest the Church be no longer able to live in the future upon the same foundations that have supported it during a past of eighteen centuries?

Why, then, do you speak of the necessity of making in the Council a new definition concerning the rule of faith, and establishing dogmatically a new rule of faith? What! Is it in our century that the necessity has arisen of putting this in question, of meddling with this fundamental principle, this mainspring of the Church's life? Have we been constituted for so many centuries, then, in a defective and incomplete manner?

After eighteen hundred and seventy years of teaching, must we ask ourselves, in Council, who has the right to teach infallibly? And that in the face of the unbelieving and Protestant world that is watching us! No; let us drop these questions, for which there is no call. Let not these foolhardy editors go on prematurely to stun and bewilder the good sense of the faithful by violent controversies, that have the semblance of wishing to force these questions beforehand upon the bishops. As for myself, Gentlemen, my opinion, with deference to my venerated colleagues, is fixed on this point. When the oak counts twenty centuries over its head, to dig down under its roots in quest of the original acorn is to unsettle the entire tree!

III. But are there not, Gentlemen, decisive precedents for this question of opportuneness that engages our attention? I shall first recall to mind the wise conduct of the Council of Trent and Pope Pius IV.

In the times of the Council of Trent, the question that agitated the public so intensely, and was even on the point of causing the dissolution of the Council, was, in substance, though in another form—for questions never present themselves twice in precisely the same form—the very one that we are handling at present.

How shall we forget the prudence with which the Holy See warded off the danger of those controversies by putting an end to the debate?

Pius IV., seeing, at last, how excited the public mind was, wrote to his legates, ordering them to withdraw the subject from debate, and declared that nothing must be discussed that could provoke wrangling or dissension among the bishops. He laid down this wise rule, that nothing should be decided but by their unanimous consent: *Ne definirentur, nisi ea, de quibus inter Patres unanimi consensione constaret.**

The Council saw that it had something else to do, in the presence of the errors of the times, besides setting up as dogmas opinions, however respectable they might be, that were the subjects of controversy among the doctors, something better than denouncing Catholic theologians. And the discussion was laid aside, without detriment to the Church.

I well remember, and more than one bishop present at Rome in 1867 can remember, that one of the chief cares of Pius IX.,

---

* See Pallavicini, Book XIX., chap. xv., and elsewhere.

before deciding upon convening the Council of the Vatican, was lest some question should come up of a kind to provoke wrangling and dissension in the episcopate. But the Pope remembered the prudent conduct of the Council of Trent and Pope Pius IV., and, hoping that it would not be forgotten in the future Council, he kept on.

Are we to suppose that, for starting and deciding so delicate a matter as that of the dogmatic definition already announced, our times are more favorable than those of the Council of Trent, and that we live in an age of livelier faith and more general submission to the Church?

Another precedent of wisdom and moderation must be recalled here—the conduct of Pope Innocent XI. toward Bossuet. When Bossuet wrote his *Exposition of Catholic Doctrine*, after having firmly established, in the matter of the authority of the Holy See, the primacy of divine right, the primacy of honor and jurisdiction of Saint Peter and the Popes, his successors, he expressly and purposely passed over, in silence, the question of papal infallibility.

"Concerning those things which, it is known, are disputed in the schools, although the [Protestant] ministers do not cease alleging them *in order to render that power odious*, it is not necessary to speak of them here, since they are not *a part of the Catholic faith.*"

Did this deliberate and intentional silence upon the subject of papal infallibility prevent Innocent XI. from approving the work? Far from it; for that holy Pope addressed to Bossuet two briefs, in which *he congratulated him on having written the book in a manner and with a wisdom eminently adapted for recalling heretics to the way of salvation, and procuring the Church the greatest facilities for the propagation of the orthodox faith.*

Bossuet, moreover, in carefully avoiding, in the wisely-expressed spirit of Innocent XI., the point in controversy, has only imitated the Catechism of the Council of Trent. I have read and re-read this grand Catechism, composed by order of the holy Council and the Sovereign Pontiffs, by the most celebrated Roman theologians; I have read it with the express purpose of finding out whether it had anything to say either for or against the infallibility of the Pope, and I have ascertained that it does not say a single word about it. Neither is the subject included in the solemn profession of faith prepared by order of Pius IV., and inserted in the Roman pontifical.

Finally, why should we not cite in this place the example of the venerated Pius IX. himself? We know that two years ago, in 1867, one hundred and eighty-eight Anglican ministers wrote to him expressing their willingness, and inquiring of him the possible terms of union. What did the Holy Father do? In an answer full of charity and wisdom, he spoke of the authority of the Church, he spoke of the supremacy of the Pope; but he did not speak of his infallibility.

At a time, then, when the Holy Father, in the inspiration of his noble and peace-loving heart, sets such an example of moderation and wisdom, do journalists, sheltering themselves behind the venerated name that they desecrate in such contests, undertake, by dint of sweeping assertions, to bear down upon public opinion, while, with the same operation, as if they wished to intimidate and silence the bishops, they hold suspended over their heads insults and attacks full of violence and gall.

I can say to them: You know neither Pius IX. nor the episcopate.

IV. We have just spoken of our brethren of the seceded communions. Truly, it is by placing ourselves at their point of view that the question of defining the personal infallibility of the Pope becomes especially grave and dangerous.

Think of it: there are seventy-five millions of detached Oriental Christians; there are nearly ninety millions of Protestants of different shades of belief.

Assuredly, if the Church has one supreme interest, if all truly Catholic hearts have one ardent wish, it is the return of so many brethren sprung from the same mother, but to-day estranged from us. That is the great cause, for which we should all be ready to give our blood, and should tremble at the bare thought of aught that might put it in jeopardy. Hence what pressing invitations from the Holy Father to the Oriental Churches! What an appeal to the Protestant communions!

Well! what separates the Orientals from us? The supremacy of the Pope. They are not willing to recognize it as of divine right. That is the point upon which it has never been possible, either after Lyons or Florence, to bring them to an earnest, effectual decision, and to bring about a permanent return.

And now, to this difficulty, insurmountable up to this day, which has kept them for nine centuries aloof from the Church and from us, it is proposed to add a new and much greater obstacle, to raise up between them and us a barrier that has never existed— in a word, to force upon them a new dogma that has never been spoken of to them, and threaten them, if they do not accept it, with a fresh anathema!

For it is not merely the primacy of jurisdiction that they will have to acknowledge, but the personal infallibility of the Pope, "WITHOUT AND INDEPENDENTLY OF THE EPISCOPAL BODY."*

Could there be, I demand—and here I merely repeat what good sense has suggested already to every one who has been willing to consider the matter—could there be, toward the separated Oriental churches, anything more contradictory than such conduct, less persuasive than such language? "We invite you to profit by the great occasion of the Œcumenical Council, to come to an explanation and understanding with us. But take notice, in advance, what we are going to do—build up a new wall of separation, a new and higher barrier between you and us. Now, a moat separates us; we are going to make it a great gulf. You have refused hitherto to recognize the simple primacy of the Roman pontiff; we are going to force you to believe, as the first step, something very different, and to admit what, up to this time, some of our Catholic doctors themselves have not admitted; we are going to set up as a dogma a doctrine much more obscure for you, in Scripture and in Tradition, than the dogma which you have already rejected—to wit, the personal infallibility of the

* Archbishop Manning.

Pope, alone, '*independent of and apart from the bishops.*' Those are the conditions under which we offer to treat with you."

Would not such speech be a mockery? Would it not also be a misfortune? Inviting and repelling at the same time!

These considerations must be still more striking if we reflect upon the intellectual attitude of the schismatic Christians of the East. When we treat with men we must really know how they stand. Now, upon this point, what is the position of our estranged brethren?

They have remained precisely where they were in the time of the schism, that is, in the ninth century. They have not gone forward one step since then. They have no knowledge of the controversies that have been raised upon this subject in the Western Church. They have not read Bossuet, nor Bellarmin, nor Melchior Cano. And whatever personal conviction we may have as to the infallibility of the Roman pontiff, we must admit that the ninth century was far from ready for the definition of such a dogma. In fact, up to that time, the Councils were the great manifestation of Church life; they were continually meeting; all the great dogmatic definitions had been made in Council. The Greeks, then, are in no respect prepared for the definition that people would have forced upon them by the Council of the Vatican. It is my profound conviction, that one of the certain, inevitable results of such a definition would be to postpone to the distant future the reunion of the Oriental Churches. Such a consideration will not seem trifling to any one who knows the value of souls.

A recent circumstance will show whether the fear that we express here is without foundation: it is the response given to the envoy of the Sovereign Pontiff by the Vicar General of the schismatic Patriarch of Constantinople. Among the reasons assigned by him for declining the invitation sent from Rome, occurs this one: "That the Greek Church cannot recognize the infallibility of the Pope, and his superiority over Œcumenical Councils."*

* The *Civiltà Cattolica*, "Chronicle of the Council." Quoted by the Bishop of Grenoble.

The Armenian schismatics use the same language, and I have had before my eyes an Armenian journal, which pretends that if Rome invites them to the Council, it is "to force upon them the infallibility of the Pope."

Perhaps it will be said: Why, what are you so anxious about? The schismatics do not desire any reunion. What matters an additional barrier between them and us? For my part, I am far from thus losing hope, and, though ignorant of God's designs for the nations, I do not believe that I have any right thus to seal the tomb of these ancient Christian nations, especially when I consider that in this tomb, beneath this Oriental soil, are reposing such ashes as those of Athanasius, Cyril, Gregory, Chrysostom, mingled with those of Paul, Anthony, Hilarion, Pachomius, and so many other saints illustrious forever.

Even were it so to be, even were neither the breath of God nor any human effort destined to recall these ancient people of the East from the error in which they are lost, even then I could not believe that it was in accordance with the charity of Jesus Christ and the mission of a great Council, to alienate them still farther, and render their return more difficult.

I have often had the good fortune to confer at length upon the welfare of these ancient Churches with the Eastern bishops whom I have chanced to meet at Rome, in our great gatherings; and, besides, an active private correspondence with several of them has enabled me to become somewhat acquainted with the state of affairs.

What I have learned from them is this: That there is a great desire for reconciliation. Yes; in this dull, lethargic East there are many souls aroused by these aspirations. And at the same time they are keenly sensitive for the slightest details of their ancient customs: how much more so, then, for anything that enters into the great dogmatic questions!

Assuredly, the Council of Trent pursued a very different course, and showed a considerateness toward the Oriental Churches far more worthy of the Church of Jesus Christ, and that too in a question of vital importance. Every theologian knows how, at the request of the Venetian ambassadors, the famous canon beginning, *Si quis dixerit Ecclesiam* ERRARE, a masterpiece of charity and theological prudence, was moderated so as to uphold the truth, and at the same time to spare the Oriental Christians.

V. The question is still more delicate in its bearings upon Protestantism. For the Eastern schism admits at least the authority of the Œcumenical Councils—those that it regards as such—and the authority of the Church, of which it is persuaded that it forms a part, whereas Protestantism does not admit this authority. Upon this precise and decisive point—the authority of the Church—turns the great controversy between them and us. Protestantism is, more than anything else, the negation of the authority of the Church. In this principle of division consists its essence, its deadly plague. And this, many of our alienated brethren are beginning to get a notion of. They feel that a principle which allows of division to infinity, which admits that one may continue to be a Protestant after he has ceased to be a Christian, cannot be the true Christian principle. Hence this labor in the womb of Protestantism, these grand and cheering conversions, of which especially England and America afford us the spectacle, and these longings after union which exist, I know, in the heart of so many Protestants.

Which one among us does not sympathize with this labor and these sufferings of so many souls? Who does not invite them lovingly? Who does not pray with them? For they are praying—I know it myself—for this great, supreme interest, the union of the Christian Churches. "There are," said no less a one than Dr. Pusey, to me, at Orleans, two years ago, "there are eight thousand of us in England, that pray every day for union."

Ah! If this reconciliation so much desired could at last be brought about! If England, above all, great England, might some day come back to us! Of all the reconciliations that the world has seen, this, assuredly, would be the happiest and yield the richest fruits. I said in my book upon the *Papal Sovereignty*, which was written, as I might say, under the fire of the struggles for the Holy See, I said confidently to such of the English as are masters of themselves and their prejudices: You have been, for three centuries, the most formidable enemies of unity: what an honor it would be for you to restore unity in Europe! How befitting it would be for your hands to upraise the standard of Christian Catholicity—for your vessels to bear it over the seas to all the countries that you visit! Happy they to whom it shall be given to see those better times, perhaps not far distant!

Well! the Council has revived these hopes among a great number of our alienated brethren and among ourselves. Ah! no doubt we must fear that they will not all be realized. But partial conversions, at least, may be witnessed, and in great numbers; above all, a powerful impulse may be given. Time, with the grace of God, would accomplish the rest.

May the Council at least, for those to whom the Holy Father but recently addressed that pressing appeal, not prove the hardest stumbling-block!

No longer talk, then, of first enjoining upon them, as the condition of their return, the personal and separate infallibility of the Pope! For this would be to forget all prudence, as well as all charity.

The new Catholics, I have heard said, are full of fervor for this dogma. Yes; certain new Catholics, perhaps. But I myself know other converts, who have been troubled by the announcement of a definition. I know certain Protestants, desirous of coming to us, whom this alone deters. I know some, whom this definition would absolutely repel.

It seems to me that one must be very little or very poorly informed as to the present disposition of our alienated brethren, not to see that thereby we should inevitably raise up a fresh barrier—an ever-insuperable one, perhaps—between them and us.

Wait, then! I would say to the impatient: schisms and heresies do not last forever. The Church has waited comfortably for eighteen centuries without this definition, and the truth, kept by her, has been well kept.

VI. There are still other perils, of another sort, which are also very grave. We must take into account the consequences that such an act might have from the point of view of modern governments; there is an expediency in this, or rather a wisdom, from which the Church may not depart. I know that many of the bishops, even the most courageous, are anxious on this point.

And truly, not without cause; for there are serious reasons for fearing, even from this point of view, that the possible disadvantages of the definition of infallibility may be very great.

Let us look at the facts; let us examine the true condition of Europe.

Out of the five great European powers, three are not Catholic—Russia, Prussia, and England. I do not speak here of America and the United States. And among the second-rate states of Europe, a large number, again, are in heresy and schism—Saxony, Sweden, Denmark, Switzerland, Holland, Greece. Who is ignorant of the grudges that all these governments still cherish against the Church? Now I merely put the following grave question: Do you believe that defining the personal infallibility of the Pope is calculated to remove these grudges? When, by reason of an inveterate prejudice, that is not to be destroyed by aggravating it, these governments regard the Pope as a foreign sovereign, do you think, in good earnest, that declaring the Pope infallible is going to ameliorate the position of Catholics in all these countries? Is it to be believed that Russia, Sweden, Denmark, will become milder toward their Catholic subjects? Will their hatred of Rome be appeased, and their reconciliation made easier?

If any one is tempted to treat lightly, as mere chimeras, these apprehensions as to the disposition of non-Catholic governments, I shall merely recite in this place facts of our own age. Why, then, were the Catholic archbishops and bishops of Ireland, and those of England and Scotland, obliged, in 1826, to sign the two declarations that I now have before me?

In one of them, the Catholic archbishops and bishops of England and Scotland, confronted with this charge—The Catholics are accused of dividing their allegiance between their temporal sovereign and the Pope—reply to it at length. In the other, the Catholic archbishops and bishops of Ireland are forced to go to the length of protesting that they do not believe " that it is lawful to kill any person whatever, under pretext of his being a heretic"—an exaggerated, yet palpable and permanent reminiscence of the bulls launched against Henry VIII.; and furthermore—be this especially noted—" that they are not required to believe that the Pope is infallible."

Cry out as much as you like against the injustice of this mistrust and these imputations—such solemn declarations forced upon the episcopate of a great country are a sufficient proof of their power. I have read that declaration of the Irish bishops, I must confess, with a flushed face. What must they not have suffered in having to repel, even in finding still alive in their country, such suspicions, impugning everything most sacred in conscience, everything most delicate in honor!

Do you wish for other proofs? You know the atrocious laws which were so long suspended over the heads of the Catholics of England and Ireland, and which it has been so hard to abolish. Well, when the famous Pitt, at the close of the last century, as an act of policy that I am willing to believe was one of generosity also, thought for the first time of delivering the Catholics from this yoke, what troubled or abruptly checked the English statesman? The papal power, old memories of the quarrels between the popes and the crowned heads. Therefore it was that he wished to know, above all, what were the Catholic teachings upon this point, and, with this object, he applied to the most learned universities of France, Belgium, Spain, and Germany.

I have before me the responses of the universities of Paris, Douay, Louvain, Alcala, Salamanca, Valladolid. Looking at the question as a question of divine law, and consequently passing over what may have been the international law of another age, they all reply in so many words, that neither the Pope, nor the cardinals, nor any body nor individual in the Romish Church, have any civil authority from Jesus Christ over England, any power to release the subjects of His Britannic Majesty from their oath of allegiance.

This doctrine, then professed by the greatest universities of the Catholic Church, might suffice to relieve Pitt's apprehensions as to the opposite doctrine, which, we are forced to admit, is professed in famous bulls by more than one Pope. But suppose the Pope is declared infallible; will not this dogmatic definition of the Pope's infallibility be apt to revive former mistrust? Certainly it is to be dreaded, and for the following reason.

The non-Catholic governments, as a matter of fact, are not going to believe in this infallibility; and this immense power having been conceded to the Pope as a matter of dogma, the Pope, in their judgment, may abuse it or exceed its limits. But— a weighty matter in their view—their Catholic subjects will believe in it, and will be obliged to submit to all its decisions, even those that are, in the opinion of these governments, the most injurious. How, then, can we fail to see that from that moment the papal power will appear to them far more formidable and odious? They already have, they still cherish this sullen mistrust of the Church with which every one is familiar; how much more will they suspect the infallible Pope, a single man, who, in their view, will afford them far less guaranty than the Church, that is to say, the bishops of their country and all countries!

VII. And the governments of the Catholic nations themselves, how will they look upon the proclamation of the new dogma? We must ask ourselves this also. For, after all, the governments will not consider themselves as having no interest in the question. Who will persuade them that it does not concern them?

Here again, in order to estimate calmly and accurately the consequences of the dogmatic definition announced and demanded so clamorously by journalists—verily, it is high time that they should desist from meddling in the most private, grave, exclusive affairs of the Church—let us come down to the reality of things, to facts; let us see what is, and what will be.

The great fact, deplorable yet incontrovertible, and never so settled a fact as it is to-day, is this: the governments, even of

Catholic countries, are full of ill-feeling toward the Church. All history proclaims this; for history is full of the conflicts between the two powers.

But why speak of the past? In the very hour that I write these lines, are not three of the four great Catholic powers of Europe—Austria, Italy, and Spain—more or less involved in deplorable contests with the Church? And even among ourselves, may not difficulty spring up at any moment? And would not even this word be too mild for the terrible eventualities of such a possible revolution?

That is the situation; the Catholic governments have been, are, or are liable to be involved more and more in conflict with the Church.

Assuredly, no one deplores more than I do these formidable conflicts, when they arrive; and, however little relish I may have for such contests, perhaps I have already shown—you will pardon my alluding to it—that I am not one of those who shrink back from them and grow faint! But that is not the question; and whether the governments are to blame, or not to blame, that is not the question either. The question is, how will the governments, to-day, regard the declaration of papal infallibility?

Is this a timorous anxiety? Ought the Church, in its Councils, consulting only the principles of its complete independence, so far as human governments are concerned, to act, decree, define, even in the most delicate practical questions, as though the governments did not exist, and without having the least care as to whether its actions would or would not wound them to the quick?

Such is not, such never was, in matters not of necessity, the custom of the Holy Church.

Ah! if, at one stroke, by a simple dogmatic proclamation, we could cut short conflicts, efface inveterate mistrust, and, by a mere decree, render the governments of the Catholic nations obedient to the Church and the Pope, like sheep, that would be worth the while!

But to flatter one's self with such an idea, especially at the present day, would be the most chimerical of illusions.

Can any one doubt that a dogmatic definition of the personal infallibility of the Pope, far from suppressing old mistrust, would only revive the causes, or, if you will, the eternal pretexts of it, by giving them additional plausibility?

In fact, what are these pretexts? Assuredly, I make no pretence here of justifying the governments; always and everywhere almost they have wanted to oppress the Church. But we must look at men and things as they are.

In the first place, there are the memories of the past.

By declaring the Pope infallible, the sovereigns may ask, do you declare him impeccable? No. The sought-for declaration not being at liberty to add to or take away from what is, and what has been, that which has been witnessed once may be witnessed again. Now, we have seen, it must be said respectfully and sadly, but it must be said—for history constrains us, and Baronius himself, the great historiographer of the Roman Church, teaches us that in matters of history we must not garble the truth*—we have seen, in that long and incomparable series of Roman pontiffs, some Popes, a small number it is true, but still a certain number of Popes, who have shown themselves weak, or ambitious, or grasping—Popes that have confounded spiritual things with temporal, pretenders to dominion over crowned heads. There is no certainty that in all the ages to come we shall have a Pius IX. on the Papal throne.

Is it not natural to suppose, if the Pope is proclaimed infallible, that these reflections will suggest themselves, of their own accord, to the existing governments? And is it not useless—I will add, is it not very dangerous, even to revive such memories? Assuredly, I am not the one that is reviving them! But why do imprudent advocates of the Papacy take upon themselves every day the pitiful mission of reviving and embittering them?

Moreover, people will ask upon what objects this personal infallibility is to be exercised. If it is to be only on mixed matters, in which the conflicts have ever been frequent, what are the

---

* We need only read in his *Annals*, the history of the tenth century, to be satisfied that he does no garbling himself.

limits of these? Who is to determine them? Does not the spiritual come in contact with the temporal on every side? Who will persuade the governments that the Pope will never, in any moment of excitement, pass over from the spiritual to the temporal? Will not the proclamation of the new dogma seem—not to skilled theologians, but to governments that are not theologians—to establish in the Pope, in matters scarcely defined, and often scarcely definable, an unlimited, sovereign power over all their Catholic subjects, a power all the more subject to mistrust on the part of the governments, because it will seem to them constantly liable to abuse?

And then, people will begin to think of the doctrines formulated, if not defined, in many celebrated Bulls.

Assuredly, I have not the least desire to defend, in this place, Philip the Fair and his imitators. But, after all, in the Bull *Unam sanctam*, for instance, does not Boniface VIII. declare that there are two swords, the spiritual and the temporal; that the second, as well as the first, belongs to Saint Peter, and that the successor of Peter has the right to appoint and to judge kings: *Potestas spiritualis terrenam potestatem instituere habet et judicare?*

And in the Bull *Ausculta fili*, he requests the king to send to Rome the archbishops and bishops of France, together with the abbots, &c., *to treat there of all that might seem useful for the good government of the kingdom of France.*

And even after Protestantism had arisen to change so radically the condition of Europe, did not Paul III., in the famous Bull that excommunicated Henry VIII., absolve from their oath of allegiance all the subjects of the king of England, and offer England to whoever should conquer it, promising to the conquerors all the property, real and personal, of the Protestant English?

Do you suppose they have forgotten that Bull in England? The declarations, of which I cited a few words to you just now, do you think that they were not demanded of the Catholic bishops of Ireland because of the still lively remembrance of that

Bull? Shall I be permitted to speak out my whole mind on this point, and ask, in accordance with history: Was not that terrible Bull, at the period in which it was published, calculated to drive off rather than to recall the English nation? Is it altogether certain that it was not a great misfortune for Christendom? In any case, I should not, by so thinking, contradict any Catholic dogma, not even that of Papal infallibility, if it should ever be erected into a dogma.

I am sad—and who would not be?—in calling to mind these great and painful facts of history; but they force us to it, these persons whose foolhardy flippancy is stirring up such burning questions. They force us to it, and it is my profound conviction that all this plunges the best minds into deplorable agitation, and that, had people undertaken to render the Papal power odious, they could not do a better thing than to perpetuate such controversies.

For, after all, will not sovereigns, even Catholic sovereigns, ask themselves: Will the dogmatic proclamation of Papal infallibility, or will it not, render such Bulls impossible in the future? What, then, is to prevent a new Pope from announcing that as a definition which has been taught by several of his predecessors, that the Vicar of Jesus Christ has a *direct* power over the temporal affairs of princes; that it is one of his attributes to institute and to depose sovereigns; that the civil rights of kings and peoples are subject to him?

Then, after this new dogma shall have been proclaimed, no priest, no bishop, no Catholic, will be able to disavow this doctrine, so odious to governments; that, in their view, all civil and political rights, as well as all religious beliefs, are placed in the hands of a single man!

And perhaps you think that governments would look on with indifference to see the Church gathering together from all quarters of the earth to proclaim a doctrine which, in their estimation, might have such consequences!

And they will be all the more induced to consider the definition of the Pope's infallibility as an implied consecration of these dreaded doctrines, seeing that these doctrines are far from being abandoned. The journals that give themselves out among us for the pure representatives of Roman principles, unceasingly parade these doctrines in their columns, establish them with a great array of arguments, and even venture to brand, as tainted with atheism, the doctrine to which both Catholic and non-Catholic sovereigns adhere so firmly—that of the independence of the two powers, each in its own sphere.

But a little while ago, we read in a French journal the following words, quoted with approbation, wherein those who maintain that the two swords are not in the same hand are compared to the Manichees:

"Can it be, then, that there are two sources of authority and power, two supreme aims for the members of one and the same society, two different objects in the mind of the divine organizer, and two distinct doctrines for one and the same man who is both a member of the Church and a subject of the State? But who does not see at once the absurdity of such a system? It is the dualism of the Manichees, if it is not atheism."

That is also what the Abbé de Lamennais claimed in the extravagances of his logic; and he set up against the first of the four articles this dilemma: *ultramontane or atheist.* These extravagances of his have met with but little success. And, to all intents, the writers in question belong, in this respect, to the school of Lamennais. But the more they reproach governments with not admitting the doctrine of the Bull *Unam sanctam*, and with holding fast to the independence of the two powers, the more they themselves will demonstrate the strength of the repugnances and the universality of the alienations that I dread.

And when I speak of the independence of the two powers, far be it from me to throw a moment's doubt upon the divine and sure authority of the Church to define, to proclaim, and to reiterate, both to government and to subject, the sacred and eternal laws of right and wrong. But everybody understands, and it is perfectly obvious, that that is not the question.

No; this old irritability is not on the point of disappearing;

passionate journalism has done all it could to revive it; and we can affirm with certainty that nowhere, either in France, or in Catholic Austria, or in Bavaria, or on the borders of the Rhine, or in apostolic Spain, or in that Portugal which but lately expelled the Sisters of Charity, is the disposition of European governments favorable to the proclamation of the proposed dogma.

Does it seem to you, then, that the hour has come for arousing animosities against the Holy See from one end of Europe to the other?

Or, rather, is not the present hour already replete with dangers sufficiently numerous and sufficiently great?

Do you wish to make the separation of Church and State the order of the day throughout all Europe?

Do you wish to force the Council into still other hazards? How little it would take, in the present state of Italy and of Europe, to bring about the greatest misfortunes!

We cannot shut our eyes to the facts; there are certain spirits who are bent upon driving the Church to the last extremity.

In what interest?

VIII. I have now come to the theological difficulties, not exactly of papal infallibility itself—this question, let me repeat, I am not discussing one way or the other—but to the theological difficulties of defining it; for these difficulties, if really serious, are an additional and a strong argument against its opportuneness.

Are the journalists who seem disposed to enjoin it on the Council to define Papal infallibility, and to define it by acclamation, aware of the conditions under which the Council would have to make this definition? Really, one would not say so, to see the manner in which they speak of it;—as if they had no idea how strange, how monstrously abnormal, how utterly impossible is the part they are laying out for themselves, especially for the last six months, meddling to the extent that they do with the most sacred matters in the government of the Church.

I am not surprised, moreover, at their extraordinary imprudence. They are no theologians. You, Gentlemen, are acquainted with all the questions that I am going to remind you of; you have been taught them in our schools. But at the same time that you are taught them, you are also taught not to discourse upon them needlessly to the faithful. As priests, you have a double duty—to study things that are obscure, to preach only things that are clear. As to the laity, let me repeat, I do not blame them for being ignorant, but I do blame them for agitating and deciding questions of which they are ignorant. They know not what difficulties they are running against foolhardily, and it becomes my unpleasant duty to give them warning, by reminding you, Gentlemen, of what you know already.

" In so *grave*, so *delicate*, so *complicated* a matter," thus, with excellent judgment, speaks his Grace the Bishop of Poitiers, " we should not suffer ourselves to be governed either by enthusiasm or by personal feeling: every word should be weighed and explained, every phase of the question examined, every case foreseen, every false application eliminated, all the disadvantages weighed against the advantages."

Moreover, the Bishop of Poitiers is not the only one that speaks thus. Among theologians, the greatest partisans themselves of infallibility admit the prodigious practical difficulties that may be encountered. The difficulties, they say, are inextricable, *intricatissimæ difficultates;* and the ablest men, they say, have the utmost difficulty in getting out of them—*in quibus dissolvendis multum theologi peritiores laborant.*

1. Difficulties arising from the necessity of defining the conditions of the act *ex cathedra*—not all the pontifical acts having that character.

2. Difficulties arising from the twofold character of the Pope, considered either as a private teacher or as a Pope.

3. Difficulties arising from the manifold questions of fact that may be raised with regard to every act *ex cathedra.*

4. Difficulties caused by the past and by historic facts.

5. Difficulties arising from the very essence of the question.

3. Difficulties, finally, arising from the state of contemporary minds.

The first thing, then, for the Council to do, before laying down a dogmatic definition, would be to determine the conditions of infallibility; for to define the infallibility of the Pope, without settling and defining the conditions of that infallibility, would be to define nothing, since it would be either defining too much or not defining enough.

How are these conditions to be determined? Theologians are at issue on this matter, whether theoretically, in the abstract, or practically, in the concrete. In a word, when and how is the Pope infallible? That is what must be determined. Yet on this point the difficulties are anything but trifling.

Is the Pope infallible whenever he speaks? Some theologians have maintained this. Or is he only infallible when he speaks, as they say, *ex cathedra?*

Now it is precisely in defining the conditions of utterance *ex cathedra* that the Council, should it see fit to take up this matter, would find plenty of study, and plenty of work.

What, in fact, is an utterance *ex cathedra?* What are its conditions? This point is discussed in all the schools; some require more, others less. Cardinal Orsi does not speak exactly like Cardinal Bellarmin, nor Bellarmin like Capellari, who was afterward Pope Gregory XVI.

Mansi speaks either of "Councils previously assembled," or of "doctors convoked," or of "Congregations appointed," and of "public supplications." "*Without these,*" he says, "*let Bossuet be indeed assured that we no longer recognize the Pope as infallible.*"*

Bellarmin endeavors to reconcile those who say, *Pontifex consilium audiat aliorum pastorum*—let the Pope listen to the counsel of other pastors—with those who say that he can define of himself alone, *etiam solus.*†

Well! in the presence of all these differences of opinion, and I cite here only a few of them—since a much larger number is estimated, even among the ultramontane theologians—how shall the Council act? Approving some, disapproving others, it must undertake the hard task of making choice in a dogmatic and

---

* De Maistre, *Du Pape*, liv. I. ch. x. 5. † *Disputationes Bellarmini.*

absolute manner among all these theological opinions. But upon what sure, clear, and indisputable grounds will it rely in doing that?

Once more, what, precisely, is an act *ex cathedra?*

Is it a simple brief? Some say yes; others, no. Is it a rescript? Is it a bull, a consistorial allocution, an encyclical?

Must the Pope, in an act *ex cathedra*, address himself to the entire Church? The greater number say yes. No, says an Englishman, a lay professor of theology* and a contemporary journalist: even though the Pope should have spoken to only a single bishop, even to a single lay brother, he may have wished to teach *ex cathedra*. And that is sufficient.

Well, then, is it necessary, as some claim, to avoid all doubt as to his intention, that the Pope should define the doctrine under penalty of anathema against error?

Or is it enough, as others pretend, that he should express, in any manner whatever, his intention of making a dogma?

Or, indeed—and this is maintained by the lay theologian whom I have just cited—can he speak *ex cathedra*, even though he should not distinctly express his intention of commanding assent? *Etiamsi obligatio assensum præstandi non diserte exprimatur.*†

Or, as others claim, must the Pope take counsel? And, if so, whom must he consult? Some of the bishops? Or, in the absence of bishops, the cardinals? Or, in the absence of cardinals, the Roman congregations? Or, in the absence of the congregations, some of the theologians, or of the doctors; and if so, how many? Would it be enough for him to prepare a decree alone in his closet? Why make any distinction, say some, when the words of promise make none?

Moreover, here is another contemporary theologian, the German, Phillips, who does not stop at this difficulty. According to him, a definition *ex cathedra* does not require that the Pope should have consulted any one whatever, either the Council, or the

---

* Mr. Ward, De Infallibilitatis extensione, thesis duodecima, p. 35. Mr. Ward is a converted Anglican minister, now a zealous Catholic, who, although a layman, has been professor of theology in the Grand Seminary of the Archdiocese of Westminster.

† Mr. Ward, *Thesis duodecima.*

Roman Church, or the College of Cardinals. The German doctor goes still farther; according to him, it is not necessary that the Pope *should give the definition any ripe consideration;*

Or that he should study the question carefully, by the light of the word of God, written and traditional;

Or that he should pray to God, before pronouncing.

Without any of these conditions, his decision would be not less valid, not less effective, not less obligatory upon all the Church, than if he had observed all the precautions dictated by faith, piety, and good sense.

What, then, is needed, according to this doctor, in order that a definition should be *ex cathedra?* This: "It remains to be said, after the above, in order to defend the validity of a decision *ex cathedra,* that it exists whenever the Pope, in Council or out of Council, VERBALLY or *by writing,* pronounces to all faithful Christians, as Vicar of Jesus Christ, in the name of the apostles Peter and Paul, or by virtue of the authority of the Holy See, *or in similar terms, with* or *without* the threat of anathema, a decision concerning dogma or morals."

According to this theologian, the Church has not the right to lay down any restriction, any condition whatever, touching the validity or the exercise of infallibility.

A French writer, the author of a recent treatise, *De Papa,* says essentially the same thing, and claims, for the infallibility of the Pope speaking to the Church universal, only one condition—not that he should have prayed, not that he should have deliberated, studied, taken counsel, but simply that he should have had the intention of making a dogma, and that he should have been free from all constraint.

Mr. Ward, as we have seen, does not even claim that the Pope should address the Church; if he addresses a single bishop, a single lay member, that is sufficient.

You see, then, how some do not hesitate, to-day, to treat these immense questions.

I say *some,* and I beg you to note this word; for I would not have all the most radical theories set down, contrary to my intention, to the account of Catholic theology.

APPENDIX. 323

Well! will the Council, in view of all these opinions, declare that there is a necessary form in which the Pope *shall be obliged* to exercise his infallibility? Or would the form go for nothing, and the Pope be infallible when and how he should see fit, without having prayed, or studied, or taken counsel, merely addressing himself to the first-comer?

And since determining the circumstances under which the Pope is infallible is also determining those in which he is not, there will then be two dogmas to define, instead of one—the dogma of infallibility, and the dogma of fallibility. It will be declared, as a matter of faith, that the Pope is infallible under such and such conditions, but that without them he is fallible.

And how, I repeat, shall we set about fixing these limits? Where are they clearly laid down in the Scriptures? Where, in the teachings of the theologians, so diverse and so contradictory on this point? What opinions are we going to establish as dogmas, what as heresies?

And if this is not done, into what *terra incognita* are we going to precipitate the Church?

IX. But this is not all. Besides the question of *law*, there will also be the question of *fact*. Who shall decide, as a matter of fact, whether such or such a decision of the Pope fulfils all the conditions of a decree *ex cathedra?* Will this always be easy to ascertain? No.

The most advanced partisans of Papal infallibility acknowledge this in good faith. The English theologian, Ward, for instance, says expressly: " Inasmuch as all Papal allocutions, all apostolical letters, even all encyclical letters, do not contain definitions *ex cathedra*, they *must be closely examined in order to ascertain in a satisfactory manner* which of them are acts in which the Sovereign Pontiff may be said to speak *ex cathedra;* and we must examine closely even the acts *ex cathedra* themselves, to ascertain clearly what he teaches *ex cathedra*," that is, infallibly.*

---

* " Circa has igitur allocutiones et litteras apostolicas adlaborandum est, ut satis dignoscatur in quibusnam earum Pontifex ex cathedra loqui, et quidnam ex cathedra docere, jure censeatur."

And this discrimination is often so difficult, even for theologians, that Mr. Ward acknowledges, with a modesty that does him honor, that he committed and obstinately persisted in a grave error concerning the nature of the pontifical acts of various kinds, denouncing the propositions designated subsequently in a recent communication emanating from Rome. He had thought, and had maintained, that each one of the acts that supplied the propositions for the collection called *the Syllabus*, should be regarded, on the strength of that alone, as having the character of an act *ex cathedra*. This, he now admits frankly, was a great error.

Ecclesiastical history, moreover, is full of similar instances. We have only to remember certain important acts of the Popes in the past, about which theologians have disputed so much, and still dispute, as to whether they are or are not *ex cathedra*.

When Pope Stephen condemned Saint Cyprian in the matter of the baptism of heretics, did he speak *ex cathedra?*

Some affirm it, others deny it.

When Pope Honorius, consulted upon the question of monothelism by Sergius, Patriarch of Constantinople, and other Eastern bishops, wrote those famous letters which gave rise to so many debates, did he speak *ex cathedra?* Theologians have had keen disputes on that also.

Who, then, shall decide? The Church. It will often be necessary, then, to resort, after all, to the Church.

And indeed, besides the two questions of fact about which Mr. Ward speaks, and which must be broached with regard to every act *ex cathedra*—Is the act one *ex cathedra?*—And if it is, what are its bearings?—there is still another, not so simple in practice as one might at first suppose. It is this:

May there not arise, in course of time, a Pope, concerning whose liberty there will be reasonable doubts?

The most zealous are forced to acknowledge this, and to admit, in view of history, that a Pope may, under the influence of *fear*, define error.

That makes, then, under certain circumstances, a third question of fact to be established—the full and entire liberty of the Pope.

Is there not a fourth? For if a Pope, even one declared infallible, might, even in an act *ex cathedra*, err through intimidation and fear, could he not err from excitement, passion, *imprudence?* The partisans of infallibility say not. God, they say, will not work a miracle in the first case, to prevent a weak Pope from yielding to fear; but he always will in the second, to prevent a passionate or rash Pope from erring by reason of imprudence; and that, some of them add, even although the Pope should not have taken any of those precautions commonly taken in serious affairs. According to them, a Pope can define error through weakness; not otherwise.

That is the explanation given by these theologians. But I submit this question: Will it always be easy to estimate the constraint to which a Pope may have been subjected? No. There may arise cases in which such a determination would be a matter of the greatest delicacy; and " every case should be anticipated."

Also, " every phase of the question examined."

Do you think that the solution of all these difficulties will be a slight undertaking for the Council? And these newspaper writers, who talk so glibly about it, because its difficulties do not make them much trouble—they do not even see them—are they authorized to lay their orders on the Bishops, as they do, to undertake this business?

X. It is easy to say that the question is already decided; but real, sound theologians know that, in fact, it is no such thing, and that if the Council is to proceed in this matter with that deliberation and gravity in which these holy assemblies of the Church have never failed whenever the question has been on the proclamation of dogmas, that its discussions may be long and laborious.

Is tradition, whatever may be its testimony, unanimous on this point? Is history free from embarrassment? It is in this direction especially that the definition of papal infallibility would involve the Council—should it feel itself under obligation to enter upon the question—in the longest and most delicate investigations.

Indeed, by defining the personal infallibility of the Pope, we should not only bind the future but also the past. For, if the Pope is infallible, he has always been so. The proclamation of this dogma would, at a single stroke, confer the character of infallibility upon all that the Popes have decided for eighteen centuries, provided they had decided under the conditions and in the forms laid down for the exercise of infallibility. I say that the Council could not have a graver and knottier subject to examine.

I reminded you, just now, of two historic facts—the dispute between Pope Saint Stephen and Saint Cyprian, and the reply of Pope Honorius to Sergius on the subject of monothelism. Well! if it were shown that Saint Stephen had pronounced *ex cathedra*, infallibly, *bindingly*, then Saint Cyprian and the bishops who resisted were not believers in the infallibility of the Pope?

And Saint Augustine, who excuses them, because, says he, the Church had not yet pronounced,* he did not believe in it either? And when he wrote concerning the Donatists, that after the judgment of Rome there still remained the judgment of the Church universal, *restabat adhuc plenarium universæ Ecclesiæ concilium*,† he believed, then, that after the judgment of Rome the judgment of the Church should go for something in defining the faith. That is a fresh instance of the difficulties which might be brought up by an examination of the facts of history.

Just so in the case of Honorius. Volumes have been written to prove that the acts of the Sixth Council, which condemned him, have been altered; volumes to prove that this Pope did not teach heresy; other volumes still, to prove that Honorius only wrote a *private* letter.

However it may be with these discussions, which it is so unfortunate to bring up again—whether Honorius was a heretic, and justly condemned as such by an Œcumenical Council that declared *Honorio hæretico anathema;* or whether he was simply an abettor of heresy, and reproved as such by the Popes, his successors, in the oath that they pronounced at their consecration, *Qui pravis eorum assertionibus fomentum impendit* (the expression

---

* Saint Augustine, *De Baptismo*.   † Epis. ad Geor. Eleus., xlviii.

in the *Liber diurnalis pontificalis*, a collection of the authentic acts of the Roman chancery)—over and above these undisputed points of history, another question, a very serious one truly, presents itself in this place; to wit—

In those times, then, did the Œcumenical Council, consequently the Church, consider the Sovereign Pontiff, while sending dogmatic letters, *literas dogmaticas*,* to great churches upon a matter of faith, as liable to error, and the assembled bishops as competent to condemn and anathematize him?

Pope Leo II. confirmed the sentence of the Council; the Churches of the East and the West accepted it. Did, then, Pope Leo II. and the Churches also believe that a Pope, pronouncing upon matters of faith brought before his tribunal, may deserve the anathema?

That is a point upon which the Council would have to decide.

I have neither the intention nor the time to do here what the Council would have to do in order to proceed with the wonted circumspection of Councils—to take a complete review of the history. I pass by the difficulties that the cases of Popes Vigilius and Liberius might occasion. But I beg leave to remind you of a single fact more. In the Middle Ages, one of the Popes, Paschal II., makes the Emperor of Germany, Henry V., such an exorbitant concession in the matter of the investiture of bishops, that a Council meets at Vienna, and an Archbishop, who was destined himself, subsequently, to ascend the throne of Saint Peter, under the name of Calixtus II., declares that the concession made by the Pope implies an actual heresy, *hæresim esse judicavimus*, and condemns his letter to the Emperor.

And the Pope himself, before the entire Lateran Council, in the presence of more than one hundred bishops, had already humiliated himself of his own accord, and the Council had overruled and annulled his concession.

Whether, then, Paschal II. was to blame or not, at all events his contemporaries, and he himself, believed that a Pope may lapse into heresy.

* *Conc.* t. III., p. 1331.

Will you say that an implied heresy (yet one worthy of anathema), in a high pontifical act, proves nothing against infallibility, when this act is not a definition *ex cathedra?* But how will you make the multitude understand these distinctions?

For here is another side of the question, one to which the Council would also have to devote its serious attention—the consequences of the definition in the view of the men of our times.

XI. We must not indulge in any illusions, not merely as to unbelieving minds, but also as to the enormous mass of minds in whom faith is weak. For my own part, I cannot think, without horror, of the number of those whom the definition now called for would perhaps alienate from us forever!

But even for the faithful, would the definition be free from disadvantages?

I find myself constrained here to put questions that are profoundly repugnant to me. But I am speaking of the past and in behalf of the future. People force us to awaken the slumbering past, and we have to labor for future centuries.

We have, then (let us suppose), the Pope declared infallible—the Pope, who, nevertheless, as a writer, as a private teacher, may make a heretical book and may obstinately persist in heresy. That is the general opinion.

Still more, we have the Pope, who can, even as Pope, when he does not speak *ex cathedra*—and even when he does speak *ex cathedra*, in whatever is not the precise subject of his definition—who can, according to universal opinion, err and teach error; and then be judged, condemned, deposed.

Now, then, let us suppose a Pope erring or accused of error; it will be necessary to prove, either that his teaching is not *ex cathedra* or that it is not erroneous: what additional difficulty if the Pope has been declared infallible! Contesting merely a matter of fact, shall we not seem to contest a matter of right? And if the Pope persists, what confusion among the faithful! It will be necessary, then, to prosecute for heresy the very man whose infallibility is a dogma.

Let some new Honorius arise hereafter, who shall, I do not say define heresy, but foment it, by means of *dogmatic* letters addressed to great churches—the declaration of infallibility will not prevent this—can you imagine the perturbation that such a case would occasion among churches and consciences?

No doubt the theologians will make all the shades and niceties of distinction, and show that there was no real definition; but how will the mass of minds who are not theologians be able to discriminate between the Pope fallible in such and such acts, even as Pope, and the Pope not fallible in such and such other acts? How will they understand that he can be infallible, and yet, by high pontifical acts, be a fomenter of *heresy?*

In the eyes of the public this will still be infallibility. Hence uneasiness for consciences which will think themselves under continual obligation to perform acts of faith; and, for the enemies of the Church, the opportunity to decry Catholic doctrine, by imputing something to it as dogma which is not dogma.

Without wishing, I repeat, to touch the substantial question, the question of infallibility itself, I cannot refrain from making one reflection here, from the point of view of men of the world. The personal infallibility of the Pope, not the absurd, unconditional, universal infallibility of which we were speaking a little while ago, citing certain theologians, but infallibility as Bellarmin, for instance, understands it, constitutes an institution, not above the power of the Almighty, doubtless, but certainly most prodigious, and more astonishing than the infallibility of the entire Church.

How does it happen—this is what will astonish the faithful—how does it happen that this immense privilege is at once the one whose definition, on the showing of history, is the least necessary, since the Church has been able to do without it for eighteen centuries, and the one the certainty of which is less established than the infallibility of the Church itself, since this latter is and always has been an article of faith, whereas the other has never been professed in the Church as a dogma?

Moreover, the greatest partisans of infallibility themselves set forth the immense practical difficulties that may be entailed by these two modes of existence of the Pope, fallible or infallible, according to circumstances. *Intricatissimæ difficultates,* they say, *in quibus dissolvendis multum peritiores theologi laborant.*

And indeed — still following their own statements — here are some of the painful questions that may arise: Does a Pope, by the act of heresy, cease to be a Pope?—By whom and how can he be deposed?—When may the Pope be said to act as a Pope, when as a private individual? &c., &c. *An Papa per hæresim a dignitate excidat? A quo et quomodo veniat deponendus? Quandonam ut Pontifex, aut ut privata persona, agere censeatur.*

Will the declaration of infallibility render all these difficulties less inextricable? On the contrary, it would, in practice, add to them enormous embarrassments.

Accordingly, certain ultramontane theologians* see only one way of extricating themselves—namely, by proclaiming the absolute, unconditional, and universal infallibility of the Pope. Otherwise, and if only a conditional infallibility is proclaimed—the infallibility *ex cathedra*—we expose the Church to EVIDENT danger. *Ecclesia evidenti periculo exponeretur.* And they prove it.

The system, they say, of papal infallibility in certain cases and fallibility in others, implies an actual contradiction. May it not happen that a Pope shall teach, as Pope, *ex cathedra,* the error which, as a private doctor, he has held to be the truth—that is, shall define the error in an infallible act, and seek to impose it upon the Church? *Posset namque ipse suum errorem definire et Ecclesiæ obtrudere.*

It is said, in answer, that this hypothesis, precisely because it implies a contradiction, will never be realized.

Then, they reply, you are forced to have recourse to a miracle: a Pope who errs obstinately, and of course uses all his efforts to set forth his error as the faith of the Church (*potest Pontifex personaliter in fide deficere, errorem suum pertinaciter tueri, et, quod amplius est, velle et conari eum Ecclesiæ obtrudere et proponere*), yet who will always refrain from defining it, and cannot come to the point of producing a Bull that no human power can prevent him

---

* Albert Pighius, and others, cited by Bannès, quæst. I, dubit. 2.

from writing; or, on the other hand, a Pope who thinks one way and defines another: *Aut certe grande miraculum esset, quod ipse definiendo contra mentem suam definiret.*

Moreover, they add, is there not in this mixture of fallibility and infallibility in one and the same man, a strange anomaly, one that reflects most injuriously on divine Providence, that could so easily have rendered the Pope infallible in every case as well as in a few cases? *Contra divinam Providentiam, quæ omnia suaviter disponit, pugnat Pontificem posse personaliter errare.*

In short, they continue, why make any distinctions where Jesus Christ has made none? *Oravi pro te, Petre, ut non deficiat fides tua.* That, say they, applies to Peter's faith in every sense; DE FIDE PETRI TUM PERSONALI ET PRIVATA, *tum publica et pastorali, intelligitur.*

Here are theologians, then, who state, who demonstrate, the perils of infallibility *ex cathedra;* who, logical and resolute, go to the very end, even to the length of the absolute, unconditional, and universal infallibility of the Pope: so that a Pope, they say, could not, *even if he wanted to,* lapse into any error public or private. *Ut non possit,* ETIAMSI VELIT, *in errorem* PRIVATIM *aut publice cadere!*

A French theologian* has set forth, at length, this whole argument, and, loading with abuse the greatest men of his country, contents himself with presenting this truly insensate Romanism as a perfectly free opinion: *De* LIBERE *controversa opinione quæ tenet Romanum Pontificem,* ETIAM QUATENUS DOCTOREM PRIVATUM, *esse infallibilem.*

What! My God! We are also free to argue, if we like, on the question whether the men at the antipodes walk on their heads or their feet. There is not, so far as I know, any definition that says the contrary, and we should be amenable, on this point, only to good sense.

It is evident that there are in the Church, at this moment, many excited people who are hurrying on to strange excesses!

---

* *De Papa,* tom. I, p. 257.

But the Council, we are sure, will not permit itself to be drawn down any such perilous decline.

XII. There is more than one point still remaining, on which it is to be feared that the proclamation of the new dogma, if it should take place, would perplex and unsettle, in the minds of the faithful, what they have hitherto believed.

How, for instance, shall we persuade them that this definition will not involve, if not in law, at least in fact and in practice, a degradation of the Episcopate?

And first, from this point of view, they will ask themselves—What will become of the Councils?

Hitherto the Councils have been one of the grandest forms of Church-life, one of its mightiest means of action. They began with the origin of the Church, with the apostolic age; every Christian century, with the exception of the last two, has known them. There have even been persons of high sanctity, great minds, Councils even, that have demanded or decreed the periodical return of these sacred assemblies. The mistrustful policy of a *régime* that has passed away, had, it is true, rendered them during the last few centuries more difficult; but modern freedom has torn down these jealous barriers—the conquests of modern science, by diminishing distances, have opened rapid communication for the bishops of the whole world with the Eternal City; and these deliberative assemblies find that while they have become easier, they are at the same time more in accordance with the ardent wishes of Christian peoples.

May we not see in all this a truly providential coincidence?

But if the next Council should define the infallibility of the Pope, would not the faithful ponder and ask the question—What is the use, henceforth, of Œcumenical Councils? Now that a SINGLE MAN, the Pope, "WITHOUT THE BISHOPS," is able to decide everything infallibly, even questions of faith, why assemble the bishops? Why the delays, the investigations, the discussions of Councils?

It is evident, indeed, that if the new dogma, once proclaimed, does not, *de jure*, suppress these great assemblies, it will at all events, *de facto*, strangely diminish their importance.

You wish the future Council, then, to make a decree that would, henceforth, suppress or weaken the Councils!

And that the bishops themselves should decree their own abdication!

But this is not the only diminution that the Episcopate would seem to undergo in the eyes of the faithful. Are not its most essential prerogatives also, about which there is no dispute among Catholics, going to be marvellously stripped, in practice at least, of their reality?

First, the bishops are JUDGES OF THE FAITH—judges with the Pope, of course, but still really judges. And hitherto they have always participated actively in the judgments and definitions of dogma; they have always, in Council, decided as actual judges. *Ego judicans, ego definiens, subscripsi.* They have ever been, in the words of Benedict XIV., *co-judices*, associate judges of the faith with the Pope.

But, under the new rule of faith, will it not seem to the faithful that there is henceforth only one judge, and that the bishops are no longer judges in earnest? Their co-operation, antecedent or subsequent, will, in fact, no longer be necessary. The infallible judgment of the Pope, as Archbishop Manning says, will be complete and perfect in itself, " WITHOUT AND INDEPENDENTLY OF THE EPISCOPATE!" If such is the will of the Pope, they will no longer count for anything in definitions of faith. Then there will be, in fact, but one single judge—the Pope.

Indeed, when the Pope shall have proclaimed, of himself, without the Episcopate and without any bishops, a dogma of faith, how shall we make the faithful understand these two things: that the Pope's sentence, immediately, in itself, independently of any episcopal assent, has the force of *res judicata;* and secondly, that the bishops still remain real judges!

What sentence can they pass?—A sentence of simple assent, you say.—But that sentence will be free, at least? No; it will not be free, for they will be obliged to assent.—Is it even required? No; it is not required in any way, for the sentence of the Pope is obligatory in itself, independently of any assent on the part of the Episcopate.

I ask myself whether, under such conditions, the faithful will still consider the bishops as real judges?

What would they think of a tribunal in which the president would have the privilege of deciding and judging everything for himself, so that all the other judges would be obliged to concur with him? The vote of the president alone would suffice; the opinion of the others would be fashioned by his, dictated by his; no one, after he had pronounced, could judge differently; and the concurrence of his colleagues would not even be required for the decision.

Evidently, such a tribunal would appear a mockery; and of judges there would be, in reality, only one.

Theologians may argue and make distinctions. But the faithful, the great public who do not understand theological distinctions, where would they stand?

Without doubt the Pope is the principal judge, and his opinion is always indispensable. Not only does he preside over the court, but he confirms the opinion of the other judges. In ordinary courts, the vote of the presiding judge commonly preponderates; but in the Church, the vote of the Pope is essential, and the judgment of the bishops, even in an Œcumenical Council, is only final when that of the Pope is superadded. In a word, in definitions of faith, the bishops and the Pope have each their necessary parts. Would that be still true of the bishops, in the opinion of the faithful, when the Pope, declared infallible, should judge alone?

XIII. Let us continue, Gentlemen—placing ourselves still at the point of view of the faithful—to seek for and examine the probable disadvantages of the dogmatic definition in question.

At the same time that they are JUDGES the bishops are also TEACHERS. All the catechisms say this. The words of our Lord Jesus Christ are explicit. It was to the Apostles, and consequently to the bishops, the successors of the Apostles, that he said, *Euntes docete omnes gentes* . . . *Ecce ego vobiscum sum omnibus diebus* ["Go, teach all nations. . . . Behold, I am with you always"]. It was to the Apostles, and consequently to the bishops, the successors of the Apostles, that Christ also said, *Accipite Spiritum sanctum*, &c. ["Receive the Holy Ghost"]; and finally, *Qui vos audit, me audit* ["He that heareth you, heareth me"]. These are all words that every believer knows by heart.

That was why Saint Paul said, *Fundati estis super fundamentum Apostolorum.* — *Posuit Episcopos regere Ecclesiam* ["Ye are built upon the foundation of apostles. . . . He hath made . . . bishops to rule the church"].*

All tradition has constantly herein likened the bishops to the apostles; and the Council of Trent, summing up all tradition, says expressly, in speaking of the bishops, *In locum Apostolorum successerunt.*

So the bishops, then, are not mere echoes; they are teachers; they constitute, with the Pope, the *Ecclesia docens.*

But with the personal infallibility of the Pope, without the concurrence of the bishops, "WITHOUT AND INDEPENDENTLY OF THE EPISCOPAL BODY," there would be, in the eyes of the faithful, but one to define, but one to teach—a single doctor, a single judge.

And the bishops are no longer voices in the Church, but mere echoes.

The assent of the teaching body counting for nothing, then, in what constitutes the essence of doctrinal judgment, how can the faithful understand that this teaching body teaches?

Moreover, Gentlemen, what is the teaching of the Church? A bearing witness. Neither the Church nor the Pope makes the dogma; they state it. Revelation is a fact; revealed truths are facts. And a doctrinal judgment is, at bottom, only the attestation of a revealed fact. Now, when the Church, assembled or scattered, pronounces judgment, that is something that the faithful understand without difficulty,—something that requires divine aid, no doubt, but still thoroughly in accordance with the nature of things, with the very harmony of the Church as Jesus Christ

---

* Ephesians, ii. 20; Acts, xx. 28.

has constituted it. It is a testimony confirmed by all those who are witnesses; the particular Churches attesting, by the very fact that they bear witness to it, the faith of the Church universal. When all the Churches, when the body of pastors united with their chief has spoken, by that act the faith of the Church is fixed; what was only implied has become explicit, and the dogma is defined, and the great Catholic maxim is realized—*Quod ubique, quod semper, quod ab omnibus*. The faithful readily comprehend that.

Whereas a doctrinal judgment of the Pope alone, without the requisition of any assent from the Episcopate, would present itself to them in a very different aspect. That would be, in a matter of testimony, one witness authorized at his discretion to supplant all the others; a single witness instead of all; one witness that has no need, unless he likes, of the other witnesses or of their testimony to learn what is the tradition and faith of their Churches.

That is to say, in place of something very simple, very intelligible, in the spiritual order, you would substitute, in the eyes of the faithful, something extraordinary, something abnormal, a perpetual miracle, and a very different sort of miracle from that of the infallibility of the Church.

In the latter, at least, if there is any miracle, the faithful understand that this miracle is absolutely necessary, and implied in the very notion of the Church—without infallibility in the Church, there is no Church. But they do not understand so readily the necessity of this miracle for the Pope alone, because the Church can be conceived perfectly well without the personal and separate infallibility of the Pope. The infallibility of the Church will always suffice for everything, as it always has sufficed.

The faithful know very well that in this grand and universal testimony of the Church, the Pope is a witness, the chief witness, the witness of the principal and supreme Church, that Church which, occupying the central position, is in communication with all the others, as all the others should be in communication with it.

But, until now, the faithful have not believed that the Pope was the sole witness in the Church.

Thereafter, pronouncing alone, he would be so, whenever he liked.

XIV. It is said, and well said—*Ubi Petrus, ibi Ecclesia.* A grand saying of St. Ambrose. But it is strangely abused at times.

To hear certain writers, whose exaggerations are certainly not pleasing either to the Pope or to scarcely any one, one might suppose that the Pope constituted, by himself, the whole Church. No. The Pope is the head of the Church; he is not the whole Church. The word *Church* is a collective word, not to be applied to any one separate individuality whatever. The Church of Jesus Christ has for its necessary head the Pope, and there is no Church of Christ without the Pope: that would be a body without a head. But the Pope is not and has never pretended to be the whole Church. The true and legitimate practical use of this saying is this, that in the divisions produced by heresies and schisms, in order to learn where the Church is, we must see where the Pope is. It is thus that we are sure that the Russian Church, the Anglican Church, are not the Church of Jesus Christ, because they have not the Pope with them; and, on the other hand, that the Roman Catholic Church is the true Church, because it recognizes the successor of Peter as its chief—*Ubi Petrus, ibi Ecclesia.*

Let us, Gentlemen, not have the appearance, in the eyes of the faithful, of putting asunder, by a definition that would be an occasion of disturbance to them, what should not be put asunder—the Pope and the Episcopate.

Certain theological schools have, for some time, been equally in the wrong on this point, in opposite directions: one set wishing to separate the Pope from the Episcopate; the other, the Episcopate from the Pope.

The Church is a living body—*Corpus.* That is the word continually repeated by Saint Paul, who employs it to show in this mystical body the relations of the head and the members, and the harmony of the entire organism.

The Pope is the head, the visible Chief of the Church.

But if we put the head on one side and the body on the other, where will be the life?

The Church is a building—*Ædificabo Ecclesiam meam;* why seek to detach the foundation from the building, the building from the foundation?

The Church is built upon the rock. Yes; but on the rock there is the building, and the rock is only the foundation by reason of its connection with the building—*Super hanc petram ædificabo Ecclesiam meam.*

There are those that say: The rock is everything. Plainly not. The head is not the whole body.

It is the foundation; it is not the whole building.

The building, without the foundation, would fall; the foundation, without the building, would be the foundation of nothing.

No separation, then, Gentlemen; neither Germanist nor Romanist, neither Gallican nor Ultramontanist—either on dogmatic definitions or on anything else; Christ would not have it so. *Unum sint*—" that they all may be one."

Let us leave the old, vain quarrels.

The faithful understand only the Church with its supreme Head, and the Head with the Church.

This conception of the Church, moreover, is in no wise detrimental to the divine authority and the supreme initiative of the Roman Pontiff.

Successor of Peter—Vicar of Jesus Christ, in whom dwelleth the fulness of apostolic power—Chief of all the bishops—Pontiff of the principal see in which all other sees maintain their unity—universal Pastor, not merely of the sheep but also of the shepherds—mouth of the Church—key-stone of Catholicity.

Such is the Pope, such the head of the Teaching Church.

And, on the other hand, the Bishops: Successors of the Apostles—Judges and Teachers, with whom Jesus Christ is always until the end of the world—Pastors of the peoples, under the superior and chief authority of the Sovereign Pontiff: *instituted by the Holy Spirit to rule the Church of God and to teach all nations.*

Such is the all-powerful economy of that mysterious and living unity of the Church, in which everything is divine because everything is one, where the arrangement and the correspondence are such that each part, when it is in its place, shares in the might of the whole.

No; let us not astonish the faithful by bringing our criticism to bear on this divine constitution; let us not dig about these sacred foundations; let no one put asunder what Jesus Christ hath made to remain eternally united.

Ah! may we rather gather more closely than ever around the Sovereign Pontiff in veneration, obedience, and love, and put far away from us even the shadow of dissension! May we all, in generous self-forgetfulness, sacrificing to the Church our personal prejudices, labor with one mind for the preservation of that peace and that unity in which God dwelleth! Then, but then only, shall we offer to the world the spectacle of that great "*army with banners*," of which the Scriptures speak; an army "terrible," because it is set in array beneath its banners.

Then, too, by our example no less than by our teaching, shall we bring to imperilled society that aid from God for which it is looking, and that last hope of life for which it is calling aloud.

XV. These, Gentlemen, are theological details that I should have been glad to avoid; I have designed them for the clergy, but they will also fall upon the highway, upon stony ground and among thorns, among chattering birds, among the unfriendly and the ignorant. But let no one be surprised at the opinions agitated in our schools. This diversity, these discussions among theologians, are a proof of liberty, *in dubiis libertas*, and also of charity, *in omnibus caritas*. But when we must come to necessary decisions, about which there should be agreement, *in necessariis unitas*, then we are no longer philosophers disputing; we are doctors teaching, and witnesses giving testimony.

It is our duty to undertake an exhausting labor in reflection, in the drawing of distinctions, in the weighing of scruples, before laying any burden upon your minds or your consciences. O, flippant men who sneer at toil entered into for you, you do not complain of the minute calculations of astronomers and navigators, before you embark, nor of the investigations of the judge that holds your fate in his hands. Theologians also merit your respect in investigations that concern your souls and the truth. Do not sneer, and do not worry. Instead of listening at the doors of our schools, enter that marvellous temple of Christian truth, from which nineteen centuries have not torn a single stone, the temple in which you find that unique combination of the divine presence and of united testimony which is called the Church; resembling, in some sort, the luminous system of the world, which is composed of one chief luminary, of countless stars, and of one and the same light spread over all.

In the brightness of an unclouded noon, the light seems to come from a single source; but if the night grows dark, we see countless stars in the firmament for man's guidance, thousands of rays blending upon his head in one single effulgence.

XVI. I would fain sum up this long series of questions, and express clearly the state of my soul.

We have our contests indeed—that is life!—but upon this great question of the Church we have peace. No Catholic doubts the infallibility of the Church; just as no one doubts the primacy of the Pope, who institutes bishops, convokes Councils, proposes decrees, confirms decisions: no one doubts the constancy, the unanimity of tradition on all these points, for nineteen centuries. Every believer, after having read the Gospel, consulted history, hearkened to his pastor, pronounces from the bottom of his heart, *Credo Ecclesiam unam, sanctam, catholicam, apostolicam.* In fact, in the testimony of the Bishops, the Popes, the Apostles, and of Christ, there is, from the very beginning, an infallible harmony, into which God himself enters.

All at once some few persons set about inquiring in whom infallibility, in this Church, originally resides. And with eyes fixed upon a marvellous fact, they commence to agitate questions. In the presence of a fact, they see fit to stir up hypotheses. In presence of a solution, they put in question the elements of the problem; and a cause that has been adjudicated, terminated by happy accord, they take up, revive, and rekindle! Straightway, as soon as the problem is enunciated, the enemy awakes and the faithful are disconcerted, the East checked, Protestants turned back, governments disturbed, the saddest pages of the history of the past dragged to light, the bishops saddened, the peace of souls compromised, and the way of salvation rendered more difficult. Wherefore? In what interest? With what gain?

To-morrow, whatever might be the course adopted, what would happen? That which was not discussed would be discussed, what was forgotten would be revived, and the habit of discussion once resumed—farewell to peace!

No, no! We are not going to assemble to substitute division for unanimity, dispute for love!

By the grace of God, the Church of France has, for two centuries, richly deserved to be released from all antiquated jealousies. That Church, I boldly say, has been and will ever be the heroine and the martyr of Unity. During the last hundred years especially, there has not been a branch of the divine tree better united to the trunk and the root, while spreading itself farther, more zealously, across all boundaries: no branch more Catholic, no branch more apostolic, no branch more Roman.

Our predecessors died upon the scaffold, that the unity might not be broken; they accepted exile and confiscation, without yielding either to the oppression of the people or the tyranny of the despot. They were to be found with Pius VI. and Pius VII. upon all the paths of exile, in the fellowship of martyrdom. It was in the French clergy that Pius VII. found his strongest consolation. The Churches of the United States were begun by French bishops. French bishops have never wearied in defending oppressed Poland, starving Ireland, the down-trodden East. Together we have demanded and obtained the freedom of parents in the education of their children; together we have defended the freedom of religious association, the freedom of charity, the development of civilizing missions. The whole Church is indebted to France for the Sisters of Charity, the Brethren of the Christian Schools, the Work of the Propagation of the Faith in the two worlds, the Conferences of Saint Vincent de Paul, the Colleges of the Jesuits and the Dominicans, the Little Sisters of the Poor, and all that incomparable army of peace, which, like our army of war, is the first in the world.

For twenty years the Papal See has been attacked, wounded, betrayed, oppressed, delivered up to implacable adversaries. The French bishops have defended, served, assisted, loved, exalted, consoled it, with a magnificent movement that time has not weakened. And is it not they, too, who in the evil days through which we are passing, gave the first impulse to that touching and now universal work, the Peter's-pence? Ah! I venture to say that such devotion to Rome and to the Catholic world gives the Church of France the right to be believed, to be heard, when it speaks of its attachment to the Holy See and to the Vicar of our Lord Jesus Christ.

What do I say! So great is the enthusiasm of France for the centre of unity, that extreme doctrines cross the Alps from France, while from Rome come forth moderation, compromise, prudence; Rome it is that arrests the *furia francese*, and refuses to push dogmas to excess. So, my brethren, be not uneasy! Men of faith, be not troubled!

If I have decided upon going into all these details with you and in public, it was because of this secret instinct, that I had rather to calm agitated minds in my own country than to forestall objections at Rome. I am convinced that no sooner shall I have touched the sacred soil, no sooner kissed the tomb of the Apostles, than I shall feel myself at peace, out of battle, in the midst of an assembly presided over by a Father and composed of Brothers. There all tumult will die away, all foolhardy meddling cease, all imprudence disappear, the winds and the waves will be at rest. We shall think of the saints in whose seats we are sitting, of the souls that we are to answer for unto God; we shall think of that God who sees us and who will judge us; we shall think of the Apostles, we shall seem to see them still in the presence of the world that is to be conquered, and the Master that is to be hearkened unto. And when in the place of that supreme Master of hearts, his Vicar upon earth shall repeat to each of us, "My brother, lovest thou me?" O believe that your old bishop will not be the last one to answer, "Father, thou knowest that I love thee!" As the gentle bishop of Geneva said: "*In the strife of love for the Vicar of Jesus Christ* I have not permitted myself to be overcome by any one. For twenty years my hair has whitened, my hand has worn itself out in thy service. O Holy Father, God knoweth that the last word of my lips and the last throb of my heart shall be given to the Church and to thee."

Accept, Gentlemen and beloved fellow-laborers, the renewed assurance of my deep and pious regards.

✠ Felix, *Bishop of Orleans.*

Orleans, *November 11th:*
Feast of St. Martin.

THE END.

☞ *The Trade will observe the prices of Irving's Works in sets as now completed.*

THREE NEW EDITIONS OF IRVING
ARE NOW COMPLETED.

"The delight of childhood, the chivalric companion of refined womanhood, the solace of life at every period; his writings are an imperishable legacy of grace and beauty to his countrymen."

NEW EDITIONS OF IRVING'S WORKS.

I. *THE KNICKERBOCKER EDITION.*—Large 12mo, on superfine laid paper, with Illustrations, elegantly printed from new stereotype plates, and bound in extra cloth, gilt top. Complete in 27 vols., $67.50.

⁎ This edition will be sold only to subscribers for the whole set. It is the *best* edition for libraries and for the centre-table.

II. *THE RIVERSIDE EDITION.*—16mo, on fine white paper; from new stereotype plates; green crape cloth, gilt top, bevelled edges. 26 vols., $45.50.

III. *THE PEOPLE'S EDITION.*—From the same stereotype plates as above, but printed on cheaper paper, neatly bound in cloth. 26 vols., $32.50.

The issue of the above several editions was commenced October 1, 1867. The WORKS are now COMPLETE as above. "The Life and Letters," condensed into three vols., is included in this edition.

Bracebridge Hall,	Goldsmith,	Granada,
Wolfert's Roost,	Alhambra,	Salmagundi,
Sketch Book,	Columbus, 3 vols.,	Spanish Papers,
Traveller,	Astoria,	Washington, 5 vols.,
Knickerbocker,	Bonneville,	Life and Letters, 3 vols.
Crayon Miscellany,	Mahomet, 2 vols.,	

The re-issue of these works in their several forms is unusually elegant. The plates are new, the paper superior, the printing elegant, and each in proportion to price, combining good taste with economy.

IV. *SUNNYSIDE* [Library] *EDITION.*—(Large type.) 28 vols 12mo, cloth, $63; half calf, $112.

G. P. PUTNAM & SON,
661 BROADWAY, NEW YORK.

PUTNAM'S MAGAZINE.
NEW SERIES—FOUR VOLS. COMPLETED.

"Calling into their service the best intellect of America, and making large original draughts upon the best known and most popular writers in Europe, the publishers have succeeded in constituting their monthly issues successive embodiments of the highest style of periodical literature, in every department. It is hardly possible to name an author whose works have rendered him familiar to the thinking public, who has not taken part in the task of rendering '*Putnam*' conspicuous among the best in an epoch which is producing so many good magazines. The three volumes of the new series contain two hundred and seventy-one original articles, and each of them is valuable in itself. These essays range the wide and prolific fields of biography, history, natural philosophy, scientific discovery and progress, art achievements, travel and exploration, religious opinion and controversy, poetry, sentiment, and romance. * * * * *

"It was said of a famous scholar that to enjoy his acquaintance was a liberal education—and the same may be remarked of the habitual reading of '*Putnam*.' The admirable plan of this publication takes in all topics of modern thought and study; while every subject is invariably treated with ability, and so as to present clearly the best ideas it suggests. We are glad to know that the Magazine is a permanent and assured success as a business enterprise, and that the energetic publishers have now under contemplation a series of improvements that will still further advance their claims to the gratitude and patronage of those who can appreciate a high order of merit in literature."— * * *Albany Evening Journal.*

"In several features *Putnam* has been preëminent among the Monthlies. The first series was without a parallel in this country for the enduring value of its contents, and a score or more of standard volumes were made up from it. The new series has been equally admirable in this respect."—*Buffalo Com. Adv.*

"This really valuable Monthly continues to increase in each issue its contributions of lively interest and solid value."—*Charleston Courier.*

"It has taken its old place at the head of the Magazines of the day, and has kept pace with the constant growth of the literature of the period."—*Norwalk Gazette.*

The 4 vols. complete in cloth, comprising 2,200 pages of the choicest reading, will be sent free to any one sending us five subscribers with the money.

Price $4.00 per annum ; 2 copies for $7.00 ; 3 copies for $10.00. Liberal terms for Clubs, or with other periodicals.

Subscribers remitting $4.00 will receive one of the receipts prepared for 50,000 Subscribers, with a Coupon attached, good for One Dollar on account of orders for any Book or Periodical published in the United States.

G. P. PUTNAM & SON, Publishers,
661 Broadway, New York.

CAVÉ. THE CAVÉ METHOD OF LEARNING TO DRAW FROM MEMORY. By Madame E. Cavé. From 4th Parisian edition. 12mo, cloth, $1.

*** This is the *only method of drawing which really teaches anything*. In publishing the remarkable treatise, in which she unfolds, with surpassing interest, the results of her observations upon the teaching of drawing, and the ingenious methods she applies, Madame Cavé . . . . renders invaluable service to all who have marked out for themselves a career of Art."—*Extract from a long review in the Revue des Deux Mondes*, written by Delacroix.

"It is interesting and valuable."—D. HUNTINGTON, *Prest. Nat. Acad.*

"Should be used by every teacher of Drawing in America."—*City Item, Phila.*

"We wish that Madame Cavé had published this work half a century ago, that we might have been instructed in this enviable accomplishment."—*Harper's Mag.*

CAVÉ. THE CAVÉ METHOD OF TEACHING COLOR. 12mo, cloth, $1.

*** This work was referred, by the French Minister of Public Instruction, to a commission of ten eminent artists and officials, whose report, written by M. Delacroix, was unanimously adopted, endorsing and approving the work. The Minister, thereupon, by a decree, authorized the use of it in the French Normal schools.

G. P. PUTNAM & SON have also just received from Paris specimens of the MATERIALS used in this method, which they can supply to order. I. The GAUZES (framed) are now ready. Price $1 each. With discount to teachers. II. The Stand for the gauze. Price $1.50. III. MÉTHODE CAVÉ, *pour apprendre à dessiner* juste et de mémoire d'après les principes d'Albert Durer et de Leonardo da Vinci. Approved by the Minister of Public Instruction, and by Messrs. Delacroix, H. Vernet, etc. In 8 series, folio, paper covers. Price $2.25 each.

N.B.—The Crayons, Paper, and other articles mentioned in the Cavé Method may be obtained of any dealer in Artist's Materials. Samples of the French Articles may be seen at 561 Broadway.

CHADBOURNE. NATURAL THEOLOGY; or, Nature and the Bible from the same Author. Lectures delivered before the Lowell Institute, Boston. By P. A. Chadbourne, A.M., M.D., President of University of Wisconsin. 12mo, cloth, $2. Student's edition, $1.75.

"This is a valuable contribution to current literature, and will be found adapted to the use of the class-room in college, and to the investigations of private students."—*Richmond Christian Adv.*

"The warm, fresh breath of pure and fervent religion pervades these eloquent pages."—*Am. Baptist.*

"Prof. Chadbourne's book is among the few metaphysical ones now published, which, once taken up, cannot be laid aside unread. It is written in a perspicuous, animated style, combining depth of thought and grace of diction, with a total absence of ambitious display."—*Washington National Republic.*

"In diction, method, and spirit, the volume is attractive and distinctive to a are degree."—*Boston Traveller.*

CHILD'S BENEDICITE; or, Illustration of the Power, Wisdom, and Goodness of God, as manifested in His Works. By G. Chaplin Child, M.D. From the London edition of John Murray. With an Introductory Note by Henry G. Weston, D.D., of New York. 1 vol. 12mo. Elegantly printed on tinted paper, cloth extra, bevelled, $2; mor. ext., $4.50.

CHIEF CONTENTS.

Introduction.	Winter and Summer.	Wells.
The Heavens.	Nights and Days.	Seas and Floods.
The Sun and Moon.	Light and Darkness.	The Winds.
The Planets.	Lightning and Clouds.	Fire and Heat.
The Stars.	Showers and Dew.	Frost and Snow, etc.

"The most admirable popular treatise of natural theology. It is no extravagance to say that we have never read a more charming book, or one which we can recommend more confidently to our readers with the assurance that it will aid them, as none that we know of can do, to

'Look through Nature up to Nature's God.'

Every clergyman would do well particularly to study this book. For the rest, the handsome volume is delightful in appearance, and is one of the most creditable specimens of American book-making that has come from the Riverside Press."—*Round Table, N. Y.,* June 1.

CLARKE. PORTIA, and other Tales of Shakespeare's Heroines. By Mrs. Cowden Clarke, author of the Concordance to Shakespeare. With engravings. 12mo, cloth extra, $2.50; gilt edges, $3.

⁎ An attractive book, especially for girls.

COOPER. RURAL HOURS. By a Lady. (Miss Susan Fenimore Cooper.) New Edition, with a new Introductory Chapter. 1 vol. 12mo, $2.50.

"One of the most interesting volumes of the day, displaying powers of mind of a high order."—Mrs. HALE's *Woman's Record.*

"An admirable portraiture of American out-door life, just as it is."—*Prof. Hart.*

"A very pleasant book—the result of the combined effort of good sense and good feeling, an observing mind, and a real, honest, unaffected appreciation of the countless minor beauties that Nature exhibits to her assiduous lovers."—*N. Y. Albion.*

RAVEN (Mme. Aug.). ANNE SEVERIN: A Story translated from the French. 16mo, $1.50.

[*Putnam's European Library.*]

⁎ "The Sister's Story," by the same author, has been warmly and generally eulogized as a book of remarkably pure and elevated character.

"By her great success, Mrs. Craven has larger power for good than perhaps any other writer in France."—*Pall Mall Gazette.*